SACRED SELFISHNESS

A GUIDE TO LIVING A LIFE OF SUBSTANCE

BOOKS BY BUD HARRIS, PH.D.

The Fire and the Rose:
The Wedding of Spirituality and Sexuality

The Father Quest:
Rediscovering an Elemental Force

Resurrecting the Unicorn:
Masculinity in the 21st Century

Knowing the Questions, Living the Answers:
A Jungian Guide Through the Paradoxes of Peace, Conflict,
and Love that Mark a Lifetime

Becoming Whole:
A Jungian Guide to Individuation
Five Lectures and Seminars

Cracking Open:
A Memoir of Struggles, Passages, and Transformations

BOOKS BY BUD HARRIS, PH.D.
AND MASSIMILLA HARRIS, PH.D.

Into the Heart of the Feminine:
An Archetypal Journey to Renew Strength, Love, and Creativity

Like Gold Through Fire:
Understanding the Transforming Power of Suffering

The Art of Love: The Craft of Relationship
A Practical Guide for Creating the Loving Relationships We Want

Bud Harris, Ph.D.

SACRED SELFISHNESS

A GUIDE TO LIVING
A LIFE OF SUBSTANCE

DAPHNE PUBLICATIONS   ASHEVILLE, NORTH CAROLINA

SACRED SELFISHNESS:
A GUIDE TO LIVING A LIFE OF SUBSTANCE
COPYRIGHT © 2002 BY BUD HARRIS

Copyright © 2002 Sacred selfishness: a guide to living a life of substance by Bud Harris

All rights reserved. No part of this publication may be reproduced, stored in a retrieval system, or transmitted, in any form or by any means, electronic, mechanical, photocopying, recording, or otherwise, without the prior written permission of the publisher. Daphne Publications, 6 Cambridge Road, Asheville, North Carolina 28804

DAPHNE PUBLICATIONS, AN IMPRINT OF SPES, INC.

Harris, Bud
Sacred selfishness: a guide to living a life of substance/Bud Harris
Includes bibliographical resources and index.

Originally published in hardcover, 2002
First paperback printing, 2005
Second paperback printing, 2015

ISBN 978-0-692-37408-5   Non-Fiction
1. Psychology 2. Jungian Psychology 3. Spirituality 4. Personal Growth

*This book is dedicated to Massimilla Harris.
Massimilla urged me to teach these ideas, then write them,
and has walked hand in hand with me through the book's
development, as she has lovingly since we first met.*

CONTENTS

Preface   *ix*

Acknowledgments   *xiii*

Introduction   *1*

Part I: Breaking the Mold and Seeking a Path

1. Captives of Normalcy   *17*
2. The Call to Transformation   *47*
3. At the Crossroads   *77*
4. Preparing for Change   *99*

Part II: Cultivating Inner Substance

5. Journaling as Inner Exploration   *133*
6. Dialoguing as Interrelating   *157*
7. Beginning the Search for Personal Substance   *193*
8. Befriending Our Dreams   *219*
9. Facing the Dark and Finding Life   *243*
10. Sacred Selfishness—Learning to Love Ourselves   *271*

Part III: Cultivating a Life of Substance

11. Relationships of Substance   *305*
12. Living the Choice   *333*

Suggestions for Further Reading   *345*

Index   *347*

PREFACE

Our love of life is the motor, the force, the magic that overrides the things we fear—birth pains, growing pains, and loss; the random disappointments and other life difficulties we encounter in our personal journeys. This love is what enables us to persevere, like a footbridge, bringing most of us across to the other side where we experience creativity and joy.

A deep love of life doesn't come to us easily. It grows slowly as we learn to truly understand ourselves, our torrents of emotions, the forces that shaped who we are, the darker destructive sides of our personalities, our denied positive potentials, the knowledge that life is a process and that love and respect must go hand in hand. Self-knowledge brings us the power to live in a balanced, fulfilling way and the capacity to deal honestly, thoughtfully, and lovingly with other people. It enables us to recognize the emotional games we play with each other, to confront reality and to have compassion that is born out of the knowledge of our own torments. Without self-knowledge our notions of love often reflect needy psychological pursuits, idealistic fantasies, or sentimental hopes.

Becoming a person of psychological and spiritual substance is a result of the committed pursuit of self-knowledge. This quest marks the timeworn path outlined by many of the great philosophers and religious figures of the past and present. In ancient Greece the philosopher Socrates enjoined us to know ourselves. One of the meanings of the word *Buddha* is "to awaken," to awaken our search for consciousness. In the Gospel of Thomas, Jesus informs us "whoever has not known himself knows nothing, but he who has known himself has already understood the depths of all things."

But in our times we have continually tried to banish this most important truth (the reminders and the very significant elaborations on this theme by Freud and his followers notwithstanding). We think we know ourselves and we do not. In spite of our best intentions, our busy, overpressured, overstimulated lives seem to make it practically impossible to find the time to learn to know ourselves. However, it's comforting to realize that we have always needed guides, prophets, teachers, and models to bring us out of our everyday selves. Religion, music, art, philosophy, and finally psychology have often directed us toward self-reflection and examination. Freud, Jung, Adler, Fromm, and other great psychoanalytic thinkers have sought to free us from the emotional shackles of our everyday lives. Jungian psychology in particular emphasizes that self-knowledge brings healing to the bruises we suffer from life's struggles, and will lead to the discovery of a truly satisfying existence. Bringing this quest to life and fruition is the aim of this book.

In the opening pages we'll consider the important aspects of growing into a fully mature person—one who has the capacity to live a life of self-realization, meaning, value, and love. From the context of this framework we'll examine the major issues in our societal character structure that affect, limit, and sometimes destroy our individuality without our knowing it.

What I present next is a program for bringing substance back into our lives. This substance depends upon our ability to learn to truly love ourselves, and it becomes the foundation for stepping onto the path toward our own lives. Living a life of substance is the heart of this book. Once we begin to realize this substance, three important aspects of how it affects our lives need to be explored: where it

PREFACE

may lead in our personal development; the impact it has in our close relationships; and the resulting relationships we will have to our culture. We mold society just as it shapes us, and we have the capacity to help heal the defects in our social consciousness in a dramatic manner.

I believe we are challenged by fate to relearn and renew our greatest values in the context of our threatening and chaotic times. In response to this challenge I hope my exploration will help you develop a clearer understanding of what it means to value and love yourself, to think for yourself, to have a life of your own, and to be able to love others without losing yourself. I also hope it will enable you to find comfort as a member of the human family, and a sense of purpose as you contribute to changing our culture.

ACKNOWLEDGMENTS

This book is the product of many years of experience and reflection. A special thanks is due to the men, women, and children whom I've been privileged to know and work with in my professional life. I want to assure all of them, who have labored to understand themselves and to grow through life's challenges, that the stories in this book are fictionalized compositions. They have evolved from my thirty-plus years of experience and are typical of real-life situations without being based on the actual experiences of any particular person.

My debt to Gail Godwin is especially keen. She has supported my writing through its ups and downs for years. Julia Cameron deserves special mention as one of the first people to generously affirm my manuscript. I also want to thank Murray Stein for his important support. Susan Leon graciously and at times vigorously challenged me to stretch beyond my limits in almost every sentence that I wrote. From the beginning to the end of my writing process, Susan Gabriel was a treasure as she helped me bring the manuscript together. In addition, Susan Snowden made many valuable contributions as my work evolved.

ACKNOWLEDGMENTS

Over the years many people have contributed to the development and refinement of my efforts and provided abundant encouragement. I wish to thank them all. Among them are Joe Kovaz, Krista Lunsford, Edward Meeks, Jim Mitchell, Gail Rogers, Dale Sargent, and Lynn Brannon Mangino.

Barbara Braun, my agent, showed steadfast faith in her effort to bring my work and a publisher together. John Nelson, the co-editorial director at Inner Ocean has steered the manuscript into a book formed with enthusiasm and humor. My copy editor Kirsten Whatley's ability to combine precision with insight quickly gained my appreciation. The team at Inner Ocean has shown the kind of creativity and helpfulness that makes turning a manuscript into a book exciting and fun.

INTRODUCTION

So in order to be able to give something, one has to be something, one has to possess, one must consist of gold and not of hunger.
—C. G. Jung

There are two general kinds of selfishness in life. One is sickly, and we often refer to it as *egotism* or *individualism.* Its practitioners are emotionally hungry for power, starved for affirmation, and driven to use and impose on us for self-serving ends. They steal our energy and vitality. Our consumer-driven society fosters *sickly selfishness* because it thrives on teaching us that we always want or need more of some product to feel good about ourselves.

Sacred selfishness is the second kind of selfishness. It means making the commitment to valuing ourselves and our lives enough to pursue the decision to become people of *substance.* Becoming this is the process of attaining what American philosopher Ralph Waldo Emerson refers to as "character—a reserved force which acts directly by presence, and without means." While Martin Luther King or Mother Teresa may picture an ultimate model of such substance, Emerson carefully points out that it ". . . works with most energy in the smallest companies and in private relationships." Sacred selfishness teaches us to love life, and its practitioners give energy, vitality, and hope to the people around them.

Sacred selfishness causes us to step outside of the everyday values of economics, busyness, goal-driven days, and pressures of getting life "right." There is nothing new about saying we are running through life like rats in a maze, that we feel like cogs in a machine, or numbers instead of individuals, that our religious institutions are empty and what we truly worship is what we can buy at the mall or buy even cheaper at the factory outlet. What is new is realizing that we can find a path with its own fork that allows us to have it both ways, authentic lives without abandoning the world.

The illusions I had to face and the pain and conflicts of my own life put me on this course. In my early thirties I was successful, yet discovered, like suddenly noticing thunderclouds on a summer day, I was depressed. I thought I had a good life but before I knew it, it seemed to turn dark and threatening. Although I didn't realize it at the time I wasn't alone in this condition, nor would I be alone today. Many people in our society have lives that seem to be working well yet find themselves strangely unhappy or suffering in some similar manner. This book has been inspired by my own struggles and informed by my work as a therapist and analyst for over twenty-five years with people who wanted, as I did, to find more in life than simply adjusting to what one's family or society describes as a "good life."

At age thirty-three I found myself restless, uneasy, and generally dissatisfied with how I was living. Everything around and ahead of me looked boring and lifeless. This feeling that I was somehow missing life had begun during my sophomore year in college when I couldn't decide on a major. The counseling center said my interests hadn't crystallized while my father's concern was that I prepare myself to get a good job. In frustration and despair I drank a great deal. I solved my increasing anxiety by getting married and starting a family. The pressure of these obligations compelled me to finish school, get a job with a major company, buy a house in the suburbs, and, in other words, seek success in a conventional 1950s manner.

INTRODUCTION

But the more successful I became, seeking my reflection in images of nicer clothes, better homes, private schools for my children, and the apparent independence of owning my own business, the more my restlessness and secret fear seemed to increase. What fear? I was terrified by the idea of the rest of my life. Was I simply going to continue fulfilling my obligations for some thirty-odd years and retire—that is if a heart attack or cancer or some other stress-related disease didn't take me first? Was my life to consist of going to work, meetings, church, soccer games, and vacations? Activities I generally enjoyed and sometimes loved, but sensed I would grow to hate as the enjoyment I took from them became choked in the smoke of my increasing dissatisfaction.

By this time in my life it was the late 1960s. Psychotherapy had become "in" and my friends were flocking to it. I, however, had dismissed therapy and analysis. I looked down on the people in it. They were "weak" and I was "strong." I dealt with reality while they mucked around in their feelings. And while I kept myself ignorant of the powers of my unconscious, I steadfastly thought that as an entrepreneur I could create my own reality, shaping my life to my will and vision. I wanted to believe that if my life looked independent and successful, I was independent and successful.

The writings of Freud and Jung had seized my interest in college, but once I had stepped onto the practical path, their ideas faded from my awareness, overtaken by concerns of making money and having a family. The next decade flew by while I was lost in work, obligations, striving for advancement, caring for small children, and starting my own business. Activity—professional, social, and personal—made it easy to forget my former uneasiness, to hide from it, and to hide from the question of what was really driving my life.

On the outside I looked great. I jogged three miles a day and was working toward my black belt in karate. On the inside, well, I wasn't so sure. I thought I should feel great, but slowly began to realize the old uneasiness was gnawing at me again, and my increasing physical activities might be an effort to avoid my inner tension. But I didn't face these emotions nor did I have a clue as to what I was really feeling. I had done too good a job repressing and denying my emotions for years to be able to simply figure them out. As I have now learned, such feelings do not magically go away. They become a hidden engine driving us into emotional and physical problems. In my case, it was a depression that began devouring my life—until it had brought both my business and my marriage into full-blown crises. My first formal meeting with a therapist soon followed.

This crises-induced meeting began my personal quest, and as this book develops, I will use the phrase *becoming a person of substance* to summarize the characteristics acquired during this quest—my own and those of whom you will read about. In mythology and legends, quest stories begin when something of value has been lost by a person, people, or kingdom. The *Star Wars* movies continue to hold the interest of young and old because they are about the themes of many of our quests. Luke Skywalker and Princess Leia must struggle to reject a political system that places an impersonal claim upon them as they search for maturity. Darth Vader depicts a father who has lost his humanity and Han Solo, a mercenary who learns the values of a hero.

I felt stagnant, impotent, and unauthentic in my depression. Nothing in my life was able to evoke spiritual meaning, passion, and unknown potentials. Entering into a therapist's office marked the transition from an everyday state of mind into an atmosphere where, with someone's help, I could search for my true nature and the source of my energy. I was fortunate he was the kind of therapist who understood that, psychologically, the healing quest I needed was for the self-awareness that leads us into a new state of wholeness, relatedness to life, and a profound experience of being alive emotionally and spiritually. These changes lead to new meanings and to a new spirit of being alive that grows into a state of fruitful completion as we approach death.

The oldest quest stories show the pattern of stepping out of the everyday world, even when we have been successful in it, to begin the journey toward a greater experience of life. In one of history's oldest epics, Gilgamesh, the king of ancient Sumer, leaves his throne and braves the wrath of angry goddesses and nature as he seeks the

INTRODUCTION

secret of eternal life. Inanna, the Sumerian queen of heaven and one of our oldest heroines, likewise leaves her throne to search for wholeness in the underworld. Odysseus struggles through the haunted waters of the Mediterranean in search of home and leaves history with a name for one of our most fundamental journeys—the odyssey. Aeneas flees a burning Troy, deserting his wife, and carrying his father on his back. He begins a journey that betrays love and ends it with the founding of Rome. Our enduring stories remind us that our searches are driven by both disasters and visions. They are lonely and difficult outer quests that are also metaphors for our inner quests. The journeys are intrinsic to human nature—and they are timeless. They are reexperienced in every age and become available to any of us who want more than conventional lives or whose conventional lives fail us.

The religious aspects of the quest frequently appear in the different mystical traditions. The image of Buddha under the Bodhi Tree is one of awakening and a journey toward enlightenment. The Hindu ascetic sitting in deep contemplation symbolizes a similar inner journey. The Magi seeking the Christ child represents the reconciliation of man with the eternal worlds, which the mythologist Joseph Campbell said pours energy into our everyday world. The Hindu and the Christian mystics often call the quest a *search for the Self*, and the Swiss psychiatrist Carl Jung named it the *process of individuation*.

The quests of the religious mystics and the legendary heroes have many psychological parallels as both seek to renew our spirits and deepen our experiences of being alive. The Quest for the Holy Grail is a legend from the Middle Ages that still has popularity. Its symbolism is straightforward and shows how a place that was once green, fertile, and bountiful has dried up and become brown and withered. The fact that the kingdom has become a wasteland signifies the need for psychological and spiritual renewal. Joseph Campbell describes the wasteland as a place where people are living unauthentically, living not their lives but the lives imposed on them by society with no courage for seeking to change the situation. In his poem "The Waste Land," T. S. Eliot brings this situation to life in another way and says:

> *I think we are in rats alley*
> *Where the dead men lost their bones.*

The Grail, the vessel that held the blood of Christ, represents the source of our lost personal and spiritual values. The remarkable thing about this search for renewal is how it guides us to realize that it is a *personal* quest. Each knight must begin the journey alone by entering the forest at a place where there is no previous path. Campbell felt the Grail symbolized the spiritual essence that energized an authentic life. Its purpose is to bring flowering and fulfillment to our beings in contrast to the more societal idea that a spiritual life is one that has supernatural virtues imposed upon it.

Like anyone embarking on such a quest, I was faced with the questions: What makes me feel and act as I do? What is my purpose here on Earth? What is my destiny? One of the biggest questions I faced was, How can I have achieved the American Dream and still be unhappy? Yet my fear and depression held firm against this question until the ancient Greek injunction "know thyself" became more than a pious platitude and more than the beginning of wisdom. Beginning to know myself was a lifeline pulling me free from pain, and transforming my desperation into a path toward a more rewarding life.

This book will outline and explain the pathway to individuation, the approach I found the most helpful in learning to know myself. It will include many of the significant mileposts on it that I experienced and that other people I've worked with have discovered. I will share some parts of these others' journeys and my own, to show how we may learn to understand and experience the individuation process—our quest for life and wholeness.

I believe that our need for renewal often reflects the pressures

INTRODUCTION

of society on our spirits and how it has molded the way we see our lives. The Grail legend supports this viewpoint by having the entire kingdom become a wasteland. In other words we are as much a product of the attitudes of our society and cultural heritage as we are of our biological makeup and childhood experiences. While in some cases either one of these forces may have greater effect than the others, both combine to influence us throughout our lives. The emotional unrest and the turmoil I was caught up in at age thirty-three were deeply rooted in the societal attitudes into which I was born. If this weren't the case then I wouldn't have become so depressed when the American Dream of a good job, success, home, and family didn't provide enough meaning for my life. In the following pages we will also take a careful look at how society's attitudes affect our development, our experiences of life, and our values.

In his classic study, *The Hero with a Thousand Faces,* Joseph Campbell teaches us that there is a timeless symbolic path that pictures the process of growing beyond our current situations. Myths and legends outline the hero's or heroine's journey, which is a metaphor for developing the personal awareness that leads to a more enlightened personality. A personality that has *substance.* The stories that disclose this path show it begins with failure. In their examples we can see that whenever a culture (an interior personal culture as well as an exterior collective one) is collapsing, stagnating, fragmenting, and declining, the mythic hero or heroine is called to leave the conventional wisdom and practices of society to undergo the trials and tribulations of becoming a person of individual *substance.* Once this substance is attained he or she must return to everyday life with new courage, clarity of thought, and a fresh perspective on reality to help revitalize the collective situation.

From the psychological viewpoint this myth is a metaphor for the development of renewed personal consciousness. Which means we must take strong action to go beyond our naive explanations for our experiences and seek out more substantive thoughts about the potentials and themes in our lives. The knowledge of this mythic pattern was comforting and challenging to me. From it I learned that what I perceived as a failing life could be a strong invitation to renewal, strength, and vitality on a level previously unknown to me. Most journeys begin with some sort of failure, threat, or feeling of vulnerability such as a job loss, marital crisis, loss of someone close, personal dissatisfaction, or deep disappointment. Odysseus, the conqueror of Troy, lost everything in his efforts to return home. Inanna, the queen of heaven, had to descend into hell before becoming her full self. And Aeneas was reduced from a powerful prince to a fugitive before he began the founding of Rome. These great stories illustrate the beauty and the utter humanity of our predicaments as well as their hidden potentials. And, they brought me hope. They gave me the knowledge that so many people in the past and present had or were having this experience in their own ways that it was part of being human. Hope, knowing I was not alone in my situation, and trusting that with work it could lead to a deeper experience of meaning and of life as well as a more substantial personality were all very helpful to me, and they continue to be.

As I've practiced over the years I've discovered that many people are afraid to look within themselves. Some fear they'll find things they won't like. Others feel that close self-examination might cause them to make radical changes that could hurt their self-images, the people they love, or their careers. This fear is primarily based on our society's idea that only concrete, outer changes in our lives can solve our problems. This idea is so entrenched in us that we aren't even aware of it. It helped me to learn that this attitude is a mistake. I discovered that taking the time and trouble to learn about myself brought about inner changes, lightened my moods, and cleared away many of my misunderstandings about how I thought life should be.

Personal renewals begin as inner journeys, and substance is built within ourselves before it begins to affect the outer world. The process of attaining self-knowledge both softens and strengthens us

INTRODUCTION

and serves to help us love and appreciate life and other people. It often affirms and enriches our choice of partners, vocations, and lifestyles. The unhappy or dissatisfied ones among us who impulsively leave jobs and relationships are not doing so from self-knowledge. When the inner quest brings change we can be comforted by knowing it's authentic, has been carefully thought through, and values our pasts and other people.

The ancient Greek philosopher Heraclitus pointed out that "a man's character is his fate." In my terms I would say that the amount of substance we build into our personalities gives us a hand in effecting our personal destinies. "Substance" is an interesting word that has dual roots. It comes from the Latin word *substantia*, which means "being" or "essence," and from the word *substáre*, which means "to stand firm." To be a person of substance means to know and stand upon one's essential nature and to be aware that there is a nature in all things that underlies their outward manifestation. The forces unleashed by modern society require that we all become people of substance, able to know ourselves and stand firm upon our essential natures or risk living inauthentic, incomplete lives.

In Western history the men and women who took first steps down new roads had to begin their journeys by stepping outside of the social character of their times. Names like Martin Luther King, Dietrich Bonhoeffer, Yitzhak Rabin, Golda Meir, Albert Einstein, Pablo Picasso, Robert Kennedy, Henry Ford, Sigmund Freud, and Betty Freidan remind us that our great thinkers, artists, scientists, inventors, and religious figures have often had to stand against the forces of their epochs. Yet they are the ones who have benefited us all with their vision and achievements. Their struggles have been admired throughout Western history, though we are often late in honoring them. But their lives show us that creative living and independent thinking bring hope and dignity to each of us, while following society's beaten path often leads to a loss of soul, a lust for power, and the destruction of human values.

Two thousand years ago the Christian faith enjoined us to love God with all of our heart, mind, and soul (Matthew 22:37–40). And to love our neighbor as ourselves. The Jewish tradition had an earlier version of this teaching that actually went a step further and suggested we learn to love the stranger as well. Along with the sanctity of the individual, these instructions are foundation stones in our religious legacy. As we progressed into modern times, rationalism, scientism, and technology ushered in a mechanical approach to life that values only what's concrete and measurable. For instance our self-esteem depends upon how we measure our success and acquisitions. How we compare ourselves to other people and appearances. The anxious eyes that parents keep on school achievement, grades, popularity, IQ scores, and SAT scores undermine the self-confidence of our children and teach them to live anxiety-based lives. In relationships, the concern with how often we make love, argue, or don't argue and how we manage as couples to get everything organized and carried out often drains the passion and love out of those relationships. The emphasis that our religious institutions have put on proper behavior as a measure of spirituality has smothered much of the heart and soul out of these organizations. It's apparent that many people have turned away from religion in their hearts even though some of them have continued to observe its forms and trappings.

However, we are born with certain necessities and potentials latent in our personalities. Among these inborn characteristics is the need for a system of orientation and devotion that provides purpose, meaning, and support for our lives. We usually call such a system "a religion" whether it has to do with a concept of God or not. This system helps us face our problems, create a vision of the future, insure our individual spiritual development, and understand the nature of joy. Without such a framework for life rich and poor alike lose their ways, experience life as meaningless, threatening, and confusing, and disintegrate into emotional illnesses, crime, and even insanity.

The practice of sacred selfishness means that we must pay careful attention to every aspect of our lives. We must seek to discover our religious or spiritual values and how they are guiding the way we live. This means we must find out if we have developed a secret religion—one that guides our lives without our realizing it. In real-

INTRODUCTION

ity the question we face isn't whether we'll have a religion or not. It's a question of what kind of a religion we'll have. As our society has lost touch with the transformational spiritual aspects of religion that lead to higher consciousness, we have left ourselves open to idolatry. By idolatry I mean having human-made secular values such as the search for satisfaction and arousal through having an enviable or powerful reputation, achievement, or material and sexual gratification, which possess us unconsciously and become our religion without our knowing it.

Whenever we discover that a child's self-esteem depends on having the latest computer game or wearing brand-name clothing seen in glossy catalogs or slick TV advertisements, we know we have lost our way and that consumerism has become our secret religion, the system that orients our lives and demands devotion. When our search for identity, self-confidence, and happiness is based primarily on what we have, our need for possessions has become our spiritual core. While capitalism is a very workable economic system, it can become very dangerous if we make it an unconscious religion. It then ceases to serve us as an economic system should and demands we serve it—and leaves us feeling overworked, overspent, and powerless. As we have become spiritually and psychologically impoverished, our search in life has degenerated into a search for thrills, indulgences, and satisfactions rather than for joy and meaning. The depression I felt and that many are feeling today has a major dimension that isn't due to childhood experience or biological heredity. It's due to the effects of a society that has lost its foundation in spirituality and the values of the heart.

The great teachings I've cited from our religious traditions are the most profound challenges to human development of which I know. To understand and live these instructions about love during the evolving period of a lifespan is a life's work in itself. This work is far more demanding than belonging to a "follow the rules" or a "feel good" religion. Without a deep understanding of human nature and our spiritual needs, religious institutions cannot possibly educate people to really figure what it means to love ourselves, our neighbor, God, and the stranger. Without the knowledge of our inner lives, psychological as well as spiritual, all that religious institutions can offer us is a superficial social structure that can't touch our unhappiness, our depression, or our spiritual impoverishment. In other words it can't touch, heal, and fulfill our hearts. I've found that Jungian psychology, which relies on the development of self-knowledge, honors and realizes the importance of love in healing, life, and joy, and proves immensely helpful when we try to understand their part in our lives.

The depth of these spiritual instructions may be greater than the scope of this book. However, one of my major concerns is how we must relearn to love ourselves, not in a sentimental, self-indulgent, or sickly selfish way, but in a manner that's authentic and that brings substance to our beings. True self-love comes from understanding ourselves and realizing how we have created a culture that requires we destroy our self-love, our very substance. When we replace it with a standard of self-alienation and self-indulgence that's needed on the one hand to keep our society functioning, on the other hand it's simultaneously destroying our finest values—destroying, indeed, our very souls.

Many theorists such as Freud, Jung, Adler, Fromm, and others have clearly seen and written about the adverse effect our society is having on our physical and mental health. I'm extremely grateful to these thinkers, and they've been a source of strength for me. Unfortunately mainstream psychology and counseling have failed to grasp the importance of their discoveries and continue to try to help people adjust to, and remain functional in, a society whose characteristics are increasingly causing their pain and suffering.

What Freud, Jung, and their followers observed and learned came from their experiences of working with people. Because this knowledge isn't obtained through statistical studies, which can never consider the individual, the prevailing attitude in professional and academic circles tends to ignore the discoveries and theories of depth

INTRODUCTION

psychology. Too often mainstream psychology and medicine are blinded by their own narrow points of view, and both individuals and society experience the suffering caused by this blindness.

The inner journey is exciting and rewarding and leads to the true capacity for loving life. I deeply regret the bias our society has developed against psychotherapy and the way therapists have picked up the jargon of treatments, disease, and dysfunction, which minimizes the fact that learning to live in a growthful way is healing. In my life and with most of the people I've worked with, I've found that while symptoms often spur us into the therapist's office or to read books like this one, seeking health once the process of self-discovery begins is exciting, interesting, and challenging. And the rewards of a more fulfilling, authentic, sacredly selfish life are treasures that can't be measured in ordinary terms.

PART I:
Breaking the Mold and Seeking a Path

Wherever a man goes, men will pursue him and paw him with their dirty institutions, and, if they can, constrain him to belong to their desperate oddfellow society.
—Henry David Thoreau

CHAPTER 1
Captives of Normalcy

For certain societies that people today like to call primitive, the dominating trait of life was not the economy—that is even true of the Middle Ages—but rather man's development.
—Erich Fromm

Whatever happiness is, it seems to wear many masks, and we have no objective way to tell whether we are happy or not. A few years ago this basic dilemma was captured in a *Calvin and Hobbes* cartoon. Calvin and his stuffed tiger and imaginary friend, Hobbes, were playing outdoors on a sunny day. Suddenly Calvin realized that it was late in the weekend and his free time was running out. As his awareness grew, his panic increased until in desperation he exclaimed, "Each moment I should be able to say, 'I'm having the time of my life, right now! Valuable minutes are disappearing forever, even as we speak! We've got to have more fun!'"

Lying serenely in their wagon, Hobbes ironically replied, "I didn't realize fun was so much work."

Calvin's creator Bill Waterson captured exactly how happiness has become an inaccessible experience for most of us. One of the most unconscious, and yet constant, of our ongoing activities is the pursuit of happiness. And, just when we think we've found it, it escapes us. Like an obsession-driven lover we discover that once our conquest is won, joy and satisfaction disappear and the fulfillment we hoped for remains an empty promise. The new car we were so thrilled over, or the boat, motorcycle, RV, appliance, or the expensive new outfit, frequently become boring or forgotten about before they're even paid for. We have become prisoners of advertising's messages that relentlessly define and redefine how we should look, what clothes we should wear, what color hair we should have, and what cosmetics we should use in order for us to be admired and envied, in order to be happy. We are bombarded with images of affluent, young, slender women and muscular men to make us think that everything from the right underwear to the newest diet will make us attractive and lead us to love, success, and happiness. Movies, TV shows, and advertisements focus on youth, comfort, and having fun, and would have us believe pleasure and contentment lie in the products we purchase.

Ironically, we have built a society that uses our desire for happiness to fuel an economy based on continued dissatisfaction. The harder we try to find happiness and fail to do so, the more frustrated we become and the more we consume. How do we find happiness? we ask ourselves. Why is it that we think everyone else knows the answer, but it continually eludes us?

When we talk about ourselves we are usually, or often, talking about ourselves in connection to others. This is only human and here, too, any product that has to do with relationships seems to have a market. Relationships, the term that really covers our longing to be known and loved and to know and love, are one of our most vulnerable areas. When it comes to relationships we are filled with hope and cynicism. The dilemmas we are experiencing in this area remind me of a comment Prince Charles made when questioned about love by a reporter around the time of his fairy-tale engagement to Princess Diana. Instead of answering the question he quipped, "Whatever love is." This appalling remark reflects the cynicism beneath our hope. But even cynicism and failure can fuel a market. We have over sixty thousand books in print advising us how to make our relationships successful, overcome their problems, and survive their failures.

A woman who had been married for sixteen years came in to see me for an initial visit. She sat down and said, "I'm tired of strug-

CAPTIVES OF NORMALCY

gling. I just want to be normal and happy!" As she finished her statement she was quietly weeping. Lisa was attractive and well dressed in a manner that showed she put care into things.

"Can you tell me more?" I asked.

Her shoulders slumped and I could see the weariness in her body and around her eyes.

"I've been married for all of these years," she said. "I think I love my husband, or at least I used to. But we argue a lot, and he doesn't seem to desire me. I don't think he even really sees me anymore. We don't talk. But we have two children and he's not a bad father. . . . I'm just exhausted. We've been to counseling. I've read a stack of books. I said it already. I'm worn-out. I want to be happy."

We talked about her situation, and Lisa felt better as she realized she was being understood and that other people had shared her experience. *I just want to be normal and happy* is a statement I hear almost daily in my practice. I hear it from men as well as women, frequently through tears. And I hear it from concerned and loving parents as they make the same wish for their children, "I just want them to be normal and happy." Every time I hear this plaintive lament I am touched by it, for it is so very human.

Wanting to be happy and normal is the result of how our society conditions us. I doubt if people in the Western world were very concerned with "normalcy" or "happiness" before the modern age. The great thinkers and teachers over the centuries have never seemed very concerned with these either. The ones like Lao-tze, Buddha, Socrates, the Prophets, Jesus, Thomas Aquinas, Meister Eckhart, Paracelsus, and Goethe were seeking more comprehensive visions of life. Their visions focused more on living a life that had meaning and purpose, one that could be fully experienced, including its sorrows. As different as their ideas often were, the Western teachers almost unanimously agreed that the development of our ability to understand and endure true suffering was necessary in order to open us to the experiences of joy and fulfillment. In general they considered happiness an incidental state, one that is sometimes here and sometimes not; they never considered it something to be sought or obsessed over.

In the modern world we have learned to emphasize practicality at the expense of much of the wisdom of the past. Focusing on science, technology, management, and the ability to learn a skill or profession to earn a living has left our system unbalanced. It is often the "non-practical" courses in classical literature, philosophy, drama, and the arts that teach us what it means to be human and what it's like to struggle with life's problems. If we really want our children to learn values we should have them seriously study these areas and the lessons they contain as a foundation for their academic journeys. Classical mythology, for instance, shows how we create our fate when we live with too much arrogance, act without self-awareness, and treat each other and the powers of life disrespectfully. Great art pictures these motifs and music expresses them. I love these studies and I'm convinced they have the capacity to teach us more than we would normally learn about what it means to be human and the values that support life rather than destroy it.

In the introduction to his best-selling book *Care of the Soul*, the former monk Thomas Moore says, "During the fifteen years I have been practicing psychotherapy I have been surprised how much of my studies in Renaissance psychology, philosophy and medicine have contributed to the work." Moore's writings grew out of the foundation begun by C. G. Jung. Jung was quick to see that the study of art, symbols, and literature led to insights in human nature and that developing a fulfilling life was art in itself.

Moore refers to Jung as "one of the most recent doctors of the soul." It was in this capacity in 1932, speaking before a convention of pastors, that Jung said, "Among all of my patients in the second half of life . . . there has not been one whose problems in the last resort was not that of finding a religious outlook on life."

If we stop and think about his statement for a moment and consider its implications, its audacity becomes clear. Imagine what it means to say our anxiety, depression, weight problems, addictions, relationship troubles, and other psychological difficulties come from the lack of a *religious orientation toward life,* instead of saying we're neurotic and dysfunctional!

Obviously Jung was a complex thinker who was not proposing a simplistic solution to our problems. Merely going to church or temple every week and ascribing to a religion that doesn't challenge us to grow, or participating in some spiritual exercises prescribed by self-help gurus, whether religious or secular, isn't what he had in mind. In fact, by the time Jung made this statement, he had long since come to feel the traditional Western religious systems no longer made much sense. His patients told him their churches and temples were out of touch with their personal needs for an experience of God and the sacred dimensions of life. My own work as an analyst indicates that this experience is as true today as it was for Jung over seventy years ago.

Awakening to Our Stories

To understand what Jung meant by a religious attitude in the second half of life, and what this attitude has to do with our emotional problems, we need to become more familiar with what he calls the *individuation process,* his model for how our personalities grow. While each of us grows and ages physically, whether we like it or not, the same fact isn't true about our psychological growth. The individuation process recognizes that after we have grown to a certain point psychologically, we have to make an effort; we have to pursue self-knowledge, to mature as people and live in a satisfying manner in our relationships and culture.

When we talk about the way we attain individuation, we are really talking about how we discover and participate in the stories we are creating with our lives. Every life in retrospect is a story and, like a story, has a beginning, unfolding events, and an end. In a narrative the story is concerned with individuals, how they feel and how people feel about them, rather than what they do or what is done to them. As I presented myself as a young man in the introduction of this book, I quickly became a character in a story and you automatically began to wonder where this story was leading. Stories become absorbing. So do our lives when we begin to look at them this way. They become stories when we are fully engaged in living them and begin to reflect on that experience.

Every life is full of tragedy and comedy, stops and starts, shaky beginnings, wanderings, wrong turns, and changes of direction. Frequently our years are marked by difficult loves, unfulfilled dreams and challenges, laughter, tears, separations, and reunions. Behind many of these events lie causes both within and outside of ourselves. For example, how our parents influenced us for better or worse and how we continue to live out our early conditioning affects our relationships today.

It may be helpful to look at some insights into stories offered by the novelist E. M. Forster. In his book *Aspects of the Novel*, he explains the difference between a simple story and a narrative that leads to meaning. In the latter we ask *why* to events. For example, "The king died and then the queen died" is a simple story. But if I say, "The king died and then the queen died of grief," we have a plot, a *pattern* that unfolds a deeper meaning within the sequence of events that happened as they did. As an analyst I would say that an unexamined life is, to a large extent, a simple story, while an examined life becomes a narrative that can lead us to understand a sense of purpose and completion in our lives and a feeling of satisfaction as we are living through them.

The process of individuation follows a pattern that gives every life a unique expression of meaning; I will discuss that pattern later in this book. Learning how to get in touch with the stories we are creating allows us to participate consciously in their development. We do this by reflecting on our lives, seeking insight into their events, and trying to understand how our feelings, bodies, and unconscious minds are participating in and responding to our stories. We will see some helpful techniques in this regard in part 2. But for now what's important to think about is this: that developing knowledge about our whole selves, expanding and deepening our self-awareness, is a key to learning about our individuation processes. And just as our stories go from beginning to end, our individuation, our psychological growth, must do the same.

By pursuing individuation with deliberation and honesty, Jung believed we could perceive the pattern or plot of the stories we are living and through this perception arrive at an understanding of a place of grace or true center in our personalities that he termed the "Self." The Self includes the unique pattern, the potential person, who is within each of us and seeks throughout a lifetime to be recognized and expressed through our conscious personalities and their actions. Therefore the Self includes our conscious and unconscious minds and our potentials.

The basic outcome of this complicated process is a growth in consciousness. As we come to know ourselves more fully and become more alert to the aspects of our stories, in the past and present, we are naturally increasing our capacities for expressing the potential people we are meant to be. Simply put, the better we know ourselves the more personal and pure our actions become because they aren't hidden, curtailed, or contaminated by the forces that shaped our early lives. Authentic actions disclose who we are to other people. Without self-knowledge our behaviors basically reflect needs common to everyone or the training and wounds of our childhoods. I recall being visited by a young college professor who told me with considerable anger that he was in trouble with his department chairman and the dean. He felt they didn't understand what a creative teacher he was.

"They make me feel stupid," he said, "like an adolescent." Pausing, he then continued, "Like my father did."

And as you may imagine his friends were the other "misunderstood" rebels on the faculty who actually invited most of the trouble they were in. In another situation a woman who consulted with me had an angry, belittling father and found she would freeze when someone raised his or her voice. By learning to understand ourselves better we can discover the negative effects of our histories, work to change them, build on our strengths and potentials, and relate to people and events in a more straightforward, authentic manner. Every time we take a step toward becoming aware of and transforming one of these past influences, we become less of a prisoner of the forces in our histories and assure that our future actions will express more of who we really are.

Generally, it doesn't take much reflection to realize that most of us haven't gotten out from under the early influences in our lives nearly as much as we like to think we have. It's difficult to fully separate or individuate from our families or from institutional and cultural influences, and for good reason. They affect us before our identities are secure; we actually use them for models; their values are the initial foundation of our values; they have power and we don't; and we're trained to make decisions and behave in a manner that meets their approval. We're taught to "color within the lines" or "pay attention," and trained to "hide our feelings." We're silenced with injunctions like, "Don't you dare talk back." Brushed off with comments like "Don't bother me I'm busy," and taught to be passive by being told to "turn the other cheek." "Forgive seventy times seven." "Honor your father and mother." In a similar vein we hear, "You're not living up to your potential"; "Men are strong"; "Women aren't good at math"—and other countless messages reflecting family and cultural influences that are structured into our personalities while we are too young to evaluate them. I remember a young woman, a physician with two children, who still felt compelled to scrub out the bathrooms the way her mother did. "The cleaning woman just never gets it done right," she would explain. In another situation a man forty years old and president of his own company couldn't tell his wife what he really wanted from her. "I think she'd actually prefer it if I did," he reported, "but every time I try to I remember how many times my mother told me to be gentle and thoughtful to women, not demanding like my father."

The expectations and values we grow up with are insidious, and even the negative ones are often seductive. How many of us try to chase away our restless dissatisfaction, despite our nice homes, jobs, and families, by asking ourselves, What have I got to complain about? How can I complain when so many other people are less fortunate? And, our ability to face dissatisfactions is complicated even further if we have reached a level of education and success beyond that of our families of origin. It's very scary for us to outgrow our families psychologically, and realizing we are doing so may leave us feeling terribly guilty and even ashamed of ourselves. It can also leave us feeling like exiles, without a home or roots or people who care about us and understand us on a basic level.

I remember a thirty-one-year-old woman who told me, "I've just felt horrible about my parents since my wedding." She had been raised in a small southern town where her parents had been good but ordinary people. Once she was out of high school she moved to a large city, worked her way through college, and after a few years in the business world became a buyer in a well-known department store. When she was twenty-nine, she married a magazine writer in a small, lovely church in the city. During the rehearsal dinner, the service, and the reception she noticed her parents were uncomfortable and didn't fit in with her friends and colleagues. She said, "I could see the distress in their eyes. They didn't feel at home with our friends and they acted like I was someone they hardly knew. I feel so ashamed because I love them but I don't even want to go see them."

She isn't an isolated case. Conway had become a gifted minister and was embarrassed by his mother's loud, opinionated way of dominating a conversation. And Karen, a popular young woman who acted as the hostess in the restaurant she and her husband owned, was terrified of being around her parents. Their ethnic prejudices, which they made no effort to hide, embarrassed her in front of her husband, in-laws, and friends and made her want to keep her children away from their grandparents. Duncan had even stronger feelings. He came from a violent, abusive family and after years of therapy is doing well while his brother and sister continue to struggle with mental illness and addictions. Duncan says he has "survivor's guilt" and is in conflict with a society that bombards him with sentimental advertisements on Mother's Day and Father's Day while he despises his parents.

In another situation a friend of mine got stuck in a pattern of conflict with his parents that lasted for decades. He is a person I have always admired as having a truly brilliant mind. It was easy for him to excel in his classes and later win scholarships to universities and graduate schools that were beyond his parents' dreams. But early in his life he began to feel that his parents were expecting more and more from him and were using his performance to bolster their own self-esteem and social status. The more they expected of him without trying to find out who he really was, the more he resented the pressure he felt from them. As a result he has spent a lifetime being a magnificent failure—making lots of money and losing it, having a lovely family and turning it into a disaster, pleasing and destroying, living in a cycle of success and defeat that carries on his early conflicts. It is easy, much too easy, to remain trapped in the expectations and values of our parents and follow the highways approved by our society, or to live our lives in rebellion against them, stuck in the swamps with other people trapped by their resentments. Yet, nature intends us to be more than the simple tales we've developed out of adaptation, fear, and compensation. We are attracted to becoming more conscious and we also fear it, because it means a journey out of our past illusions into personal responsibility for ourselves.

All of this complex psychological language is, of course, only a tool to help us examine our lives and find that "story." Our stories must be unraveled from our tangled personal histories and the pressures of our lives—and then lived as fully as possible. The individuation process guides us in living our stories with meaning, a sense of honesty and destiny that is unique and our own, while remaining part of life's greater story.

If we stop and think about this process it will make sense. We feel more secure once we realize that it isn't necessary to struggle to be like someone else or meet another's ideals. As we feel more complete, at home within ourselves, free to explore our creative abilities, developing our strength and authority, it becomes natural to seek the ways we resemble the human "family," and how we can relate, belong, and contribute without again losing ourselves.

It is our lot, the Jungian author Robert Johnson tells us, to live through the dualities and conflicts in our inner and outer lives until we become conscious of the underlying unity within us that is the source out of which our complexity and vitality flows. The Self is a metaphor for this unity. Whether we want to follow our mind or our heart, or are stuck between them, they both have the same source.

However you look at us—body, mind, spirit, conscious, and unconscious are all parts of the same whole. The Self is a kaleidoscope that recognizes all the aspects of our being and all the potentials within us that may develop and emerge into a unique pattern of life. The unity experienced by an illuminated person, one who has lived and attained a level of consciousness above the ordinary, is often thought of as a knowledge of the soul, of the image of God, the divine or transcendent within each human life. The path toward the Self, the individuation process, goes hand in hand with the development of consciousness.

Individuation: The Path to Growth and Authenticity

In understanding the individuation process and how it can work for us, it helps to know a few basic things about the levels of consciousness we can obtain. To begin with, our levels of consciousness or psychological maturity become increasingly based on self-awareness rather than age after we have reached adulthood. Unlike our physical growth, which is generally automatic, our growth in consciousness requires intentional effort, and is a process that takes us through four general stages:

- *Simple consciousness*
- *Complex consciousness*
- *Individual consciousness*
- *Illuminated consciousness*

Our development in the first two general stages of consciousness, first simple and then complex consciousness, relies heavily on the modeling done by our parents, families, and other people, and on training, education, and the development of skills. The two stages that follow, individual and illuminated consciousness, depend upon attaining a deep knowledge of ourselves and the transcendent aspects of life. For example you may have a Ph.D. in psychology, which means you are highly trained in the area of complex consciousness.

But it doesn't mean you automatically know very much about your inner life. The same thing can be said if you have a Ph.D. in theology. It doesn't necessarily mean you have had an experience of the divine. Higher consciousness requires more than education.

No one begins life as a "conscious" individual capable of making self-responsible decisions. That identity, known in technical terms as *ego-development,* comes much later, and develops in stages from childhood through adulthood. *Simple* consciousness covers the period of time that begins at birth and encompasses the years of our early lives when our ability to learn and act responsibly is a potential slowly being fulfilled. Our parents, families, schools, churches, places in society, and the media introduce us to life in the world. They teach us that the world is safe or threatening, abundant or impoverished, educated or ignorant, a place to give to or to take from. They also teach us their perceptions of reality—for instance, "This is a vicious dog-eat-dog world," as well as other basic attitudes covering a wide range of topics such as racial or ethnic groups, religions, and virtues.

The second stage, *complex* consciousness, develops as we grow through adolescence into adulthood. During this stage we become aware of and attempt to undertake the social and personal tasks that generally define adulthood. In my generation in the late 1950s, graduating from high school or college, getting married, and owning a home generally defined adulthood. My father told me, "When you get married or reach twenty-one, you're a man and on your own." In primitive societies, elaborate initiation ceremonies marked this transition from childhood to responsible adulthood. These ceremonies often culminated with the initiate receiving a new name and public recognition as an adult. As an official adult, the former initiate was no longer dependent upon or subservient to his or her parents and had to carry an adult share of tribal responsibilities.

Growing into adulthood includes forming and testing our identities in the temperamental forge of adolescence and young adulthood. It is a crucial period when we begin to more closely observe the world around us and the world immediately outside our parents' sphere of influence. As we pass from adolescence into adulthood we need to discover a sense of "who we are" that we can rely on. One that has some competencies, and can persevere enough to go through whatever has to be gone through. We need to become secure enough within ourselves to separate from our parents, become self-reliant, and develop our own personal and social relationships. Technically, we refer to developing our sense of identity as *ego-development* and developing our ability to get along with other people at work and in relationships as cultivating our *public face* or *persona*.

Trying to work out an identity begins with models because we have to have something to identify with to get us started. Hopefully, we will discover models that fit our abilities and strengths, but this process is never easy. When I was bogged down in my sophomore year in college and couldn't choose a major, I eventually became so desperate I chose the basic social model of getting married and thereby getting "serious" about life. Suddenly my friends and family became approving and supportive instead of worried and concerned about me. In other words I now had an identity that people could understand, not necessarily the right one, but one that could get me started and represented the "social clothes" most of us need to wear at this age.

As children we tried out grown-up identities by pretending to be doctors, teachers, nurses, and so on. We were alert to the effect the games had on the adults in our lives—whether they brought approval or disapproval. Interested uncles and aunts asked us what we wanted to be when we grew up. By age seven or eight, I learned to reply "a lawyer," which assured a favorable response. While I enjoyed the response I had little idea what lawyers really did. I only knew it brought me validation from "big" people, and I now realize how much power this process had in affecting how I saw careers, social graces, manners of dress, and other attitudes.

By the 1970s, life had become more complicated. Few adults were asking children what they wanted to be when they grew up because the adults were either dissatisfied with their own careers, frustrated with their relationships, or rethinking their own places in life. Parents often copped out on helping children seek adult identities by telling them they could be anything they wanted to be. Children are smart enough to know that's not true, and the lack of adult expectations and guidance often left the children floundering and unable to get on the track toward adult identities and a sense of responsibility.

Our parents' views of their unrealized opportunities also play a role in our identity formation. My father, for example, spent a rich career as an educator. As time went by, many of the people he taught became very wealthy. On the one hand, their success gave him a gratifying feeling of accomplishment in his work. On the other hand, however, part of him began to feel wistful that he could have been more successful in business—that he could have made more money, had a higher standard of living, enjoyed more respect in the eyes of society. Part of him felt fulfilled and part of him felt resentful. As a result of this conflict he urged me to go into business rather than academics, without considering what might be the most personally meaningful career for me. We are all shaped by these two models: family and society.

A few years ago I worked with a middle-aged physician. Fred was a highly skilled doctor who was board certified in three areas. But he was wondering if he should have been a writer. In exploring his past Fred felt he had been guided toward medical school by his mother, who was a nurse. Because he was so convinced that his mother was the dominant influence in his life, I wondered about the role of his father, a retired contractor, and his hidden effect on Fred. I shared my thoughts with Fred and suggested he ask his father what he thought had guided so much of Fred's early ambitions. A few days later Fred had a surprising conversation with his dad. He discovered his father had wanted to be a doctor but hadn't pursued his dream after he got out of the army at the end of World War II because his wife was pregnant. His dad said that it may have been his quiet endorsement that influenced Fred more than he imagined. And, of course, everyone in Fred's extended family and in the small community he had grown up in was thrilled with the choice. Once Fred understood the motives and circumstances that had molded his course, he felt a sense of freedom.

Instead of changing careers he set about figuring out how to transform his career into one based on his values and how he wanted to live them.

Fred discovered that he could practice in a manner that fulfilled his needs to find meaning in his work by becoming more concerned with people and less science oriented. He let his intuition and feelings become part of his work on a regular basis and soon left his prestigious, high-profile practice group to join a smaller group whose approach to medicine was more compatible with his new ideas. He also realized he could spend more time with his wife and family and still make a good living.

Stop and think about these situations for a moment. Who do you know that might have been guided to live their parents' unrealized ambitions? What about yourself? How many of your choices were influenced by this often subtle but sometimes not so subtle pressure?

Erich Fromm believed that character determined behavior. In his studies of how society affects our development, he concluded that every society shares a common character structure, meaning a common set of traits that motivate us to behave in ways that fulfill the goals and ideals of our culture. For example we are taught and conditioned to believe our self-worth depends upon our achievements, our financial value, the things we own, how productive we are, and how other people evaluate us. Fromm called this collection of traits our *social character*. Society from its largest institutional units down to its smallest, the family, endeavors to teach us these traits.

In many ways the social character of our culture operates like a tribal mind-set, a collection of basic beliefs to which every member subscribes. This "social character" continues its efforts to contain us as adults just as it attempted to mold our earlier growth, just as it has always. Even primitive people identified with their tribe's model for living and its values, beliefs, and customs. To be a member of the tribe meant to have security, acceptance, and to be considered a human being. To violate a tribal value resulted in expulsion from the community, which in turn cost that person his (or her) identity in a real as well as a psychological sense; it turned him into a nonperson with little hope and little chance of surviving in a harsh world. Even today events that threaten our identities and self-images may touch this place of primal fear in our heritage, and cause us to dread feeling alienated and alone.

The feeling of belonging in our families, peer groups, and communities is a powerful sensation. To be with people or family with whom we feel spiritually, emotionally, and physically comfortable makes us feel secure and that life is manageable even if our circumstances could be a lot better. People stay in bad marriages and poor jobs to hold onto this security and because they are afraid of the loneliness and disapproval that change could bring. The power of fear, the implicit threat of denouncement or disappointment, makes many of us afraid of crossing the boundaries set by the conventional values and beliefs we have internalized and on which our self-images rest.

This fear blocks our development and makes it difficult to break free of beliefs that no longer serve our growth. It's difficult to shed the old skins made of familiar or hardened beliefs and attitudes. We can even get stuck in this process. In other words fear can block our growing past the stage of complex consciousness into that of individual consciousness. We fear the prospect of divorce, the embarrassment that may come with the loss of income, the criticism by our partners, families, or close friends. We even fear going to therapists and analysts because we want to feel we are OK and don't want other people to see us as needy, flawed, or crazy. That is when we feel stuck. Overwhelmed by the fear of what we might lose rather than inspired by what we might gain. The core of this book will revolve around the problems of this crucial transition point in our lives and the promise it offers.

When we approach the third stage, *individual* consciousness, it's as if a door were opening, inviting us into the experience of personal authenticity and of feeling truly at home within ourselves.

CAPTIVES OF NORMALCY

Individual consciousness moves us beyond the mind-set of social norms. During this stage we begin to become aware of our unique natures as something *separate* from the forces and values that have molded the roles we are living. In fact this may be the first point at which we realize we are actually living roles. This awareness, unless it is quickly repressed, will lead us into a swirl of conflicting emotions as we begin to question ourselves about who we are, and to ask ourselves if this is *all there is*.

If we are unable to confront our earlier choices at this point, we may be devoured by our disappointment and resentment. Sometimes these feelings bring some people into therapy while the fear and denial they stir up keep others away.

The "midlife crisis" that bruises or ensnares so many of us is a collision of just this: a point where we come into conflict with social norms and expectations. The values we have been living by begin to seem repressive, and being "responsible" feels dull and unsatisfying. We long to step off the never-ending treadmill of obligations.

At this time I want to pause and ask a question. What happens if we have reached age thirty-five or forty and *haven't* been able to fully form workable adult identities? The answer is that sooner or later we will also find our lives breaking down and coming to a stop. But this crisis won't be a midlife crisis, although they have many similarities. Rather it will be an *identity* crisis that too needs to be resolved in order for us to become actual adults, no matter how old we happen to be. This situation isn't unusual because starting in the 1960s our society has become complex and the guidelines for figuring out when we have become adults have broken down. At the same time society is doing less to foster self-responsibility. The following example portrays a grown-up who hasn't fully grown into adult consciousness.

I first met Sam at one of my workshops on dreams and creativity. He was quiet, but also jovial and warm, and gave the impression of being very sensitive. People were surprised to find out this quiet fellow with a ponytail was a lawyer. But they smiled knowingly when he disclosed he worked for the legal aid society. As he shared bits and pieces of himself, he mesmerized the other participants with his enthusiasm for Tai Chi and other Eastern spiritual practices. Everyone pictured Sam as perceptive and caring.

One morning Sam phoned me for a private appointment. When we sat down together a few days later he said, "I've got to find a life." As Sam's story unfolded I found out he was forty-three. He had gone through adolescence in the 1960s and '70s. Sam had been married twice, had two daughters, and his current wife was threatening to leave him if he didn't quit smoking pot.

Sam said his wife felt like there was "just nobody at home" inside of him. His teenage daughters were embarrassed that their dad smoked pot and by their comparatively shabby standard of living. Sam's life was in crisis, but his was really a deferred crisis from his adolescence. At that time he took the path of going to law school to satisfy his parents. But inwardly he identified with many of the rebellious values of his adolescence. He has remained stuck in that quandary for almost twenty years, working for legal aid in order to defy his ambitious parents' values and using pot to medicate his feelings of self-alienation. Sam's self-analysis was correct. He needed to find a life, one based on an adult identity and a self-responsible place in the world of work and relationships.

After two months of analysis Sam recognized his addiction and began an outpatient drug treatment program in addition to analysis. His wife decided to stay with him as he began the quest to rediscover himself. In Sam's case, taking up the struggle for a stronger adult identity had to take place before he had a real foundation for seeking *individual consciousness,* and for seeking further self-knowledge.

Once we have achieved adult identities we must face another turning point that is just as significant as moving from childhood into adulthood. It is one of the most important periods in our lives, and when it is simply known as "midlife crisis," it may become one of the most misunderstood. It is misunderstood because we are so oriented toward practicality and toward our outer lives, that it is difficult for us to hear our inner spiritual events and understand them. The discontent with life that causes our midlife crises is a call to develop higher consciousness that we no longer know how to recognize as an epiphany, an awakening. Families, friends, co-workers, and even our children often want us to get back to normal and keep soldiering down life's highway. Instead, we should *welcome* this call as a time to deepen our lives, as a spiritual turning point, and an opportunity to redirect our energies inward, to reclaim parts of ourselves that we lost or never found as we were growing up. This call, if we have the courage to answer it, demands that we look back and ask, At what point did I betray my own existence and begin turning my energy against myself?

Because of its paradoxical nature this is a perplexing time for us. It frequently comes at a time when we may think our lives are working the best they ever have. We are no longer young. Our identities seem secure. We have earned our way in life, have given up some illusions and fantasies, and feel grounded in reality. Little do we realize that instead of preparing a sure highway into the future, we have prepared the ground for our next transformation. Sometimes, our inability to recognize the spiritual turning points in our lives frequently forces them to appear covertly as illness, emotional problems, and other crises. Sometimes the restlessness and vague feelings of fear and unease we feel may reappear in external forms such as affairs, divorce, the loss of a job, the illness or death of a loved one—symptoms, and not the cause, of an emotional hemorrhage we are not ready to face. And sometimes there are small ailments like headaches, anxiety attacks, fatigue at work, and increased moodiness that, if left unattended to, may escalate into alcoholism, obesity, use of tranquilizers, sexual difficulties, heart attacks, and repeated changes in jobs and spouses.

Whatever the symptoms, something has happened to shake our values in the old systems. We may seem to have everything a person in the conventional world would want, but we are miserable. Our lives seem to lack meaning; we can't figure out what our partners want from us, or we can't control our teenagers, and everything we try to do seems to make matters worse.

When these events come along we have a choice.

We can listen to them or shut them out. We can choose to ignore them and go right on driving ourselves down the well-travelled interstate of social convention, being good lawyers, doctors, businesspeople, ministers, homemakers, college professors—typical normal people. But the Self I discussed earlier (the whole personality including the inborn urge to grow) may not stand for this kind of stagnation. This Self is determined to create psychological growth and will continue to repeat certain calls and escalate predicaments and ailments until they get renewed attention. Of course, we have additional options: We can stiffen and rigidify our attitudes, cling to the highway, and perhaps even become pillars in the community—in effect pillars of the past. Or we can try to placate our restlessness by following the latest trends in self-help and health while others choose to become more rigid in their religious and political attitudes. These health-promoting activities may seem appealing, but we have to be careful we are not using them in the wrong way, to avoid facing our deeper selves. If we are going to confront our lives and grow into them, we must accept our emotions and begin to ask ourselves who we are and how we are living.

These kinds of questions open us to new ways of looking at life and the conflicts we experience when we try to live as individuals within a social group. They also compel us to examine the principles steering our lives and to look at the ways we have interpreted our religious teachings and to assess the degree to which our modern experiences of religion can restore our souls and guide our existence. Thinkers like Sir Laurens Van der Post, Carl Jung, Joseph Campbell, James Hillman, and Paul Tillich have agreed that we have misunderstood our religious figures like Buddha, Moses, and Christ. They suggest that these figures exemplify the pattern of individuation—the journey to the true Self and how to live in an authentic manner that expresses our wholeness and fulfills our best potentials. They would emphasize, for example, that the great fallacy in theology is to take the life of a spiritual figure like Christ literally rather than in its full symbolic meaning. The results of this mistake lead us to advocate a blind imitation of his life and teachings and miss the real message, which is that we should live our lives to the fulfillment of our natures, gifts, potentials, and destinies, as truly as Christ lived to the end to which he had been born. The same points can be made about the lives of other spiritual leaders such as Buddha and Moses.

The Jungian analyst Edward Edinger in his moving book *Ego and Archetype* uses the story of Christ as seen from a psychological perspective to amplify this point and to outline how we may grow in self-awareness. When we look at Christ's teachings in this manner, many of his seemingly paradoxical statements take on new meanings. One of his admonitions symbolizes part of the pattern our growth must follow: "Do not suppose that I have come to bring peace on earth: it is not peace I bring but a sword. For I have come to set a man against his father, a daughter against her mother, a daughter-in-law against her mother-in-law." (Matthew 10:35, 36). That is, if we are going to have our own lives, we must become self-responsible and independent from our parents and their influence. The paradox in this teaching is that psychological and spiritual development call for us to accept the contradictions and sufferings that occur when we break with conformity in a manner that ultimately leads to a higher level of fulfillment.

Our foes, in terms of our struggle to become individuals, are the members of our own households. It makes sense. They are the ones closest to us. The ones it was natural for us to have identified either with or against, whose approval and acceptance we sought and whose criticism we feared. Establishing our own individual lives is the very foundation for psychological development. Abraham had to leave the country of his father. Buddha had to leave his father's palace. The disciples of Christ had to leave home and vocations. The symbolic pattern is clear. Our growth depends upon our ability to muster the courage and awareness to separate ourselves from the group mind-set of our families and the conventional wisdom they embody. Which is not to say their values are wrong. We must disentangle ourselves from them and then decide how we want to relate to them from our own standpoints.

The symbolic image of the sword represents the power, the self-awareness we must develop to make these difficult discriminations. It also suggests the amount of strength we need and the pain that may result as we cut away our deepest ties in the service of beginning a new journey in life. Many of us have fooled ourselves into believing we have made this step when we actually have not. In my own case, for instance, I thought I'd outgrown my father's aggressive sports mentality and felt superior to him, only to discover in my own inner search that I had a very strong, but hidden, competitive drive that everyone was aware of but me.

In many ways this passage into individual consciousness is the hardest of the four stages. This is because, in general, we have the social and emotional support of our families, friends, and communities as we struggle through the first two stages. The passage into the third stage is lonelier. Often we must work by ourselves on ourselves and seemingly against the values and popular attitudes promoted by our society. But the next stage, *illuminated* consciousness, makes the journey worthwhile. It is that place we reach when we have realized our individual personalities and recognized the existence of a greater Self, or the image of God or the divine, that is within us.

As children we often saw the path to illuminated consciousness illustrated in fairy tales, where a young man or woman begins in poor or humble surroundings, passes through a series of trials and adventures, and ultimately becomes a king or queen. Their adventures and close calls cause them to rise above their previous selves, and summon unknown and helpful potentials within their own personalities (often pictured as helpful animals, wise old men and women, brothers and sisters, and even villains) until their journeys culminate in their ability to unify their kingdoms. Translated into psychological terms, they've brought a sense of wholeness, prosperity, and uniqueness to their personalities.

It's a good idea for adults to read fairy tales as well. Once upon a time, in fact, they were indeed listened to by young and old alike, and helped many generations to learn about life. With the same complexity as myths, they refer to many different levels of experience at once. In an Italian fairy tale, which I found in a collection by Italo Calvino, there's a story that shows the pattern of a woman's journey into fully becoming herself. The story is "Silent for Seven Years," and it begins as a tired, angry father returns home. When his sons run to him in excitement he impatiently curses them and they immediately end up as tormented prisoners of the Devil. While these events are happening the children's mother stands by passively, failing to help her offspring. Then the boys' sister leaves home in an effort to find and rescue her brothers. When she meets the Devil he tells her that to free them she must remain silent for seven years.

During these seven years she faces many trials and conflicts that tempt her to speak. In her first adventure a handsome prince discovers her in the forest and marries her. Later the jealous mother of the prince betrays her by accusing the poor girl of giving birth to a dog. Unable to speak for herself she has to flee for her life as the angry old mother of the prince wants to execute her. Next, she assumes a masculine role as a soldier. Finally she finds herself part of a band of outlaws and murderers. Even on the verge of her execution after being captured, she keeps silent and at the moment of her impending death, the seven years are up, a reprieve comes, her brothers are freed, and the king recognizes her and, having learned of her innocence, takes her back as his queen.

The tale is one many women who have successfully made the passage into individual consciousness can relate to as they consider their past experiences. Leaving home, redeeming lost aspects of ourselves, trying and sometimes failing at different roles, persevering until we find our strength and voice prepare us to face our true selves and live authentically. Becoming a king or queen means that we feel good about ourselves, competent, whole, and enthused about life, ready to discover more about where our stories are taking us. Isn't that a happy ending in itself?

The Individuation Process as Stages of the Development of Consciousness

Stage	Description
1. *Simple Consciousness*	The naive, developing consciousness of childhood
2. *Complex Consciousness*	The consciousness required to fulfill the societal tasks of adulthood
3. *Individual Consciousness*	The awareness of ourselves as separate from the forces that molded us
4. *Illuminated Consciousness*	The realization of our unique personalities and their relationship to our deeper selves and all life

Society's Illusion of Normalcy

Part of our task as we are growing is to develop personalities and identities that assure us we can take care of ourselves. We need the education and training that will enable us to make a living, along with the personal capacity to make friends and have other relationships. Our society is complicated, and we need the social skills that will enable us to interact with various institutions ranging from the grocery store and local schools to government agencies and medical facilities. We also need to develop a foundation of social ethics that will guide our relationships and minimize our conflicts. The way we experience the world and the shape our personalities or identities take as we grow up are informed by primary forces. They are: the effects of our biological characteristics; the wounds, traumas,

CAPTIVES OF NORMALCY

and inspirations we experienced during our childhoods; and the social character of our times.

Both our biology and our childhood experiences may present serious issues with which we have to learn to deal. For instance, biological concerns may range from such things as being born into a minority or having birth defects, physical handicaps, or other genetic problems. If our personality development was injured by traumatic experiences such as the serious illness or death of close family members, alcoholic or otherwise damaging parents, or harmful social situations, we may have to be willing to retrace our steps in psychotherapy or in some other manner to heal these old hurts before our growth can continue. Frequently we find these old wounds becoming more focused, more challenging, more insistent as we approach middle age. The poet Rainer Maria Rilke points out that we all leave childhood unprepared for adult life; that childhood is a helpless, complicated time whose struggles mark us all; and that we must continually come back to our histories to integrate them further into our destinies. Whatever our biological inheritances are or however we were wounded growing up, we also need to realize that the social character of our eras dramatically affect who we become, usually without our realizing it.

Every society develops a model for the character of its members. This model is made up of collective attitudes that are so common we have trouble naming them, and once we can name one it's terribly hard to get out from under its influence. They make up a cluster of social attitudes that inform the ways we evaluate ourselves. The adages that women should be thin, that eating soothes emotion and so does buying, that we judge ourselves in relationship to others and to advertising images, and that we can always be more efficient and get more accomplished are all particular and familiar mind-sets that continue to drive most of us. These attitudes strongly affect how we act, feel, and think—and how we believe we should act, feel, and think.

Society develops such mind-sets in order to keep its values and structures operating. Its institutions such as families, schools, churches, the media, and advertising attempt to mold our development so we fit the model of the social character. This model is imprinted on us so thoroughly and so subtly that we generally take it for granted that its attitudes and values are our own. Erich Fromm points out that when we define ourselves by what we have—by the cars we drive, the neighborhoods we live in, the logos on the shirts we wear— we are actually increasing our feelings of powerlessness at a deeper level. By living in this way he says we are committing what the Old Testament claims is one of our greatest mistakes: living without joy in the midst of plenty (Deuteronomy 28:47).

Looking back over the last few hundred years can help us see how our social character has changed and how it now operates in a self-centered, sickly selfish manner. In the seventeenth century when goods were scarce, self-denial and thrift were central themes in our social character structure. As time progressed so did the importance of economics in society. By the nineteenth century the economic force driving society needed capital to fuel it and saving money became a widely recognized virtue. The money saved allowed the banks to fund the capitalization of our industrializing nation. During this period of our history it was considered irresponsible, even immoral, to spend money we didn't have. Today the opposite is true. We subscribe to the notion that spending money we don't have is the proper thing to do. Imagine what our lives would be like without credit card or bank debt. Even our government supports and sanctions indebtedness and consumer spending. Would home ownership, the foundation of the American Dream, be even possible without the tax incentives both political parties vow to protect?

We teach people to spend in order to create demand and employment, and to drive our economy. These imperatives have progressed so far that a marketing orientation governs our entire lives; we have to consider *ourselves* as commodities that should be sold or marketed—just think, for instance, of the free agents market. Think of the many things we do to enhance our credentials and resumes by creating a seemingly endless array of awards, honors, certificates, degrees, boards to serve on, continuing education requirements, publications, and professional associations. In addition we are taught to consume everything immediately, compulsively, or as our old friend Calvin reminded us in the opening scene of this chapter, "Valuable minutes are disappearing . . . We've got to have more fun."

This pattern of accomplishment and frenzy, acquisition and emptiness has become one of our most insidious and unconscious driving forces. But when we lose the ability to pay careful and patient attention to our inner lives and the process of cultivating love with the people we value; when we emphasize competition, success, self-sufficiency, individualism, and material progress over the development of the integrity and spiritual quality of our lives, we put ourselves, our inner as well as social selves, at risk. Because of this emphasis, our self-worth rests on our achievements and our possessions rather than on our moral character, compassion, and wisdom. The advertising media portrays the successful person as organized, on-the-go, and in control of a complicated lifestyle. Self-validation is a constant process of comparing ourselves, especially those in our peer and friendship groups. In this world of brands and brand names we are what we possess.

The forces of the culture shape our personalities in such a way that we want to do what we must do for society to function. The traits of our social character become transformed into our personal needs as we come to believe that success, feeling better, and self-regard are based on having and consuming things.

Our indoctrination into this code begins at an early age, when we teach our children to define themselves by the grades they make, the awards they achieve, and clothing they purchase. J. Crew, Abercrombie, Tommy's, and Calvin's are code words by which our children rank each other, and appraise themselves. Our opinions, most especially of ourselves, become based not on our substance, but on continually comparing ourselves with the changing images of the media and the achievements of other people. While the achievement of a friend, classmate, relative, or colleague may not affect our position of success at all, it may make us envious, cause us to feel we are dropping behind or not living up to our capacity, and in the end, like the changing images in advertising, make us think less of ourselves.

Once we are caught in this unconscious cycle of living it then becomes natural to think that if we feel bad we should consume something to feel better. Our feelings become an excuse for consumptive self-indulgence on a material level. If we feel anxious or depressed we consume medications. If our marriages grow stale we may remodel our houses, buy new ones, or purchase vacation homes. Our social character teaches us that consumption is the key to happiness and the answer to most of our problems.

In this climate we cannot help but think of ourselves as commodities. The great vocations of medicine, law, psychology, and the ministry have all turned toward marketing themselves. In today's world we find that efficiency, cost effectiveness, and doing things in the easiest, most convenient way are more important than the effect these approaches to life may have on our souls and health. "Who I am" has become less important than "what I can do," whether it's at work, in relationships, or at church. Even the vocabulary for romantic attachments has fallen into this same, cynical idiom; comments like "my partner doesn't fill my needs" or "I've invested so much in this relationship" underline this perspective, as if human relationships could be calculated, measured, and exchanged, rather than nourished and cherished.

I've often heard people trying to find good reasons to do something they value that is not valued by our social character, such as taking time off from work for a child's field trip at school, an important anniversary, or enough time to truly mourn the death of someone close to them. Most people I know are reluctant to take all of their vacation time and sick days. We feel that we must justify these things to ourselves and to the people close to us. We have trouble justifying spending money on our self-development, on reserving time for quietness and reflection, or even in allowing ourselves to realize we're tired and need to relax without feeling angry with ourselves and guilty about not being productive and working toward our goals. The confusion and uneasiness we feel about investing in the subjective values of honoring ourselves as human beings, with psychological and spiritual needs and potentials, reflect how we have become estranged not only from ourselves but from the value of life.

CAPTIVES OF NORMALCY

As we develop through childhood and into early adulthood, the attributes of our culture's social character are structured into our personalities by our parents, families, teachers, and other institutions. This process is so subtle and powerful that we do not become aware of its influence on our lives until suffering, conflict, or illness may cause us to question the meaning of the values we are living by.

We all want and long to be part of a world that will understand and support us. But the truth is the model of our social character only allows these things at a price. When we remain unconscious of its effects we are guided by false authorities that reside outside of ourselves. Our need to be accepted, to be a meaningful part of society can leave us feeling more and more estranged from ourselves, from our own hearts. Because the model of our social character defines what we think of as normal, to be *normal* actually means to be alienated from ourselves.

When we examine how out of balance, dehumanizing, and self-alienating our idea of normalcy has become, it's easier to understand many of our personal and cultural problems. For example our society teaches us to solve our problems by overcoming them. Therefore when we are faced with a difficult situation we attempt to gather our strength, develop a strategy, and try harder. In addition our news and entertainment media make it appear that only powerful people succeed. The simplistic approach to problem solving erodes our self-esteem because it simply doesn't fit many human situations that range from being shy or overweight to being physically or economically handicapped. When a culture supports such a power-oriented perspective it should come as no surprise that people who feel powerless will become enraged and turn to violence as a way to seek empowerment. We see signs of the symptoms of frustration and feelings of powerlessness: road rage, race rage, militia groups, school shootings, or the violence against ourselves—anger turned inward in the form of depression, self-mutilation, self-starvation, suicide, or family violence.

For most of us, our cocktails of frustration take subtler venues such as restlessness, overeating, drinking too much, or losing our spirits and our desire for intimacy and closeness. While we may not turn actively violent, we may be slipping into a pattern that implies giving up on life. I want to emphasize that by learning to know ourselves we can complete the process of achieving adulthood and attain a level of individual consciousness that will free us from the "model of normalcy"—the constricted patterns and perspectives of the culture; help us develop our inner authority; and in our small ways help change society. Destructiveness comes from self-alienation, feelings of powerlessness, boredom, and a lack of love. The creative solution for achieving a fulfilling existence requires developing the kind of self-knowledge that leads to love and a deep respect for life. Our choice is to either grow in consciousness or to see our lives and society become more alienated and destructive.

Moving on, I will continue the exploration of society's influences on our personalities and the meaning of the individuation process—and I will begin to outline how we can participate in life with more conscious awareness. Conscious participation in life requires a religious devotion to the search for self-knowledge because we are usually trapped by our model of normalcy into believing we are conscious when we haven't even begun to understand the forces shaping our lives.

CHAPTER 2
The Call to Transformation

One thing I did learn from Freud, which has never diminished and has indeed grown with the years, is a habit of careful observation, of heedfulness, in my relationship with the rest of the world. To learn to see what is right in front of one's nose, that is the task and a heavy task it is.
—Robertson Davies

We begin our lives saturated in the belief patterns "everyone" considers normal. The word normal by its nature describes things based on the characteristics of a group. If enough people think it or do it then it's considered normal. Parents, relatives, teachers, religious leaders, politicians, and the media cooperate in training us to be normal, to value what society values and to want to become functional, productive members of our consumer-oriented middle class. Although many families and religious groups may have alternative ideas, our mainstream culture still stresses this central theme as a way of life. Most of us are proud when our children excel in their honors classes and in competitive sports. While they're learning to base their self-esteem on the results of competition and achievement, we feel affirmed as parents if they do well. Our families and ever-widening circles of friends, well-wishers, and colleagues want us to assume the roles and characteristics they think are normal—as loving husbands, dutiful wives, caring partners, ambitious hardworking colleagues, all with a positive attitude. On the one hand these pressures help us grow up, form identities, find work, gain some security in the world, or decide security isn't so important to us. For most of us it feels good to be accepted, worthwhile, and part of a community. Having friends, going to parties and family gatherings, organizing cookouts, participating in "the wave" at the ball field, attending soccer and Little League games, and celebrating holidays, anniversaries, birthdays, and promotions join together to enrich our lives.

On the other hand enjoying being part of a community or family has a price. If we accept their values without sufficiently questioning them and cultivating our individuality, we may never learn how to develop our own value structures and live in a manner that satisfies us rather than those around us. These remarks remind me of Wade, whose story was told to me by a concerned associate. He described Wade as a wealthy, but deeply unhappy orthopedic surgeon whose joy in life came from playing tennis, watching sports events on his giant TV screen, and drinking. Wade's father was an appeals attorney who wanted his son to follow in his footsteps and have a good life. As an attorney in a highly specialized field he felt his career was personally and financially rewarding. Wanting the best for his son, he groomed him to become a physician and sent him to the finest schools. In medical school one of Wade's favorite mentors convinced him that becoming a surgeon suited his talents and would be financially rewarding. Now in his mid-forties we can say that Wade is very rich and very poor. He is emotionally alone. His children by his first wife consider him harsh and distant; they don't like him and they rarely visit. His second wife is frustrated and depressed. At a recent party Wade's colleague suggested he try analysis. "Why?" Wade retorted. "Perhaps understanding yourself might bring some important changes for you, make your life more enjoyable," his friend responded. "I don't have time to contemplate my navel," Wade snapped. "A life that has to be examined is already off track, and my life is on track!" he continued as he moved away from his friend.

When we simply accept the roles and values that are handed to us, we don't think we have to be responsible for the consequences of how we're living, or to think through what they mean. It's easier for Wade to blame the kids, the times, his wife, the litigious nature of our society, the disrespect of insurance companies for physicians, the decline of values in society, or anything else when his life isn't suiting him.

Society and its subgroups are always seeking to define our lives, and as long as we meet their expectations and don't get sick or break down, they will reward us with their model of the good life. Wade, who makes money faster than he can spend it, is our social character's idea of success. But the longer we live by external definitions, the less *personal* our choices become and the more impotent we begin to feel. Often we end up living cover stories authored by others that cause us to avoid the possibility of creating our own stories. Wade's perfunctory dismissal of his colleague's well-meant overture is typical, and even understandable: We want to get away from the few people we know who may actually challenge us to take a more honest look at who we are. I sympathize with Wade because I faced the same dilemma. But I also feel sorry for him because he's missing the chance to grow intellectually, spiritually, and lovingly during some of the most important years in his life.

Whoever we are—whether teachers, ministers, doctors, lawyers, homemakers, or something else—it can be alarming to sense even for a moment that there might be a disparity between the cover stories we're living and our inner realities. Getting to know ourselves, *really* know ourselves, can be frightening. Scary dreams can reflect our self-alienation by being filled with wars, storms, and violent or seductive figures, and our fantasies may follow story lines of grandiose sex, fun, success, and power. The startling pictures, metaphors, and plots used by our unconscious minds in their response to how we are living are frequently upsetting because they picture people and events that may be far from what we consider normal.

Eventually Wade's wife, Carolyn, surprised me by coming to see me, not so much because of her husband, but because she had a dream in which she and Wade were asleep in their bedroom and an angel awakened her by touching her shoulder and saying, "Wake up and get out of bed. It's going to be struck by lightning." This dream was so forceful that she wanted to talk to someone who was trained in understanding dreams. I wasn't surprised when she reported that Wade thought dreams were worthless and seldom remembered them. "He does have nightmares though. Once or twice a month he wakes up thrashing and terrified. In the last one a vampire was holding him like a lover in an embrace he couldn't break free of. But my dreams are usually different," she continued. "In my last one I was back in college. I was late for an exam and couldn't find the building it was supposed to be in. I've had several of these kind of dreams lately. Once I couldn't read the exam questions because they were in a foreign language."

"Questions scare me," she elaborated after a little prompting. "We have a great house, a great life. Wade financed my business. We should have everything we want. But whenever I let myself think, the questions come, What the hell kind of life is this? Am I happy with Wade? Why does he criticize me so much? Is he drinking too much? How much is too much? Why am I so frightened? I wasn't when I was younger. Why am I depressed? Why do I feel so damn lonely? You see why I don't like questions. They can wreck my life."

Like most of us, Carolyn would rather pretend her life is working than face the potential trauma of changing it. Change for her means that she will have to set it in motion herself and face the consequences. She may have to tell Wade she's unhappy, that she's now working in analysis, and that they both need help. She knows this conversation will threaten him and make him furious.

It takes more courage than we realize to look for help when our lives aren't working or satisfying us. Carolyn has courage and it's by no means rare. Those who find it generally discover self-knowledge liberates our minds and spirits, and there is meaning in our emotions that illuminates the reality of our lives.

We all know that we have a darker nature, that we can be cruel, ruthless, aggressive, and antisocial. Generally we're taught to suppress and control these characteristics and if we don't, society will attempt to control them for us. What's more important in terms of getting to know ourselves is to rediscover the more positive and creative aspects we learned to deny early on because people close to us disapproved of them or approved of other things.

THE CALL TO TRANSFORMATION

For instance if we think about Wade as a child, it isn't too hard to imagine his legally trained father telling him to stop daydreaming and study. "You'll need the grades to get in the right college." With such pressure and approval shaping his life I doubt if little Wade ever had much of a chance to fantasize about being something else—an artist, a professional tennis player, or a teacher. If he ever expressed such a thought I can easily hear his parents saying, "You'll never amount to anything that way." "Get real." "You won't make any money doing that." No matter how independent or rebellious we may have appeared while we were growing up, approval and disapproval structured much of what we activated or denied in ourselves.

We learned early to see life through the lens of our generation's social character as it was interpreted by the groups and influences that guided our development. Even the parents who said, "You can be anything you want to be" didn't really seem to mean it because they still wanted us to fit in, be successful, and have high self-esteem. Our desire to be reclusive, write, paint, act, muse, work with our hands, or lose ourselves in spiritual pursuits often ended up being denied due to the influences of well-meaning teachers and parents. Children at the extremes—those who are highly introverted and like to be alone and reading all of the time, or those who are very extroverted and want to talk and interact continuously—feel the shame of being unable to measure up to the moderately extroverted, achievement-oriented, compliant model rewarded in our elementary schools.

I've known a number of people who illustrate these points and you probably have, too. One of them is Debra, who is intensely introverted and spiritual. She wanted to become a nun but her family was aghast at the idea, so she became a successful, but unhappy, therapist. Brian is another person who really wanted to be an artist but drove himself to become a well-known architect. And I think of Ariel, who yearned to be a set designer and work in the theater, but feared taking her creativity seriously. She got married and became a part-time interior decorator. Like many of us, Debra, Brian, and Ariel chose to live cover stories that left them with a sense of missed purpose and unfulfilled promise. In these kinds of situations we often think we're making responsible choices and are self-directed but this feeling is an illusion: Our actions are still being governed by the beliefs, values, and preconceptions that structured our formative years.

People like Debra, Brian, and Ariel show how we learn to deny our faith in ourselves and our creativity by the time we begin making career choices. When we overly rely on the conventional path into life, we give up not only our power, but also the urge to understand ourselves better and to make our lives ongoing creations. The world we live in still believes that the sensible approach to life means to have a "cool head." Passionate emotions such as hate, rage, anger, and even passionate love are seen as dangerous states that can easily get us into trouble. But avoiding them out of fear can also be dangerous because we can't be fully alive without them.

Can you imagine how different Debra's life might have been if just one relative had understood her passion and encouraged her, "If you think you love it, give it a try." Or how Brian's choices could have been different had an inspiring teacher been able to explain to him the fury that drove Picasso, or that compelled Cezanne to paint straight through his mother's funeral even though he loved her dearly. And how might Ariel's life have been different if her mother shared Thoreau's skepticism of group values and had urged her to march to her "own music?" Creativity and creative living depend upon our emotional relationships to life. They require passion and persistence and the ability to respond to life instinctually and with the heart as well as the head.

Maturity means that we can experience the power of our full range of emotions. Emotional maturity means we experience vitality, strength, and the enjoyment of becoming who we are. When we don't feel, can't or won't feel, we are usually depressed. We have become overwhelmed and trapped by fear, anxiety, and live like a deer immobilized in the headlights of a speeding car. If we are seeking self-knowledge, emotions are among our best teachers. Anger can be a call to action or it may teach us where our boundaries are, alert us to when they're being violated, or when we're not being treated with respect. It urges us to respect ourselves, to stand up for ourselves and our values. Emotions usually become destructive only after they've been stuffed back within us to accumulate in some wounded inner space we try to keep buried. We saw this in the drunken anger of Wade, the rich but miserable surgeon whose bottleneck of feelings hurt and frightened his wife and damaged his marriage. Very likely his anger came from a lifetime of feelings and personal integrity being denied. However, if Wade was willing to explore the meaning in his anger, as some of my examples later in this book do, it could open a passageway to growth and change. Carolyn denied her anger as well and covered it with her depression. But, as we'll see in later chapters these destructive feelings and our emotional suffering can actually become transformative in the right circumstances.

Fearing Change

When we surrender ourselves to the values of our culture and the limited perspective society considers normal, our lives can become emotionally and creatively grim. However, individuation and growth in self-knowledge bring hope because they join our efforts to grow up and become effective members of society into an overall pattern of personal development that goes far beyond what it means to be normal. This process turns our crises into epiphanies, our struggles into inner teachers, and our mistakes into potentials for change that all lead to a more complete and satisfying life. It also teaches us to honor our difficulties and realize that our ability to experience joy is measured by our willingness to search for meaning in our suffering.

There is an important point that can be made about success and its relationship to the individuation process. It's summarized by a wonderful statement that Jung made that says, "If you do the wrong thing with all your heart you will end up at the right place." I believe that he means we're better off pursuing the wrong path as hard as we can than becoming lost in indecision or working halfheartedly at something and feeling sorry for ourselves. When I went into business it was the wrong career for me. But because I had a real desire to grow up and become somebody, I worked furiously. Once I had the mental security of success, events forced me to step back and look at myself in a way that I'd been too fragile and unformed to do earlier.

In the process of proving myself, many of the old wounds to my identity development had been healed and I'd established the inner strength for starting a new journey. I felt assured that I could take care of myself and my family, and if I took risks that didn't work out I could find starting over a challenge that would open new opportunities and stretch my abilities to new levels. I also learned not to linger in jobs, relationships, and environments that diminished my soul. It took more than success for me to learn these things. It required my inner work as well. Through self-awareness, age and experience can bring courage, confidence, and wisdom. Without self-knowledge we can end up more timid, afraid, and trapped in later years than we were in our youth. What appeared to be the wrong early choice for me in terms of my temperament and long-term potentials was actually the right choice for my psychological growth. Pursuing my business career with determination and later being willing to see therapy as a potential turning point based on a process of self-examination transformed my life.

Debra, Brian, and Ariel are on track for the opportunity of transformation. They're becoming successful in the careers they chose because they couldn't really see another path. Eventually their satisfaction will dry up, as Debra is already finding out, and their old dreams will begin to catch up with them, will stir up their dissatisfaction, and may even open them to the possibility of new ambitions. If they seize the opportunities before them, they'll have a chance to reclaim their old interests or build new ones from a standpoint of strength.

Wade, however, is an example of someone more trapped in his identity. There is no apparent missed purpose or unfulfilled promise with which he has ever had to deal. His programming was too strong and began too early in his life. Working his way free from the inauthentic life he is stuck in and the problems it's causing should start with the kind of psychotherapy that will help him develop the knowledge of his emotions, how to live and relate from his heart, and how to use his mind to help him separate from the role he's living. To go further in his individuation he will need to carefully revisit the story of his childhood in order to reawaken the potentials he never knew he had. Will he have to change careers? Maybe. Maybe not. It's too soon for him to figure out what it will take to renew himself and his marriage.

The more people are trapped in their identities the more they fear change. They fear they're too old or the work will take too long, or won't be worth the trouble. We all have these fears to some extent and they're often difficult to overcome. Nevertheless, it's even more difficult to see the reality that's "right in front of our noses" and ask ourselves: What kind of future are we currently facing? Most of us need some help and support when we initially start the process of facing ourselves and the future we are building. We are all fabricating a future that is beyond appearances and will reflect how we are growing or failing to grow in creativity and concerns of the heart and spirit. If Wade would let a skilled therapist or analyst help him to realistically see the future he's constructing—a lethal concoction of marital problems, health problems, drinking problems, and professional difficulties, he might be more open to considering whether the question of growing and changing is as fearful as it appears.

How trapped we are in our identities often depends upon the power of the messages we internalized from our parents. The more negative they were the harder we have to work to overcome them. Michael has been an accountant for almost twenty years. He was the only son of a couple who had owned a jewelry store in a small Southern town. His parents had a clear idea of what they wanted him to become when he grew up. Michael often joked that he could have been a doctor, a minister, or a failure in their eyes. He admitted that he didn't realize until he was in analysis that he might be allowed to have ambitions of his own.

By the time Michael was forty, he felt like he was losing control of his life. He ate too much. He felt very little sexual desire for his wife and he didn't particularly like being around his children. His wife sensed his tenseness and accused him of having an affair. His parents said he had a better life than they had at his age and he was stupid not to enjoy it. In other words he got little support or sympathy for his feelings of distress. Eventually Michael found his way to me.

At a certain point in exploring the story of his childhood, we began discussing the influence his parents have had on his life. I asked him what he'd wanted to do with his life as he was growing up.

"To become a professional man, get married, and have a family," he answered.

"You did that very well," I said. "But you're still not satisfied. Have you considered that maybe that's not really what you wanted?"

"Yes, I've considered that a lot in the last year. But it's not just that my parents forced me into a profession, it's how they did it that hurt me so much. . . . I was smart and I was good. But the words they used to motivate me were 'stupid,' 'lazy,' and things like 'you'll never succeed, you'll never be worth a damn.'"

"You mean they taught you to drive yourself to excel by the use of extreme criticism."

"Exactly. I learned their system so well I actually developed a mantra to drive me through my homework. I would say to myself, 'You're stupid, you're stupid, you're stupid,' until I forced myself to finish my work. It's still the same. I make a mistake and say, 'You're an idiot' or 'It's all over now, you've fooled the world as long as you can. You are going to lose everything.' I don't dare even talk to my kids about school—I couldn't stand doing this to them. . . . I just hate myself. . . . You see, I'm doing it again."

Michael used all of the old normal excuses for not dealing with how he felt about his parents: They're too old to change. Confronting them would only hurt them. They wouldn't understand. I'm not sure I want a closer relationship with them anyway. They did the best they could at the time. Finally the excuses ran out and the surface reality was penetrated as he leaned forward in his chair. "I hate them so much! They should have known better. I was a good kid. I worked hard. I made good grades. Why didn't they like me? Why weren't they proud of me? Why didn't they hug me, encourage me, brag about me? If I really think about all of this I'm afraid I'll be so angry that all I'll want to do is hurt them, and hurt them, and hurt them."

This was the truth that caused his anxiety about talking to his parents. He was afraid that his rage was so powerful, so real, that he would become out of control. But here in my office, where we were able to crystallize and bring this rage out into the open in a safe atmosphere, it took some of its power away. The objective here wasn't to change the past or to reconcile Michael with his parents. Dealing with his parents was a topic for future sessions. Our immediate concern was to help him stop trapping and driving himself with harsh self-criticism.

As Michael's analysis proceeded he continued working as an accountant but eased up on himself. He also became a part-time sportswriter for the local newspaper. He never had a talk with his parents because his father died of a heart attack before he decided whether he wanted to make an attempt to express his feelings more honestly and thereby risk either making them angry or getting closer to them. Michael ended up being very clear about one thing: He wanted to get to know his children better and hoped they wouldn't be reluctant to talk openly with him.

Our past experiences, like Michael's, cause us to numb our feelings. Our society teaches us we must honor our parents and respect our elders without holding them responsible for how they dealt with us, which is a great contributor to the numbing process. This numbness covers anger and hurt. It causes us to shut down emotionally, to say to ourselves and even to others, "It doesn't matter." "I don't care." "It isn't worth the trouble."

When we say such things what we're really saying is: "I don't matter." "I'm not worth the trouble."

If we deny our feelings, we're giving up the ability to feel good, to feel bad, hurt, angry, or sad, but also happy, joyful, loving, and passionate—the emotions that tell us how we're experiencing life, how we feel about what we're doing and what's being done to us. Without feelings we don't know if we're living authentically or in bondage, whether we value something or not. My parents have been dead for many years yet I think about them every day. The strongest feeling I have when I remember them is one of longing. I yearn to have known them better, to have heard more about their hopes, fears, dreams, struggles, and triumphs. And, I wish they had known me better. I wish they had lived long enough for me to have developed the inner strength it would have taken to risk their anger, to risk upsetting our workable relationship, and to talk openly with them about my childhood and my disappointments, hopes, and dreams. I long to know them deeply and to be known by them.

"Honor your father and mother" was an injunction that served me badly. I have since learned that we must carefully question everything we've been taught to believe as right or wrong if we are going to live the truth of our own lives. To me, honoring them meant not taking the risk of upsetting them, and this shallow interpretation of the commandment kept me from challenging myself and them into a deeper relationship, one that could truly have honored all three of us. Nor do I think anyone should "honor" abusive parents because they have already dishonored the sacred trust of being a father or a mother. We must learn to look deeper into how we are living and to listen to how we feel about the principles we're trying to live by.

Paying Religious Attention to Our Lives

Developing what Jung called "a religious outlook" in the second half of life requires careful self-questioning and ongoing attention to every aspect of life. It's easy for many of us to misunderstand this statement because our early religious experiences were often quite the opposite of questioning ourselves, life, and especially the particular dogma to which we were exposed. Organized religions appear to ask us to believe a lot of things that don't seem true in our experience, or to follow a code of behaviors that not only look unrewarding, but undermine the self-esteem we struggle to build in adolescence.

But as Jung framed it, being "religious" does not mean believing or following rules. The word *religious* means to pay careful attention, to pay heed, or to give careful thought to something. It comes from the Latin word *religere,* which is the opposite of *neglegere,* from which the word *neglect* comes. To have a religious outlook means to be attentive, careful, to try to look at things clearly with integrity and intuition in an effort to see beneath their surface appearances.

Developing a religious outlook requires that we grow beyond the stage of complex consciousness, the limited self-awareness of normal adulthood, that we examine everything and no longer focus solely on our goals and whether we're progressing toward them or not.

Albert Einstein once said that a real scientist was a truly religious person because he must train himself to neglect nothing, to set nothing aside as trivial, because the truth may be hidden within a considerable body of trivia. The careful study of our "stories," especially the parts we prefer to gloss over or the feelings we have denied, will often provide the meaning, the context, and the perspective for where we are today. Once we understand today the future becomes less veiled.

When Michael paid close attention to his story he discovered how brutal and inhuman his way of driving himself to success was. How it was now failing and how his life was breaking down. Then he was able to detect the anger deep within his soul that he was turning against himself rather than facing. Each new bit of self-awareness he achieved seemed to invite further exploration, and following this process has begun to free him for a future that isn't a prisoner of his past.

If we want our lives to be those of growth and unfolding, we must give religious attention to every aspect of our experiences and be willing to see every part of them as manifestations of the human spirit. Learning that we have to seek the experience of life firsthand rather than avoid it or transcend it, that our feelings, problems, crises, struggles, and pain are teachers and not just things to be overcome and avoided, will help us pay attention to areas we normally neglect. In the Western tradition the mystics consider these things manifestations of the transcendent God, our higher power, or whatever name we wish to give it. The religious outlook trains us to try to see everything as clearly as we can—our strengths, our weaknesses, our foolishness, our hopes, dreams, loves, and fears, even when what we're observing seems still shrouded and ambiguous. Obviously we can't understand everything, but every new piece of self-awareness brings us a step closer to feeling at home within ourselves.

In terms of our growth, the decision to pay attention is a commitment to becoming personally involved. It means to listen to our thoughts and feelings and also to our unconscious as it expresses itself—whether through dreams, fantasies, intuitions, or artistic expressions—and to respect our physical and emotional symptoms. Involvement means taking them seriously and personally, rather than ignoring them or blaming them on something outside of us. My bad dreams don't come from how highly spiced the food I ate at dinner was. My bad mood isn't really my wife's fault. My fantasies of moving to Alaska often alert me to how stressed and tired I am, how overwhelmed I have let myself become. The religious attitude of paying close attention to ourselves mentally, physically, emotionally, and spiritually prepares us for change and growth, as we shall see when we move ahead to discuss the process of healing.

Paying careful attention to the *nuances* in our lives and relationships is a path the great mystics discovered long before psychological theory evolved. They realized that paying attention to the minute aspects of life and its personal issues led to a deeper experience of being alive and that we find spiritual meaning by knowing life, not by fantasizing about cosmic consciousness. The Buddhist monk Thich Nhat Hanh describes the religious attitude I am talking about as "mindfulness." In her book *The Artist's Way,*

THE CALL TO TRANSFORMATION

Julia Cameron points out "that creativity is grounded in reality, in the particular, the focused, the well observed or the specifically imagined." New awareness is born in the moments we encounter life, for in them we can meet our truths, meet ourselves and our lives as expressions of who we are. The religious outlook connects us to the forces and currents of life through our emotional responses and thoughtful reflections. The more aware we become the more we discover that our awareness determines how we experience life.

Most of the time our culture, families, friends, and religious organizations prefer to keep their mind-sets intact. They don't want us to upset the assumptions by which they've defined their lives. Nor do they want to hear any troubling little voices, however truthful, as the little boy in the fairy tale "The Emperor's New Clothes" prompted when he pointed out that the beautiful apparel everyone was admiring didn't exist at all, and that the emperor was naked—as were their illusions. But individuation—the process by which we grow—rests on our continuously developing awareness. Not so we can point out to others that they are wrong, but so we can break the mind-sets that entrap us and live lives that are expressions of our best promise.

Heeding the Call: Becoming Ourselves

To feel a sense of self, a sense of personal identity that, like our fingerprints, is immutably ours alone, is part of living a full life. As we grow into our identities the influences of our families and society help our development. Our sense of identity initially depends upon our places in society and how we identify with the group. Many members of the health care professions think this is as far as our development needs to go; that is, they focus on reducing the symptoms of anxiety, depression, addictions, relationship problems, and stress without considering the true source or meaning of these symptoms. They then try to help us cope or learn better skills in order to return us to the limiting world of normalcy. They base their treatments or efforts to help us on the values of society, which they have uncritically accepted. In their eyes happiness is a result of our adaptation to life's circumstances.

However, Jungian psychology as well as many approaches to spiritual development assert that life is a continuing process of becoming more fully who we're meant to be, and of forming an increasingly intimate relationship with the spiritual aspects of our existence. These two directions—authenticity and reaching for the awareness of our highest values—have an attraction for each other and when they're joined, they bring a deeper sense of unity and meaning to our lives. From the Jungian point of view these two paths are the most powerful psychological healing forces we have.

In one form or another the great civilizations of the past honored the powers in life that affect our destinies and that are beyond our control. The ancient Greeks and Romans consulted the gods through sacrifices and rituals designed for revealing their will. The ancient Hebrews relied on dreams, prophets, and the interpretations of the Bible to connect them to the guiding will of God. The Chinese developed the I-Ching to help them meet life in a manner that balanced the individual with cosmic principles. All of these civilizations sought to align themselves with the transcendent powers and cosmic principles. In depth psychology we observe ourselves, and attempt to develop relationships with the powers that affect our lives, which we cannot control but often find within our unconscious minds. The old tempestuous gods of ancient Greece are now seen as the psychological complexes that toss us around emotionally. The potential richness of our lives is hidden from us by our lack of awareness, and the destinies we have failed to open ourselves to accepting stand outside of our doors like unknown angels disguised as beggars.

The promises of our present and future growth join with increasing self-knowledge and lead us into new visions of ourselves, where the love of life becomes the measure of our values. Following this path requires a religious attitude and religious devotion. This path, which I've called individuation, expresses a desire for continual psychological and spiritual rebirth during our lifetime and is a fundamental part of human nature. Because individuation brings us toward wholeness we may find that there can be a rebirth of our

THE CALL TO TRANSFORMATION

suppressed natures, the ones we were encouraged to limit in order to find practical places in the world, as well as a rebirth of our spiritual perspectives, which seek to see life as transformative and holy.

Dissatisfaction with career choices frequently opens the door to self-discovery. We may have been encouraged into medical school because we're smart, into sales because we're personable, or, like myself, into business to support our families. But it's even more important to remember our culture has valued rationality and material things in a manner that's brought the scientific and mechanical aspects of our lives to an apex of which we can be rightfully proud. And yet to do this, many of us have had to repress our sensitivity, our ability to develop the personal values that bring us meaning, and the art of cultivating love and friendships. These losses leave us lonely, discontented, and dissatisfied with our lives. Giving special attention to the discovery and nurturance of these aspects of ourselves can renew our ability to feel at home in life, enriched by our relationships, and to see our jobs as vocations.

Life is a process of growth. Because life's a process and we're wonderfully complex beings, we can't change ourselves all at once. Growth is incremental, step-by-step, with each step leading to the next. The more we get to know ourselves the more we discover what there is to know, what potentials are undeveloped or perhaps even unknown. If we're extroverted, we must learn that there's an undeveloped part of us that longs to be introverted. If we're concrete in our perceptions, a hidden part of us seeks to look at things intuitively. If we're trained in thinking, life will challenge our feeling values. The many inner elements in our personalities continually want to rise up, be recognized, and in some way be lived. Initially it may appear frustrating to have to grow in such a manner until we begin discovering the hidden rewards within ourselves.

I think of Cecilia as an example of how wanting to grow too fast could have become destructive. In her late thirties she was anxious to get her life "on track." A decade earlier she'd become a pharmaceutical salesperson because she was attractive, extroverted, and persuasive. Cecilia felt overstressed and unhappy and quickly concluded she should either change careers or give up her career and devote her life to her family. As she explored her inner life more carefully by coming to analysis, by journaling and listening to her dreams—techniques for learning to know ourselves more fully we will explore later—she discovered a spiritual side of herself that wanted a career oriented toward helping people rather than simply making money. Assisted by this new knowledge she was able to find a smaller company to work for that specialized in a certain disease area. In this position she worked more closely with physicians, helping to keep them up-to-date on research and treatments. By following a careful process of self-exploration she found out what she really needed was work that gave her a deeper sense of meaning rather than the choice she was trying to force on herself of either changing careers or staying home.

Forcing our choices and changes can also happen too fast in relationships. Many times, the problems we see in them come not because we're with the wrong people, but because we haven't explored ourselves well enough to know how to cultivate our ability to love, respect, and be friends with our intimate partners. We will examine relationships more completely later.

In Cecilia's case it took a while for her to understand that the fatigue and unhappiness she was experiencing meant that she needed to find a new level of meaning to her work. Unfortunately some people think they can accomplish the same thing with a quick fix. But as life will usually teach us, it isn't that easy. I'm often surprised at how many people come to me knowing I'm an analyst and yet want quick answers to their dilemmas. I remember Bill, a man in his fifties who came to see me for an hour's consultation and began our meeting by saying, "Listen, I don't want any long-term analysis. You're the expert. I want you to tell me what to do and I'll do it." As we began to talk, Bill explained that years ago, when he'd finished college he'd wanted to go to seminary and become an Episcopal priest. Instead he'd gone to Harvard Business School to satisfy his parents. As his life progressed he'd become a successful financial advisor, married, and had three children, who were currently attending expensive colleges. About a year before coming to see me he started becoming depressed. His old dream of returning to seminary returned and as his discontent increased, his income began to fail and he lost his edge at work. At first his family was alarmed to see him so unhappy. Then they became angry at his inability to pull himself together. Bill's unwillingness to explore himself with me also indicated he hadn't thought his situation through enough to be able to discuss it with his wife. I can imagine how she must have felt confused, threatened, and all alone. It was no surprise that she soon became angry.

Bill wanted my advice as to whether he should try to go to seminary or simply continue taking the antidepressant medication his physician had prescribed, and try to get his life back on track. He did not like my answer. My position was that he was seeking a solution to his problems without fully understanding the questions they were asking him about his life. To search for these questions Bill first needed to develop a careful attitude of reflection and self-exploration in order to listen to the inner aspects of himself.

I explained to him that the willingness to be reborn—in his case, to become a man capable of discovering and living from his deepest needs and values—requires courage and faith. Conventional wisdom says for us to go to an expert and solve the problem. It takes courage to stand outside of this perspective and consider that the source of our problems may come from a poorly developed sense of values or a failure to come to grips with how to find meaning in our lives. It also takes courage to risk leaving the comfort, care, and social standing of the life someone like Bill is living. But that wasn't the real issue at this point. In fact his depression was already threatening that part of his life. Bill needed the courage to face himself and to search for the truth behind his depression and the dilemma he was in.

Courage, I told him, can often rely on faith. By faith I didn't mean the blind, unconscious piety of the fundamentalist, but faith in its Old Testament connotation, where the word means "trust" or "certainty." In Bill's case, this kind of trust meant he needed to know himself well enough so that he could rely on his thinking, feeling, and perceptions of his inner life to recognize how they could guide him in his relationship to life and God. If we don't have the courage to face and understand ourselves, every major life transition we make will lead to further dissatisfaction and conflict.

Bill wanted to jump from one career to another, hoping a past dream would fill a current need, which would have been a leap of desperation rather than one of faith. In addition, he'd boxed himself in with an either/or decision for which he wanted to be "advised" on, rather than go through the process that was needed for him to be able to own it. To make a change based on trust we must learn to know ourselves well enough to be confident in making that change, and to realize that even if the change fails to bring fulfillment we'll search what happened and ourselves deeply enough to discover the next step.

After our talk, Bill decided on a compromise. He still felt he wasn't ready for taking a deeper look at himself, but he decided to reduce his workload in order to study theology on his own and enrolled in a study course offered for laypeople in the Episcopal church. Bill's choice seemed a reasonable way to investigate a career change decision. Even so, I didn't feel that it had the inner foundation to become the answer to the questions of meaning and fulfillment his depression was asking of him. However, like many of us, Bill may have to evolve at his own pace in his own time. He may need even more time and possibly more struggle and suffering to strengthen himself before looking more intensely into himself and his current values.

Most of us are not sufficiently aware or brave enough to willingly embark on the journey of individuation. But life puts us on this path, and the first two stages of consciousness that we must face virtually without personal choice are the beginning of this journey. In this sense life is like a bicycle ride. Once we learn how to pedal, we get started and head into adulthood. But all too often we're more concerned with who's passing us than with our direction or even why we're riding in the first place. Most of us hope to coast for a while after having worked so hard to establish ourselves in life, whether we're fully satisfied with what we have or not. It's difficult to consider starting another journey without knowing

THE CALL TO TRANSFORMATION

whether we'll be headed for even higher hills or into lush, green valleys.

Usually, it's some kind of conflict, such as a midlife crisis, that sparks the recognition that some part of our lives has stopped working, and we find ourselves forced into further development. Children may become rebellious; they may exhaust or disappoint us. Jobs or marriages may grow stale or wear away; stress may wear us out; job loss, heart attack, or other illness may upset the patterns of our lives. Or we may simply feel depressed, anxious, or burned out for reasons we dimly understand. Frequently these feelings are accompanied by guilt. On one level we feel guilty because we're not functioning to full capacity in our social roles at a time when our culture tells us we're in the prime of our work and family lives, when our income potential is highest, and when we can or have to spend on ourselves. So why aren't we happy? It's like that old expression, "Are we having fun yet?"

On a deeper level we feel guilty because we know silently that we've betrayed ourselves by denying some of our "better" characteristics. We keep these thoughts buried in that deep sloshy pit inside us called "self-doubt" or "self-loathing." And to paraphrase author Mignon McLaughlin, we know this is part of the price we pay to get what we used to think we wanted, or should want. We know that somehow we've lost our best selves, like a parent and child whose hands accidentally unclasp. The child has wandered off, and so has our personhood, our vitality, our tenderness. Where has it gone? All lost and repressed in service to the idols of our social character.

The juncture between the first half of life and the second half of life, when complex consciousness begins to evolve into individual consciousness, is a critical point in our growth. Frequently its arrival is heralded by dreams that reflect the uneasiness we're feeling. We may dream we're on a trip or a journey, staying in unknown hotels. A woman I worked with facing this passage had such a dream that began in a luxury hotel. She was traveling with her mother. "It was a beautiful place," she said. "But we kept traveling and traveling. I never went home. I reached a point in the dream where I no longer knew where I was from." Her dream was quietly but emphatically telling her that she was losing touch with the ground of her own life.

The more fixed we are in our identities and the more attached we are to our self-images, the more turbulent our dreams may become. We may dream we're back in college taking a final course or exam we somehow missed. Or, like Carolyn, Wade's unhappy wife, we may dream we are back in college taking a difficult class and not being able to find the classroom on final exam day. Back-to-school dreams are common and they often recur when we don't listen to them. Another woman I was working with tried to dismiss her dream's importance by remarking lightly, "It's my old anxiety dream." Her comment reminded me how easily we categorize our dreams and fail to listen to them. I was left wondering what she was anxious about today, what test was she unprepared for, or if her inner being was preparing for a new life transition that she wasn't keeping up with consciously?

We may also face stronger images, such as storms and tornadoes, that threaten our inner landscapes. One man I knew, who was also at the midlife junction, was beginning to feel restless. Then one night he dreamed he was on the seacoast, where the land was hot and humid (he'd never been there). Suddenly the air was deathly still, the sky turned black, on the horizon over the ocean he saw a hurricane approaching. He awoke wondering if he could get his wife and family into the storm shelter in time. Can we make it through this turbulent time safely? is a question many of us ask ourselves. In most cases the answer doesn't seem clear and we may freeze or try to deny what's happening. Then we may get stuck, unable to move. For many people it becomes a transition too difficult to make.

Our conflict is twofold. On one side we have the duties defined by our conventional roles, the relationships we have built while in these roles, the obligations we've taken on, and the self-images we've created under the influence of the social character that makes us feel like worthwhile people. On the other side of the conflict is the duty to ourselves, to our one life to live and our need to live it genuinely, personally, and to have it become a creative expression of our uniqueness rather than a reflection of other people's perspectives. There are many conflicts of duty between being a successful, "normal" person and having a life of one's own.

When I first met Porter he told me about the following dream: "I was in the big, old house I grew up in on the river outside of Charleston. It was dirty, dusty, full of cobwebs. The furniture was collapsing, the whole place was a mess. It looked like some set designer's idea of a haunted house. And it was. I was maybe twenty years older than I am now, around sixty. I entered an empty room, there was nothing on the walls or ceiling. The window panes were shattered. But I couldn't get out of the room. Suddenly I realized there was something else in the room. It was my father's ghost or spirit. (In reality he's still alive.) Wherever I moved he followed me. I heard him breathing heavily. Was he mad at me? I struggled and struggled to wake up. Was I struggling against him? I woke up screaming, 'No! No! No!' That was six years ago," Porter concluded. "That dream started everything."

Porter's father had been a self-made man who had built his carpet store into a million-dollar business. He came from a poor background, worked hard, drank hard, worked his family as well as his employees hard, and enjoyed intimidating just about everyone. By the time he was forty, Porter was president of the company while his "retired" father still actually ran everything. "I've built this business from nothing and made every one of my children rich," the old man would boast. Indeed he was right. Porter lived in a big house, belonged to a country club, and his wife ran her own interior decorating business in conjunction with the carpet stores.

After this dream Porter began a troubled path that led him into an affair and through a bitter divorce, hurtful times with his children, and several years of analysis. He finally realized that his life was devouring him. With the help of his new awareness he told his father he was leaving the business. To his surprise his father answered, "Congratulations, you're finally as tough as I am," showing that he actually respected him for leaving. After his decision to leave the business and his father's surprising validation, Porter decided to expand his efforts to reclaim his life through delving into other aspects of his emotional experiences.

A few months after our consultation, Bill, the financial advisor I mentioned earlier who had been stuck between his successful life and a desire to study theology, came back to see me. He felt his life was sinking out from under him. At home his wife and children continued seeing his unhappiness as weakness. At work it came across as indifference. Bill finally concluded that by trying to live two lives, he was failing at both of them. At the same time his disgust and despair was increasing as his dream of truly studying theology seemed more remote than ever.

It's not surprising that at this juncture our growth often gets stuck between our conventional values and our real-life obligations and our need to grow. At this point our problems or the hold they have on us intensifies; we may feel neurotic; we may become symptomatic; we're in conflict and it can only be solved in one of two ways. We can defensively regress in our conscious development and seek pleasure and comfort in the conventional world—that is, we can buy new things, take vacations, look for hobbies, and enter into affairs and new relationships. Or we can go on with our growth and develop a level of consciousness that's outside the norm but is our own, a standard that seeks a higher level of values—one which we'll choose to live in devotion to.

Bill's road to the life he needed to live began with an experience that surprised him. He went to talk to the dean of a well-known seminary about returning to school. The dean informed him that even with his academic credentials he couldn't just enroll and begin studying. He would have to go through a process of discernment that would convince the admissions committee that this course was actually a calling for him. Such a process of discernment is one of self-examination, and to Bill's amazement the dean suggested he begin Jungian analysis. The dean took Bill's desires and conflicts seriously. He told Bill he should treat what he was experiencing as something important, and that his struggles were not neurotic from a spiritual perspective, but were an effort to bring a deeper meaning to his life.

As Bill's analysis got underway he learned that developing a respectful attitude toward his interior life was his first important step. After a year of analytic work he began to pursue the deaconate, an ordained position in the Episcopal church that requires study and discernment, but not seminary training. He considered this move an outward manifestation of his inner work. Bill also concluded that it was best for him to live one step at a time, listening to his unconscious, seeking to know himself better, and allowing his vocation to unfold. As he was able to develop self-knowledge and a sense of trust in the path he was following, Bill also became strong enough to confront his wife and children about spending less money and treating him with greater love and understanding.

Bill's inner work introduced a new and deeper note into his life and as he rediscovered his self-respect, he experienced a return of his family's respect as well.

Paradoxically, as I've said before but it's worth remembering, it's often our breakdowns in health or conventional consciousness that lead to breakthroughs to more genuine levels of growth. Bill's depression forced him into self-development, and his family into broadening their views of a meaningful life. A friend of mine underwent open-heart surgery at age forty-nine. His pain and fear pushed him into facing the stress and depression he'd denied for years. Another friend's scare over the possibility of having cervical cancer led her to reexamine her attitudes about love and sexuality. The road to enlightenment may appear to begin in the form of an affliction or hardship. When we encounter such situations, it's not unlikely we will need help to understand and resolve them because we're experiencing them so intensely, it's difficult to also question them deeply without outside support.

During his open-heart surgery my friend needed the help and support of his family. He considered himself lucky to feel the healing warmth of his parents, friends, wife, and children. Once he came home they continued expressing their concern by helping him pay attention to his diet and exercise as well as taking more time off from work. However when he began to share his concerns that something more profound was out of kilter in his life, such as some of the values he had been living by, he was disappointed because his family began to feel threatened and his parents criticized him for not getting himself back together. It's human nature for people to have more difficulty giving us support for inner changes than for outer crises. The people around us want us to get back to being the same people they knew how to deal with, who lived in ways they understood. They want us to rejoin the belief systems we shared, which have defined us. If we begin to change our belief systems, the values by which we've been living, we threaten the identities and security of those who shared those systems with us.

Author Reynolds Price in his book *A Whole New Life* explains how cancer transformed him and shares his experience with us as he says: "Your mate, your children, your friends at work—anyone who knew or loved you in your old life—will be hard at work in the fierce endeavor to revive your old self, the self they recall with love and respect." Whether our need for transformation is caused by an illness, a breakdown, or simply because we feel frustrated by a life that isn't working for us anymore, the people around us will have difficulty understanding what we are trying to do unless they have had similar experiences. Generally the people closest to us will attempt to stall our efforts to learn who we need to become, rarely realizing that we can't resurrect the ruins of our old selves in a manner that will give us deeply satisfying lives. It may be because our change threatens them or they liked who we were, but in either case I've found they will often accuse us of being arrogant, self-centered, and irresponsible as we press on toward self-growth. These responses add to the pain of our transformation, but also teach us that part of what we must give up is the approval—the very approval that pleased us as children—we get from others by meeting their needs and expectations.

When we're stuck in the conflict between transformation and the expectations and social values of others, we generally need the assistance of someone who understands these treacherous passages.

THE CALL TO TRANSFORMATION

Finding help in this situation is difficult because the person who supports and encourages self-discovery seems to be defying the values of our families and culture. Reynolds Price says that as soon as he'd finished radiation therapy he wished someone would have looked him squarely in the eye and said, "Reynolds Price is dead. Who will you be now? Who can you be now and how can you get there?"

Transformation periods are also tough to deal with because we may discover that the values we esteemed, and that served us well, have lost their potency and must be let go of for future development to begin. When I left the business world I had to give up my "take charge–be in control" attitude. Bill had to realize there were values in life more important to him than his lifestyle, and my friend who had the cervical cancer scare realized that if she continued to use sexuality carelessly, her body might turn on her. The best help we can have as we negotiate these experiences often comes from the guidance of people who have been through them and have learned, like Reynolds Price, the value and necessity of transformation. And as I have mentioned before, some of my most important help has come in books and particularly in myths, where Joseph Campbell reminds us that the heroes and heroines throughout history have walked this path, proven its value, and that we can find the support we need within ourselves.

Becoming conscious of the effects of the wounds and traumas of our childhoods and the influences of the social character on our development is the first step toward attaining individual consciousness. The completion of this step means that we increasingly experience ourselves as authors, actors, and subjects of our lives. When we can trust that it's we who think, feel, and act rather than the ghosts of our parents or well-trained robots, we learn that we can also love, be in relationships, and be in the world without losing ourselves. Personal values and meaning support our activities and make our lives expressions of uniqueness. When we have attained individual consciousness, we will find that we've created personalities that are solid and we're no longer footballs kicked around by our inner emotions or external expectations.

Picturing Wholeness

To a significant extent, the journey into individual consciousness parallels the spiritual pilgrimage of many mystics. The mystics subject each initiate to a process that's psychological in nature and that aims to purify and regenerate the personality. Their purpose is a profound transformation of one's identity. The process is intended to rid the initiate of everyday wants and needs, and to transform him (or her) into a purer state of being that's no longer dominated by personal desires or family and cultural influences. The power of this initiation, which includes a painful ordeal of self-examination and self-denial, calls forth the potentials of one's best characteristics. Its goal is to open and strengthen the initiate in order for him to have a personal relationship with the divine, or one's inner Self in Jungian terms, and thereby to be able to serve greater values.

This process begins much like analysis, with self-examination and reflection, and helps the initiate become more fully conscious about how he has been living. It requires the initiate to examine every aspect of his attitudes and behaviors, the acts (sins) that separate one from the divine. The initiate must also consciously choose to make the sacred the center of his life rather than worldly values and aspirations. Each mystical tradition has its own imagery of the transformative process of life, death, and rebirth. The spiritual exercises of Saint Ignatius of Loyola, for example, outline one of Roman Catholicism's approaches to spiritual development. They begin with self-examination and carry one step-by-step through a process of purifying oneself from the effects of the past, secular life and ultimately to choosing God as the center of one's life. Whatever the tradition, initiates meditate on the transformative process until it's internalized as a vision of their own processes of growth and becomes experienced in their lives.

Psychologically, this intense process may be interpreted as a series of steps that take us through the experience of suffering as our "normal" or everyday identities become transformed by experiencing the death of an old way of life and the rebirth of a new one. The process of self-examination and reflection consolidates our

THE CALL TO TRANSFORMATION

experiences of who we are by enabling us to acknowledge the power of our denied emotions, strengths, weaknesses, and potentials and to free ourselves from the needs and constraints of the previously unexamined forces that shaped who we were.

It's only at this point, where individual consciousness has developed, when we've awakened to what we really think and feel, that our speech and actions become genuine. It's only at this point that the sanctity of ourselves as people becomes the measure of all things, where humanity matters more than the societal mandates of economics that depersonalize us in so many ways. This is the kind of consciousness we need in order to develop a society that serves us rather than forces us to serve society. In this way, the development of individual consciousness is the foundation for having free will.

The conscious choice to serve values greater than ourselves and to seek to know and serve the Self begins at this point. However, our ability to actually *do* this depends upon our having traveled through each of the previous stages of consciousness—simple, complex, and individual—or we'll simply misunderstand the process, and in our confusion will look for a manual, a theory, or an "expert" to tell us what to do. But listening to our inner voice cannot be reduced to a tidy formula any more than the experience of listening to Beethoven's Fifth Symphony can be reduced to sitting in a chair, although many of the suggestions I will make later can be helpful.

Self-awareness and self-discovery that come from carefully paying attention to every aspect of ourselves pave the road to living authentically. It evolves as we turn our energies away from looking for the answers and trying to control everything to developing self-knowledge and allowing ourselves to "live into the questions" as the poet Rilke suggests. How do we know when we're living this way? It's something we know instinctively. We feel "at home" in life. In all of its aspects, including misfortunes, life has meaning, purpose, and dignity. We realize that our dark moments are teachers, they strip us of what we thought we needed before, they humanize us and open us to love and joy. We feel less of the anxiety of modern life and more whole within ourselves and the world.

Joseph Campbell summed it up with his version of a Buddhist saying: "We can joyfully participate in the sorrows of the world."

Individual consciousness leads us out of self-centeredness and allows us to see others as they actually are, to see their personhood just as we're first beginning to see our own, and to accept their shortcomings and shadow sides because we *know* our own. As we move further into illuminated consciousness, the process brings us truly and fully into the world. We experience ourselves more completely in relationship with others and to the process of life. We realize suffering and joy are equal facets of life and both bring value to us. And we learn to give and receive love without the contamination of our former needs and projections.

People who can live at this level help us all to appreciate life's vitality and to see how much of our suffering is brought on by our own lack of consciousness. Out of this suffering an urge for life, for spiritual fulfillment, and a strong drive toward love may grow.

CHAPTER 3
At the Crossroads

Do you remember how life yearned out of childhood toward the "great thing"? I see that it is now yearning forth beyond the great thing toward the greater one.
—Rainer Maria Rilke

The ancient story of King Midas, as narrated in the *Metamorphoses* by the Roman writer Ovid, is not just a simple tale of greed. It carries many subtle details and levels of meaning. For instance the story begins with a kindness and generosity. Selinus, the foster father of the god Bacchus, has become lost while in a drunken state. As he is wandering around, some peasants find him and take him to the king. Midas recognizes Selinus and treats him with hospitality, caring for him for ten days and nights. In these opening details we begin to get the true flavor of the story, a message that our most serious problems often begin with good intentions.

As the story goes on Bacchus offers King Midas a reward for his kindness to the old man. Midas, rejoicing in his good fortune, asks that everything he touches be turned to gold. With his wish granted the king happily returns home. But he soon finds out that when he touches a piece of bread it turns into gold. The same thing happens with meat, vegetables, and wine. Everything turns to gold. Finally starving and dying of thirst, he prays to Bacchus for relief from his "blessing." In response to Midas's prayers, Bacchus sends him to the headwaters of the river Patolus to wash himself clean of his affliction.

But this isn't the end of the story. Midas, who had become disillusioned with wealth and splendor, goes back to nature. He begins to live in the fields and worship the nature god Pan. He becomes so enthralled with this opposite way of life that he compares the music of Pan to that of Apollo, the mighty sun-god and the god of music. In anger Apollo turns the ears of King Midas into the ears of a donkey.

In this phase of the story we see Midas go from one extreme, that of wealth, to the other extreme of nature. Apollo is also the god of the "golden mean" of keeping life in balance and doing nothing in excess. The donkey ears make it clear how we end up when we lose our balance between materialism and nature. But the fate of poor Midas continues. In embarrassment he covers his ears with a turban. Only his hairdresser knows of the king's humiliating secret, and he is strongly advised not to reveal it. But the secret is so compelling that the hairdresser is overcome by it. He goes out into a field, digs a hole into the ground, whispers the story, and covers it up. Before long, reeds grow from the freshly turned earth and begin whispering the story into the wind. Ovid concludes the tale by showing us that no matter how we try to hide our follies, whether it be behind appearances or by burying them, the truth is in the wind around us.

As a society we are caught like Midas when he could turn everything into gold. The civilization we have created that brings us so much opportunity also brings harm and illness and makes it difficult to understand exactly what's happening and how we can help ourselves.

The nineteenth-century religious philosopher Soren Kierkegaard attempted to summarize the despair modern life brings along with its benefits as a spiritual and emotional sickness—a "sickness unto death." Today the cardiac specialist and writer about healthy living, Dean Ornish, describes heart disease as an epidemic of emotional and spiritual sickness brought about by the breakdown of our social and religious networks, which formerly gave us a sense of connection and community. Dr. Ornish emphasizes that people who feel stressed, lonely, and isolated are more likely to smoke, overeat, abuse drugs, work too hard, become aggressive, and die prematurely. They are also more likely to have anxiety, panic attacks, depression, and destructive relationships.

The works of Freud, Jung, Fromm, and their colleagues have supported the position that loneliness and alienation have been causing our illnesses for over a century. The breakdown of our social and religious structures makes the appearance of our economic success a hollow achievement. It was Fromm who named the values in our societal mind-set as our social character and pointed out that it provides the lens we look through to define ourselves and how the world should be. Unless we develop enough consciousness to grow beyond the values of today's culture, we will find as King Midas did that it is our own well-intentioned actions that are causing our problems. This result happens because even good intentions must be based on thoughtful considerations and carefully understood values and ideals, or they may cause more harm than good.

These observations remind us that we need to understand ourselves on a deeper level and become aware of the damaging side of the forces affecting our lives. Yet recognizing the harmful influences of society on our physical and mental health, however, doesn't relieve us of having to deal with our illnesses and difficulties. And yet, this awareness does have strong implications for all of us. To begin with, our society is so biased against emotional problems, labeling them a form of weakness, that when we experience them we often are made to feel even more isolated and alone in our struggles.

Actually, we aren't alone. Many of us are having similar struggles that range from feeling harried and pressured to more severe forms of depression and marital conflicts. To some extent we all feel driven, anxious, depressed, and dissatisfied at times. One of the questions today is whether we understand our feelings well enough to even be aware of our emotional conditions before they go so far as to cause other physical illnesses. Frequently we are so caught up in plunging through our everyday business, we don't realize we are depressed and worn-out. Nor do we recognize that life isn't fulfilling or that our spouses have become strangers until some kind of attention-getting breakdown occurs. However, if we work to understand our emotions on a deeper level, we will have to slow down and take a closer look at who we are, how we're living, what values are driving us, and how our relationships are affecting us. This process increases our awareness of life and reality. As our self-knowledge grows, we'll change and mature emotionally—and so will society. Personal growth will cause a ripple effect as the growth in consciousness of enough people, one by one, can create general change, and lasting social improvements.

As our world has become dominated by the ideals of performance and efficiency, we have internalized these as guidelines in our everyday lives. Recently a friend explained to me how he had planned, organized, and set mental goals and schedules for his Saturday yard work. "I've finally realized," he said with a grimace, "that I'm making my weekends as stressful as my job." I've heard similar complaints about organizing housework, paperwork, car pools, golf games, shopping, and other hobbies and household chores. These tasks have become so insidious that we're increasing our stress and leaving little room for fun, spontaneity, and creativity, not to mention love, sensuality, intimacy, and reflection.

I once asked a woman who consistently over-jammed her life with goals and deadlines how it would feel to take a day off, spend it in bed reading, napping, and watching TV. She looked aghast. "I'd feel so guilty I'd probably get really sick," she replied. I think we've become so used to making demands on ourselves that we eliminate self-compassion from our very lives. We live, instead, to perform.

Let's Be in Life Together

Jungian analyst C. A. Mier, who spent his life studying ancient healing practices, observed that in older cultures and until the Middle Ages it was well known that raising a disease from a personal to a cultural and spiritual level had a curative effect. This approach makes me wonder how our lives might be changed if we took our current epidemic of depression and raised it to a cultural and spiritual problem rather than treating it as an individual problem that's primarily based on biochemistry or childhood disturbances.

The growth of support groups for illnesses, addictions, and other problems shows we're developing a new awareness of how we can help each other grow and heal. Before the modern age of medicine everyone felt vulnerable to disease and the priest or shaman was as important to the ailing person as the physician. In many cases the sick person was thought to have offended a god or to be out of harmony with the transcendent powers. In the early days of our Western religions the whole community participated in the search for spiritual meaning in human vulnerability and suffering, which gave both a network and the ritual support of spiritual practices to sick people. The Jewish tradition of the Lamed Vovniks, the ten "just" (morally perfect) men whose suffering supported the world, and the Christian tradition of Christ's suffering that redeemed the world, gave a sense of meaning to people they could identify with when they were in pain. This point of view brought them a deep feeling of support from the community and from within themselves.

The scientific approach to medicine brought forward the idea that an illness should be treated and cured by itself. Yet for all the gifts that modern science has given us, it's also made it difficult to figure out how to take a personal or spiritual attitude toward our illnesses. When we're sick, we like to know where we stand, but our technological approach to healing leaves us feeling isolated because our fear, anger, vulnerability, and need to find meaning in our suffering are ignored. It's amazing how much pain and hardship we can bear if we believe we have a good reason for doing so, and if we think we're carrying our share of a common burden. Sharing our stories of suffering and hearing those of other people help us find meaning and feel we have burdens in common. This process is healing and even galvanizing when we discover we have access to a greater wisdom within us than we realize.

During my years of practice I have been surprised at how often people in social situations say to me, "I don't see how you can listen to other people's problems all day." To begin with, that isn't what I do. Such questions reflect the public bias and misunderstanding of analysis and much of psychotherapy. I rarely listen to problems and then try to help people solve them. I listen to stories, the stories of people's lives, of their struggles, their inner stories told in dreams and fantasies, and we dialogue with each other. I am seldom bored and more often moved profoundly by how many ways life is struggling to heal these people and reenergize their growth. By taking time out from the pace of the world and by being human together in this way, the healing process becomes far deeper than a simple problem-solving approach can be.

In our efforts to understand and regenerate ourselves it is often helpful to listen to other stories that have evolved out of the experience of being human. Fairy tales, myths, legends, and traditional religious stories and parables have evolved over the centuries to support and map out our experiences. Our enduring interest in these stories, I believe, has to do with our need for depth and substance in the way we *understand* life. Fairy tales from around the world vividly explore the fundamental patterns and themes of our lives. The imagery may be specific to the culture in which they were born, but the issues are universal and teach us how much we have in common. Joseph Campbell explained how these themes are going on in the lives of everyday people and how we are all living these motifs in our own ways when he said: "The latest incarnations of Oedipus, the continued romance of Beauty and the Beast, stand this afternoon on the corner of Forty-second Street and Fifth Avenue, watching for the traffic light to change."

The fantastic imagery in these stories is essential to their purpose because, like the images in dreams, they are meant to switch our focus from the realistic particulars of life to how we are experiencing and interacting with its deeper aspects. Because the tales reach beneath the surface of our everyday activities into the description of the universal ways in which our lives play themselves out, they can be indispensable guides to self-understanding. And self-knowledge brings healing, while realizing that our difficulties are very human brings comfort.

AT THE CROSSROADS

I once had a woman write to me about a year after a fairy tale seminar I'd conducted. In her letter she shared that for several years before the seminar she had been feeling increasingly exhausted and seemed to have some kind of cold or infection most of the time. One of the fairy tales we had discussed during the seminar was "Bluebeard." She thought that our interpretation of this tale had opened her eyes to the hurtful things she was doing to herself without realizing it.

I'm saying "our interpretation" because fairy tales may be read as referring to many different levels of experience at once. In this seminar we had discussed "Bluebeard" as a story picturing a destructive interaction that goes on in a modern woman's psyche and how she can become more aware of it.

As the story opens a young woman finds Bluebeard to be a very unattractive man. Furthermore it is well-known in the kingdom that he has been married several times though no one knows what has become of his former wives. Soon, however, the young woman discovers he's very rich and powerful. As you might imagine he then becomes more attractive in her eyes. Shortly thereafter they are married, and Bluebeard generously gives her access to all of his riches and to every room in his mansion except one. He warns her sternly that she must stay away from this room.

One day while her husband is away on business the young woman becomes overcome with curiosity and unlocks the door to the forbidden room. Inside the room she's horrified to discover the bloody bodies of Bluebeard's former wives. Quickly she flees the frightening scene. When her husband returns she tries to act innocent. But he's suspicious and spies a drop of blood on the key to the forbidden chamber. In a rage at her disobedience Bluebeard tells her that he's going to cut off her head and throw her body into the room with his former wives.

Knowing that her brothers, who are soldiers, are coming for a visit she stalls for time by pleading and praying. At the very last possible moment her brothers arrive, size up the situation, and kill her vicious husband.

Bluebeard represents a dark masculine attitude that we can

develop. It's an attitude that values power, control, and accomplishments more than love and compassion. I've known many men and women who gave the appearance of being warm, outgoing, and successful but behind these masks were controlling and perfectionistic. One woman's mother compulsively straightened her house to perfection as a ritual to placate her anxiety. She passed on both the anxiety and the ritual to her daughter by screaming at her children whenever they created disorder. Another woman I knew was the daughter of a teacher and felt she had to make perfect grades to please her father. A third grew up in a family that lived on the fringe of an affluent neighborhood. Although she attended the same private schools as her wealthier neighbors, she always felt inferior around her friends and their families and worked hard to put up a perfect front to protect herself from these feelings.

Men in general are still taught to wall off their feeling sides and aren't brought up in a way that cultivates their emotional capacities. I remember Mike, an architect who worked harder and harder building up his firm, overseeing every project and working nights and weekends to be sure all the firm's work was up to "our firm's" standards—his anxious standards of perfection. Finally he realized that the only time he was happy was during the evening after having played racquetball and before going to bed. As we reflected on his situation he remembered that he'd developed a deep sense of inferiority as a boy. He was more artistic than athletic and felt his drive had originated in order to prove his worthiness in a competitive male world.

We unconsciously surrender our authenticity to dark attitudes for a variety of reasons. It may be because we've internalized a very limited idea of what a worthwhile person is all about. But more often we learn to do so as a way to cope, protect ourselves, feel worthy, and excel. The earlier story of Michael and how he learned to drive himself with self-criticism illustrates this process. Eventually living under the influence of such an attitude will exhaust us. While this process is taking place, our own state of fatigue can frighten us, make us think we're losing control or that we're failing. And, it can cause deep anxiety as we think that everyone *else* can do the job faster, better—but we can't. This leads to more self-doubt, self-hatred, and intensified effort.

In our society these driven attitudes are often admired and rewarded. And while they may lead to early success in our lives they will eventually begin to consume us—usually with inner criticism that makes us feel inferior or fragmented when we fail to meet our own unrealistic standards. As the fairy tale revealed, it was the power and riches of Bluebeard that initially made him attractive to the young woman. But she had to live with him for a while and develop a bit of forbidden awareness—to look behind the facade that appeared so impressive—in order to discover the reality of the price she was paying for her position. The room full of bodies suggests the way we kill parts of ourselves when we make compromises and lock our pain away in some inner compartment. We may marry for wealth, status, or to please our families; stay in relationships for security; make career choices that are "safe"; or live in other ways that deny our hearts and creativity for the sake of appearances.

Opening the forbidden door in fairy tales depicts how fate eventually leads us into new awareness. The story of Bluebeard teaches us how the decisions we make that don't consider our deeper needs and values can hurt us. Once we can see things more honestly, we have to confront our old attitudes and the patterns of living they support, and struggle to replace them with more helpful ones. The woman who had written to me explained, "As soon as I heard the story and you began discussing it I knew 'This is me.' I've got to stop being so ruthless with myself and learn to use my strength for self-protection and nurturance. I'm learning to look for the ways I drive and criticize myself and when I catch myself I say, 'OK Bluebeard, that's enough, get out!' It isn't easy but it's giving me a sense of power I never felt before." She soon felt strong enough to take a year off from her job as a communications consultant in order to rest, write, and think about how she would like to live in the future.

When we carefully reflect on these stories it's surprising how many bits of ourselves we can find in so many of them. Most of our problems are common ones clothed in the fashion of our particular circumstances. Marrying the prince or princess reflects our hope for maturity and wholeness. "Cinderella" shows how much we want to find out how to live beyond the mundane. "Beauty and the Beast" shows that love can transform life, and "The Frog Prince" exhibits the way hidden potentials can evolve. Every story explains a journey and reveals an archetypal example of human nature. But when we're in their grip, we usually lose our ability to see ourselves clearly. A tale like "Bluebeard" can mirror our experiences back to us in a manner that opens our eyes and helps us see our struggles as part of the human condition instead of a neurosis or dysfunction.

Thomas Moore reminds us of the importance of the commonplace in our lives as he observes: "To the soul, the ordinary is sacred and the everyday is the primary source of religion." Modern theology has made the mistake of allowing our religious stories to lie fallow in the past rather than bringing them up-to-date in a manner that seems relevant to our own stories. For example, in the story of Christ's birth Herod is pictured as a mean old debauched king who is threatened by the birth of a potential rival. However, this story, which is so rich in religious symbolism, could be looked at in another way. Like Bluebeard, Herod could be seen as a picture of a dark attitude within ourselves. A character who wants to maintain the status quo in our personalities, the dominance of the cultural mind-set, and who will try to kill our ability to grow, transform, and live into our true spiritual potentials.

In many cases we've whittled these stories down to fit some acquired standard of social and spiritual acceptability. Buddha, as an illustration, isn't simply a saintly figure. He was first a man of the world who had a wife, concubines, and a child, a life uncommonly secular (he was also born a prince) before beginning his saintly journey. Moses and Abraham have similar stories as does Jesus, who was a carpenter before becoming a religious leader. In other words our great religious figures didn't disdain the human condition. They grew fully into it and through it, using it as a foundation for illumination. Their journeys were filled with doubts and inner conflicts. They questioned the voices directing them and had to battle the temptation to use their inner strengths to gain personal power, wealth, and fame. They endured suffering and deprivation and bore the tensions of compassion and dying in disappointment, as Moses did, without entering the Promised Land, and as Jesus did, cruelly crucified without seeing his kingdom come to life on Earth. Saints and prophets live out similar story lines.

For centuries these patterns brought consolation to the people who listened to them in story form and could see a comparison between the suffering of a religious figure and the suffering of ordinary life. We can do the same by revitalizing these stories and making them relevant to modern life. In this way, we can compare our feeling lost or confused as the "Dark Night of the Soul" that precedes a new revelation, or in fresh and more resonant terms, a new vision of how we can live. Or we might compare our depression to the dark events approaching Good Friday that are calling for the dawn of a spiritual or psychological rebirth in our lives.

The darkness in religious stories reminds me of the heartbreaking account of Abraham on the journey to sacrifice his son, Isaac. Initially Abraham had been called by God to leave the security of his past, "Your land, your kin and the house of your father," by the promise he would father a great nation. Then in that magnificently told story in the Old Testament, Book of Genesis, God directed Abraham to give up this future promise by sacrificing his only son, Isaac, to God—Isaac, the son born to his parents in their later years, the son who symbolized carrying his father's life into the future. Step-by-step the story carefully describes the preparations for the sacrifice and the tense conversation between father and son. At the last moment, divine intervention saves Isaac and rewards Abraham's faithful devotion with a renewed promise for the future.

This is a story that has always meant a lot to me. Many years ago when I sold my business and returned to school, I often thought of this story for I felt in some ways that I was sacrificing my own sure future, the future I imagine Isaac represented to Abraham.

Abraham's trust in God, in life, eventually brought him a reprieve and he went on to found a great people. I felt that my own trust in life and the voice leading me would likewise lead to a meaningful future beyond my previous vision. I found great comfort in this story that so few people seem to understand today.

The tragedy of the Holocaust is filled not only with stories of great sadness and suffering, but also with incredible efforts to find spiritual meaning during the darkest of nights. One of the most moving stories is that of Vienna-born existential psychiatrist Viktor Frankl. During World War II, Dr. Frankl, along with his entire family, was sent to a series of concentration camps, which included Dachau and Auschwitz. His description of the life in these camps is of unforgettable intensity. At the end of the war he returned to Vienna to discover that no one else in his family had survived. By reflecting upon his experiences in the camps and the slow, painful rebuilding of his life, he enriches our understanding of suffering. In his classic book *Man's Search for Meaning*, Dr. Frankl tells us that if we can turn suffering into a search for meaning it transforms our experiences, that we are most human when we are living in a manner that is pointing to something or someone beyond ourselves. Whether we find a purpose to fulfill, another person to encounter, a cause or vocation to serve, or someone to love, suffering can open us to new experiences and the awareness that we can shape our characters and how we face life. The great lesson learned and shared by Viktor Frankl can help us understand the value of looking for meaning in our struggles and suffering, whether they are large or small.

Like Jung and his colleagues, Frankl believed that depression, anxiety, addictions, and our other emotional problems in adulthood are primarily the result of living lives that lack the meaning necessary to fulfill them. And yet, he reminds us through his own painful past, we have the capacity to find the meaning we need to sustain us in even the most dangerous circumstances. However, we have to search for meaning through the development of self-knowledge, and stories can be a great help, a wise yet probing counsel, in this search.

AT THE CROSSROADS

From Breakdown to Breakthrough

Sometimes it's very difficult to understand what's happening to us. Losing control of our emotions can be a frightening experience. One morning Janice, who had been a sixth grade teacher for seventeen years, began weeping in her classroom and was unable to stop. One of her friends brought her to my office, hoping I'd be free during the lunch hour.

Choking back her tears Janice said, "I'm a fake! I'm supposed to be a professional, but, but . . . I just can't do it anymore. I can't get my life together. I yell at my own children, my marriage stinks, and I'm supposed to know what to do about it. Well I don't. I don't like my husband. I don't like myself. I hate the way I look. I hate my body. I feel stupid and the harder I try to . . . fix everything, the worse it gets." And the tears began to flow again.

As you would expect, Janice was scared and ashamed of breaking down in public. She was also shocked at the vehemence of the exclamations that poured out as soon as she sat down in my office. A little later when we were discussing the anger in her outburst, we discovered it had a deeper dimension. She said, "It seems like the whole world conspires to make me feel bad about myself. Every time I pass a magazine rack I see all those articles about losing weight, improving your sex life, looking attractive, feeling empowered, and being happy, organized, and successful. Just seeing them makes me feel like a total failure, and I hate myself. Sometimes I even buy the magazines, read the articles, and then feel even worse."

I've met many women who share Janice's distress over the messages the media sends to them. And yet, we know better—or at least we should. For in spite of all the research and best-selling books that remind us about the negative effects our culture's messages have on women and adolescent girls, the stream of them continues—preying on their desire to feel good about themselves and turning life into a process of never feeling good enough to be satisfied.

After a few days when Janice returned to school, many of her colleagues asked how she was doing. Several of them even shared their stories of depression, marital tensions, and experiences in therapy. These gestures of compassion and understanding were precious to Janice, because thanks to these friends she no longer felt like a total failure and all alone. The openness of a few friends also made our work together easier because they helped her realize that many competent people in our society are having similar difficulties.

When Janice was able to ease up a bit on blaming herself, she was able to begin exploring her anger in all its fullness. Previously, she had only directed it inwardly. Now as she retraced her childhood, for the first time she began to get angry at her parents. She resented the way her father had criticized her as a young girl, demanding good grades and behavior but rarely rewarding her with praise, warmth, or understanding. And, as she grew into a young woman, her developing femininity seemed to scare him rather than please him. She also resented her mother's never-ending concern with appearances. The more Janice talked the more she realized she was discovering new things about herself. In the past she had described her early life as an average childhood. Now she was beginning to understand that it was full of life-shaping events that seeded the direction of her life's story. In fact, the more she learned about herself the more she began to grudgingly respect her depression as a turning point that forced her to begin the efforts to open up her life. She decided to talk to her family doctor and with his help, she requested disability leave from her job. Janice wanted the time to recover, which meant time to fully understand what her "breakdown" was all about.

Learning to value her depression didn't mean she immediately began feeling better. There were still days of tears and of not getting off the couch. Days when she would proclaim, "It's no use. I'm ruining my life and my children." And, "I'm too old to change and God knows nobody else is going to." But she remained in analysis, coming to see me twice a week and in every session she spoke from and about her depression. We lived in it together and never treated it like a disease.

During that time I simply listened to her with interest and acceptance. We also discussed the memories, feelings, and frustrations she was discovering as she reminisced and explored her psyche. Like most of us, she knew at some level she'd held in many feelings during her life. But when they began to emerge she was surprised to find out how far back in her life they went and how strong they were. While her feelings were coming out on their own I urged her to pay careful attention to them. I simply wanted her to appreciate and share in the previously unacknowledged part of her story that was now coming into expression. And as we went along I observed the slow, subtle shift in tone and vitality that was taking place in her.

In her lowest moments Janice frequently said she should never have become a teacher. I didn't take her statement literally because I realized how much being a teacher had meant to her previously and how respected she was in her community. Then one day she said, "I'm a good teacher and I know that. And I need to learn, too. I need to find my center and stay balanced, and not be thrown by all the pressures of accountability and the threats of complaining parents when their children aren't doing well. Or when they're not doing enough. Or when it's too much." Janice raked her slender fingers through her hair. "I always feel I'm doing something wrong. That it's my fault."

Janice uncovered piece after piece of the sacrifices she'd made to become a good teacher, a choice she made initially because she couldn't figure out anything else she wanted to do. Early in her career she wanted to impress her supervisors, and this desire led her to teach children what they needed to know to do well on standardized tests rather than what she thought was important for their educational foundation. The more she let her need to please and impress authority figures dominate her judgment, the more she regretted her career choice. But at the same time she couldn't help talking about her concern for children and our educational system. Janice was finding out that deep down she really is a teacher. She was also recognizing that her anxieties about having her classes excel on test scores, pleasing the parents of the children she taught, and impressing her school's administration were stealing the enjoyment from her work. While she was discovering that teaching was her heartfelt vocation, it was becoming obvious that the anxious, perfectionistic aspects in her were being replaced. She was becoming a stronger, more independent, and less driven woman.

Early in her depressed state Janice could only see her experience as a breakdown, the ending of a familiar life and the collapse of long-held values and viewpoints about how life is supposed to be. However, as feelings poured out of her and she began to get a sense of her life as a story, she saw that her depression was forcing her to broaden her perspective and to become more complete as a person. In reality it had made her stop and reassess her life. It was telling her that things weren't going well at all and she had better find out why they weren't and how she really felt about the way her life was affecting her. To her surprise she discovered that being a hardworking perfectionist was a condition driven by anxiety and instead of being a strong character trait it was destroying her, while working with her depression was strengthening her and giving her a new sense of self-confidence and solidity.

Janice is continuing to work and grow. Her story thus far shows that no matter how ashamed and alone we feel in our difficulties, we are not so isolated after all. And that the expectations and pressures of our society exacerbate our pain. Furthermore, Janice's breakdown marked the necessary end to an old way of life and the potential for a new one. The experience became its own teacher and a preparation for change.

It shouldn't require a personal crisis to illustrate the value of raising our experiences to a general level once we've stopped to think about it. As human beings we share similar feelings in many circumstances. If, for instance, a reasonably well-off person living in a nice suburb encounters business reverses and goes bankrupt, he or she will feel terrible—ashamed, stupid, and a failure. If, however, there's a general economic depression or a natural disaster and everyone in the neighborhood loses everything, they will certainly feel unhappy about their economic misfortune, but they'll feel better because other people are sharing their circumstances. We feel differently in a group than when we face things alone. This simple reality explains why support groups help so many people in their healing process or why television talk shows are so popular. Part confession, part populist renewal of the community covenant, they allow the audience and viewers at home to feel relief that they're not alone in their despair, that they're at one with the rest of the human race. Janice originally thought her friends and colleagues were better at managing their lives than she was. When she found out several of them had been to therapy for various reasons, that her boss was understanding, and that several well-known public figures had suffered from severe depression, she no longer felt so estranged from everyone else.

My analytic work with Janice wasn't as much about depression as it was about self-alienation that had progressed to the point of self-hate. The pace of modern life and society's images of how successful, high-functioning people should appear seem to foster an inner voice that constantly drives and criticizes us. Many of us experience this voice as a relentless *inner critic* that is observing, measuring, and telling us how we're failing to measure up to our own, usually perfectionistic, standards. We can't seem to keep our kitchens clean enough, our bodies toned enough, our bank accounts filled enough. Our lives are like our refrigerators—never stocked full enough, always in need of replenishment. We can't keep our paperwork up-to-date, our checkbook balanced, our thank-you notes sent out, or our credit cards paid off. Too much inner criticism results in self-alienation, even self-hate, and the symptoms of this condition are often depression and exhaustion. I believe that our epidemic of depression reflects our animosity toward ourselves, and I agree with Dean Ornish that alienation lies behind much of our medical distress.

A general principle we can take from Freud is that love and destructiveness are equally available to us. To understand our vulnerability to self-destructive attitudes and to learn how to reverse these attitudes into ones of love require that we look carefully into the process of how we form our adult identities. And this exploration returns us to our efforts to understand how society affects our growing up and molds many of the expectations and fears our parents brought to our early years.

Reassessing Our Values

Janice concluded that her parents' overconcern with her behavior, grades, and appearances reflected their own insecurities. However, their anxiety affected her and prevented her from building up the self-assurance she needed in order to face life confidently. The stories of our families and how they affect us is to a large extent a smaller version of what's taking place in our culture. As our culture fragments, our families fragment. If our society values achievement and productivity more than developing individuals who are secure in themselves, confident in the future, and looking forward to the challenges of adult life, then our families will have trouble living in ways that provide this kind of foundation in life for their children. In other words when our society overemphasizes competition, we become anxious and this anxiety invades our families.

Recently I witnessed a small but dramatic example of how our collective attitudes seep down to the personal level. I saw a grandmother standing outside of a church playground next to her daughter-in-law. In the playground were a number of toddlers walking, sitting, crawling, laughing, and looking quizzically at each other. It was a beautiful sight. Then I heard the grandmother whisper, "He doesn't seem quite as big as the others, or as *fast*." The young mother's face tensed in response as the grandmother's anxious comment made a hurtful impact.

It won't take too many situations like this one to begin undermining the young mother's ability to give her child the sense of security he needs to begin his life with confidence. There is something more going on here than a cliched expression of mother-in-law criticism. Anxiety and comparisons are generated by our social character and its value structure. When they invade our homes, undercurrents of worried, apprehensive comparisons begin replacing expressions of love and joy. And if parents and grandparents are anxious about their offspring, comparing them to fantasies of "normalcy," the children they raise will become adults who have a core of self-doubt rather than self-confidence.

Another example comes to mind. Close to my home is a group of soccer fields that are filled with children's competitions during spring and fall weekends. The coaches of these teams have recently banded together to ask the parents not to yell any instructions or comments during play. The angry, aggressive instructions from parents are distracting and humiliating to the small players. It doesn't take much reflection to realize that these parents are mirroring the angry, competitive nature of our culture and how it frustrates and frightens us with the fear of failure or not "measuring up."

Competition, evaluating ourselves in comparison to other people and media images, winning, aggressivity, and consuming material goods have all become traits of our social character. We're taught that they mark the path that will lead us to a successful place in the world. Our institutions rarely teach us to cooperate, foster creativity, or be empathetic. Even our teams foster competition for playing time and reward individual stardom. Schools and businesses likewise teach us to be independent, objective, competent, and analytical. This one-sided emphasis in our social character structure leaves us struggling to recover other values, values of the heart such as love, compassion, gentleness, and community that are needed in order to bring health and equilibrium back into our lives.

When I think about how we overemphasize independence and individuality, I recall a man in his late fifties who was talking to me about the problems he was having in his second marriage. He had done well in the arena of competition and achievement, but couldn't realize why his wife wanted to leave him.

"I just can't understand what else she wants," he said. "We talk, we go out, we enjoy each other's company. We have more than enough money to enjoy our lives. What's missing?"

"Does she feel needed?" I asked.

"Needed?" he responded. "Needed?"

"Yes. Isn't it important to feel needed? Think about it for a minute, don't you want to feel needed? What makes a relationship important?"

"I didn't think we were supposed to be needy.... No ... maybe I don't need her. I think she actually said that once."

If we put too much emphasis on performance and competition, it teaches us to overvalue being self-contained, and if we do that, how deep and how human can our relationships be? Can we expect to have love, growth, and intimacy if we can't admit to ourselves that we need to be needed, and that needing other people actually fulfills part of our beings? There's no doubt in my mind that I need my wife, my children, my friends, and my colleagues, and my life is richer when these needs are filled.

We have traditionally used our religious institutions to uphold the moral aspects of our social character. This means their job has been to remind us that we must act ethically and responsibly. They also served as community centers where people met, celebrated the events of the life cycle and the seasons of the spiritual year. As their influence has diminished we've been left more isolated and vulnerable to the trend makers in advertising and the entertainment industry. When we live within an active religious system, it gives us a context for living, a map, so to speak, that provides us with a picture of life in general, our place in it, and an idea of how to live purposefully and consistently.

I remember during one of my seminars a woman asked, "Isn't the whole system of capitalism destructive and selfish?" I answered that I didn't think so, and I still don't. The problem isn't in our economic system. It's that our economic system has become our unconscious religion, and we've lost our sense of values to a system that should serve our values.

The power of unified beliefs in a society, whether they are right or wrong, secular or sacred, makes it difficult to be at variance with our culture. At home and in school we're generally taught to make choices of which our culture approves in manners, social graces, how we dress, and the attitudes we support. Symbolically our adaptation reflects our membership in the group. This feeling empowers us to act, and as long as we make choices in line with the group, we feel a sense of belonging and security.

As churches and temples have declined in use as community centers, we've also lost a forum and support for questioning social values and for trying out other values and ideas. We're left alone to face the gods of commerce, the fire and brimstone of media advertising and image making that mandates like Moses on the Mount who we should be and how we should live. Charge cards and ordering from slick catalogs or over the Internet have become our baptism into the tribe of chosen people.

One of the most difficult tasks we face in individuation is facing and working our way out of the web of cultural influences. Most of us have been hearing about the things I'm discussing for a long time but haven't quite figured out how to confront them effectively. Accepting a full awareness of our reality is the first step in being able to change it. While our families and society have molded who we are, we must use our awareness to break free of the belief systems that limit and fail to serve our personal growth. And, by doing so we help our culture to grow as well.

There is nothing simple about developing self-understanding, independence, and self-respect. It begins with carefully searching out the effects our families and society have on us in order to awaken, to become aware of the forces that shape our lives. We must learn to see many of our adult crises and problems as symbolizing our need to break free of these old patterns. Blaming society, capitalism, or our parents isn't the goal. Awareness is the end we're aiming toward. Then we can use our self-knowledge as a springboard into higher consciousness and a life that is free of its former limits as old habits and self-images die. The path of individuation, of developing true self-reliance and maturity, is much more than an act of psychological health. Becoming adept at the process of self-inquiry and symbolic understanding is a vital spiritual task that leads to growth of faith in ourselves.

CHAPTER 4
Preparing for Change

And there we have it; the fundamental contradiction and challenge of creativity. If we practice it we enter the inner world, we find ourselves outside the perimeter of conventional society—outsiders feeling all the loneliness of that disconnection. And yet we are simultaneously as far as we can get from loneliness because we are, finally, with ourselves.
—Deena Metzger

The search for gold has been a force that's lured Western civilization for centuries. Gold is the most precious and incorruptible metal. It symbolizes wealth and power, the good life; and for older civilizations it has represented the highest values of the human spirit. This quest has taken many forms: searching out and exploring new lands, engaging in various kinds of warfare, and braving unknown hardships. Strangely enough, the quest has also included medieval alchemists, working in their mysterious laboratories, seeking to put primitive materials through a careful process of heating, cooling, and distilling. Their goal was to produce an end product they referred to as gold, or the "philosopher's stone." The true gold they sought was a metaphor for the heart of life and illuminated consciousness.

The alchemist or "goldmaker" was concerned with the transformation of primitive material into more highly evolved substances. Carl Jung viewed the alchemical process as a metaphor for the individuation process, one that symbolized the steps in our personal development that transform ordinary life into higher levels. Two kinds of gold were sought in the alchemical process: The first one is *common gold*, the symbolic substance required to leave the world of childhood and become a functioning adult. Common gold may be further refined until it becomes *true gold*, the essence of life. True gold is the symbolic substance that represents the illuminated personality.

Understanding the refining process that has shaped us makes it easier to accept our inborn desire to explore our creative abilities and develop our inner strength and authenticity. This desire energizes our efforts to grow in self-knowledge and to search for the true gold. In my introduction I told you that this process leads to "living a life of substance," and the heart of my efforts is to lead us in the direction of an enriched life. At this point it may be helpful to first consider the kind of substance that comes when we've attained common gold, the state I referred to as *complex consciousness* in chapter 1.

Complex consciousness, you may remember, is all about becoming competent in the world and in relationships, or what I have summarized as the tasks of growing up. I've referred to the kind of substance we need to become adults as *secular* substance. Secular substance is simply a more modern name for common gold, and it's based on forming identities capable of having partners, friends, and colleagues, being socially responsible, and finding an occupation. Secular means worldly. But these characteristics and their values, no matter how good they are and how well they are developed, can't bring into our personalities the substance that comes from our essential natures. Deeper, more profound, and animating, this kind of substance comes from inside us through knowing ourselves deeply and living life fully. I call it *sacred* substance.

The way we deal with religion can illustrate these two kinds of substance. A faith learned in childhood with values and beliefs can help guide us into adult life. Such a structure can be taken on in adult life as well, and for some of us it can provide a feeling of community with other people who share the same values. But despite its value, and even though it may have included an emotional conversion experience, this religion is still one developed from the outside. Any religious institution will have its own social character that insists on its version of the revealed truth; and when the beliefs of the institution are threatened, its members respond as negatively as any group does when its belief system is threatened. But it is still *secular* substance, and for many of us leads to a sickly form of selfishness that teaches us to admire ourselves at the expense of judging others.

When a religious faith is more personal, however, and based on inner experience, on the process of formation and discernment, it's built of essential spiritual material that's difficult to threaten. This kind of faith, rooted in personal and sacred substance, responds to threats with laughter and compassion, and can lead to a more sacred form of selfishness. In her book *The Interior Castle,* Saint Teresa of Avila reflects the thoughts of most of the great mystics in all religions when she writes that developing self-knowledge is a fundamental aspect of spiritual growth. The first of the seven mansions in her symbolic description of what she calls "the interior castle of spiritual growth" is the mansion of self-knowledge. She says, "Knowing ourselves is something so important that I wouldn't want any relaxation in this regard, however high you may have climbed into the heavens . . . enter the first rooms where self-knowledge is dealt with rather than fly off into other rooms."

Revisioning the Good Life

The best stories have many meanings and these meanings change as our capacity to understand the complexities of life increases. Revisiting folktales over the years has often left me wondering why I couldn't see their meanings all along, and yet, experience has taught me to also wonder about what meanings future readings may reveal. When I was a young man reading them to my children, I saw them as children's stories. Today, I agree with the simple statement that the great Italian writer Italo Calvino made after compiling a book of fairy tales. He said, "Now that the book is finished, I know this was not a hallucination, a kind of professional malady, but the confirmation of something I already suspected.

Fairy tales are true. Taken altogether, they offer . . . a general explanation of life . . . the infinite possibility of a metamorphosis of all that exists."

And their truth grows as our ability to understand the patterns of life grows. The novelist Robertson Davies says that fairy tales only seem irrational or unreal to those who haven't grasped what life is all about. These people, he continues, "live under a spell—too often a spell they have brought upon their own heads."

"The Emperor's New Clothes" is a story I referred to in chapter 2. It's a tale that has always resonated with me and it grows as one of my favorites. In the story two swindlers claim they can create the most beautiful fabric in the world, a fabric so fine and so sheer that people who are incompetent or "unpardonly stupid" can not see it. The king and his entourage of counselors are caught between admitting their stupidity and acknowledging the reality that the emperor's new clothes are a hoax even after a child has pointed it out to them. Rather than confront a humiliating reality they persist in carrying out an illusion they know is false. The story shows it takes more than just awareness for us to change. It takes courage and humility and the willingness to occasionally feel like fools and laugh at ourselves.

The story is about illusion, appearances, swindling, and the refusal to acknowledge reality even when it's obvious. In fairy tale language the emperor can picture the governing attitudes in our lives or in our culture. We can imagine that he represents a view of our social character, one that's only concerned with appearances. His sole desire is to be well dressed and admired. The emperor shows no interest in the essential meaning of his position, administering his cabinet, supporting the arts, or caring for his soldiers and people. Nor is he interested in the values of the heart. We can infer this because the presence of an empress in the story and his interactions with her would have shown his relation to the values of the heart in the vernacular of such stories. But there is no empress, and therefore no life of the heart for this emperor.

At first glance he appears vain and to love himself too much. However, it's clear that he doesn't know how to love and more likely lives in fear, needing affirmation all the time. The story, with its emphasis on how we can be swindled by crafty illusions accepted as real by powerful people, reminds us that what we admire or subscribe to, what may appear to be the very best according to image makers or to any authority outside of ourselves, may also have no substance at all.

Jung has proposed a valuable framework that will help us to see and understand the role of the child here in symbolic terms. The emperor's mistake and the dishonesty of his advisors were pointed out by an innocent child as the emperor paraded proudly through the city. In his studies of archetypal symbolism Jung suggested that the image of the child that shows up in dreams, fairy tales, and myths, represents everything that is abandoned, exposed, vulnerable, and yet magically powerful, full of weakness and full of potential. In other words, children represent the unknowing, unindoctrinated, and not yet adapted parts of ourselves. When the child calls attention to the reality of the emperor's illusions and the common people all agree, I don't find it difficult to imagine what these images could symbolize in our modern lives. The feelings of the heart and the potentials of our future are calling attention through our symptoms, our angry children, and our unhappiness to the illusions we may be stubbornly and fearfully clinging to as the basis for how we live.

Talking about the image of the child reminds me of a dream I had in my early thirties when I was struggling with the decisions my life changes were about to require. The dream began with a wistful scene, one that continues to move me, that showed a young, golden-haired boy standing on a hillside in the morning mist. He was beckoning for me to join him. I was too far away to hear what he was calling but I could see him clearly. I was standing in the hallway of a large old house. The inside of the house looked the way I imagine an old English men's club would. The walls were paneled in a deep mahogany and the carpets were richly colored. Gentlemen in suits and ties were sitting in the leather club chairs smoking pipes and cigars while reading newspapers. As I sought to leave the house and join the boy I felt a powerful force grabbing me around the legs and pulling me back. I awoke struggling for freedom. How hard it is, I later thought, to break away from the traditional values of success and from the rich sense of belonging to see through the spell of that enchanted domain and seek new life.

Lifestyle, a word popular when I was younger, was the rich illusion that tempted my generation. While I've said that achieving success strengthened me personally, I also discovered that continually increasing my standard of living—by moving into more expensive neighborhoods, joining a country club, attending more cocktail parties, and taking expensive trips—wasn't fulfilling. During my late twenties while I was pursuing a corporate career, I had a boss who was a mentor I admired and wanted to emulate. One day I was shocked to hear that he'd resigned. A few days later we had lunch together and I asked him why he was leaving. "Bud, I worked toward this job for years. But you know what? It isn't fun up here and it isn't creative." His honesty and his ability to see through a miasma of success caused me to rethink my own future and to question my illusions. By speaking directly, and being willing to frankly state that he found being successful in the conventional way boring, stressful, and unsatisfying, he was kind and inspiring to me. His integrity saved me from years of working without questioning my assumptions about the "success" I was trying to achieve.

We are just as vulnerable as that old emperor was to the golden carrots dangled in front of us by our marketeers, image makers, and the purveyors of conventional wisdom. Rarely do our counselors—wise and well intentioned though they may be and who may include our parents, trusted friends, and colleagues—acknowledge the illusions with which we live. Like those counselors of the emperor they may be too afraid of appearing stupid or incompetent to question what's called reality. It's safer to support the spell cast by society's values.

Without realizing it we work hard to keep each other inside the boundaries of the life defined by our social character. Conventional wisdom defines the mainstream approach as to how society or our peer groups believe we should live. When I decided to return to school at age thirty-three, I was a husband and father of three. Not one person in my life, other than my therapist, even attempted to understand or support what I was doing. It dawned on me that I was experiencing more peer pressure to conform than I had ever felt as a teenager.

As adults, keeping our jobs, our marriages, and our friends often depends on conforming to what the people in these groups believe is the proper way to live. Advertising has become more sophisticated as it makes its appeals to different age, socioeconomic, and ethnic groups. The images we compare ourselves to are everywhere and range from business wear to sportswear, from wine to restaurants, from vacation spots to entertainment events. The things our peer groups admire make up a collective set of values that have a strong influence on us because we want their approval and acceptance. However, whether you own a Lexus or a Ford, a dishwasher or a big screen TV, cultural pressures are still cultural pressures that are economically driven and generally go against individuation.

Image continues to be a powerful shaper of our social existence, which ignores not only our inner selves, but also reality. The ideal images that society holds up for us and that we accept without question perpetuate our feelings of self-alienation because they always leave us playing for approval.

Mapping the Territory

Our personalities are much more unique and complicated than we realize. Freud and Jung developed their perspectives of human nature by studying their experiences with their patients. In Freud's case, the patients were primarily men and women suffering from various neuroses. But Jung frequently worked with people who were in good mental health and wished to enlarge the range of their understanding. In the Freudian tradition the realm of the unconscious is generally seen as the dwelling place of unruly instincts symbolized by demons and monsters. Jung added that the unconscious is also the home of our muses, angels, and our undiscovered potentials, perhaps even our best selves.

One of Jung's well-known contributions to psychology is his

concept of the *collective unconscious*. It's very similar to the concept that theologian Paul Tillich refers to as the "ground of our being." Fairy tales show the basic story patterns of life as they are contained in the collective unconscious and as we will live them out in certain circumstances. These stories have the same foundational themes in every culture throughout the world, and studies show they represent universal patterns of life fundamental to human nature. Every society in fact can have its own version of the emperor, of what it means to be more concerned with appearances than substance in that particular culture. And understanding such a story helps us see ourselves more clearly. Based on these facts Robertson Davies concludes that "fairy tales are nothing less than the distilled truth about real life."

The tough-minded patterns and sometimes cruel logic of these stories before they were Disneyfied remind us we live in a difficult world with its own logic and paradoxes that we all experience. The term *collective unconscious* signifies that we, as human beings, have a common psychic structure just as we have a common physical structure. This is a common ground of humanity out of which our psychology and imagination work. In his book *The Hero with a Thousand Faces,* Joseph Campbell shows how the theme of growth and transformation is pictured metaphorically in mythology throughout the world. Whether the myths are from India, Greece, China, or from the African Bushmen, Eskimos, or Native Americans, the mythological patterns are the same. And in their folktales we find ourselves encountering an international panoply of heroes and heroines, wicked witches, wise old men and women, powerful wizards, strong enchantments, sagacious animal helpers, ogres, lucky third sons, and yes, Cinderellas and lost princesses. What is important here, besides the remarkable confluence of the human unconscious, is that frequently the story patterns in our dreams will reflect one of these common themes. And, once we've learned to understand our inner lives enough to feel secure and complete within ourselves, it is natural to seek to further understand the values, interests, and essential qualities that bind us together as human beings.

Robert Johnson refers to the unconscious, including the collective unconscious, as the *original mind* of humankind. In this sense it's the original source from which our conscious minds evolve, which means that every human capacity, every feature of our personalities that drives or motivates us, has found its way from our unconscious into our conscious experiences. Our growth is nourished by a continuing stream of potentials from the unconscious gradually rising to consciousness, seeking to form a more complete conscious person. We consider this stream the archetypal urge toward individuation, and it requires that we develop a strong enough personality to refine and integrate its contents.

By the time I had married and become a businessman, my personality had become strong enough to grow further, to recognize the new potentials within me that were seeking to be developed. My restlessness and the crisis that followed it were telling me that I needed to break free of the goals, assumptions, and beliefs that were limiting me. Like a snake that had outgrown its skin, my unconscious was urging me to grow into a larger personality.

If we behave in ways that block this stream by ignoring or repressing its messages, as I did at first, or if we act on them impetuously, we begin to cause ourselves to have emotional problems. For example a woman I knew had a dream where she went into a murderous rage and strangled her mother. The image understandably terrified her and she simply, like most of us would, tried to forget it. But the image wouldn't go away. When she mentioned it to me she wondered, "I suppose that means I need to confront my mother about all the ways she belittled me when I was young?" "Maybe," I replied. "But I wouldn't move too fast. The first thing you might want to do is just accept the image, mull it over in your mind and see what kind of thoughts and feelings come up."

We have a tendency to rush into action too fast. If something is unpleasant we want to either banish it quickly or move to an oversimplified solution. In either case the woman I was working with would have missed the message from her unconscious. After a week or two had passed, this woman returned to the subject of that dream. "I've thought about it for several days. Then I remembered a confrontation I had with my daughter. I treated her exactly the same belittling way my mother treated me when I was a teenager, and I just hated it. I've got to stop doing that." At this point I believed she understood the message from the dream, which was that she had internalized her mother's belittling attitude. She needed to become aware of this attitude within herself and eliminate it. With a little thought and patience it's surprising how many of these communications we can come to understand that are meant to help us grow in ways that are both large and small.

In many myths and dreams what we think of as our personality, our sense of "I-ness" or our conscious mind, is symbolized by an island. Like an island people in an island world, our personality sets up a little state of its own—a system of order and a set of assumptions about who we are and how we should live. According to Robert Johnson this metaphorical island rises out of our collective unconscious and grows through several supporting layers that represent the influences of our personal and cultural heritage. Normally we grow into our full adult identities with little awareness of the entire universe of realities in our unconscious, which supports us in the same way the earth supports an island and the sea provides much of its nourishment.

Deep beneath the surface of the system of order on our island, stormy forces are at work. Mythical kingdoms represent the deeper forces in our personalities such as those of the tempestuous Greek god of the sea, Poseidon, or the passionate lord of the underworld, Hades, and his bride, Persephone, who preside over the kingdom of the past and the ghosts of our ancestors. Legends show dwarfs, dragons, mermaids, nymphs, and other magical creatures carrying on lives parallel to the daily lives of our conscious personalities. These little kingdoms of alternative consciousness, emotions, values, and ideas maintain their existence, often waiting to be acknowledged by an inquiring mind.

Jung tried to help us by bringing some organization to how we understand the unconscious. He included much of our unconscious lives in what he called the *shadow*, a term now becoming well known. There are two aspects of the shadow. The first one consists of the possibilities in our potential personalities that we have rejected because of the forces that shaped our adaptation while growing up. The people we have learned to be create dark doubles in our unconscious—people with the characteristics we have denied. This compensatory shadow varies from person to person. Thomas Moore suggests that for some people sex and money have a lot of shadow energy while for others they are simply a part of life. The second aspect of the shadow is the potential for evil and destructiveness in human nature. Evils like racism and the Holocaust have taught us how easily evil grows one step at a time among normal people until hate and violence are justified. Jung was convinced that the only solution to evil was self-knowledge, "because we are the origin of all coming evil." Failing to recognize evil as a reality leaves us naive and incomplete in our development.

In our "normal" state of adult maturity we're still sitting on our islands, living the conventional models of existence we learned from our families and society. The purpose of learning to understand ourselves in a more profound way isn't just to resolve our conflicts or deal with our neuroses. It's to join forces with the deep troves of renewal, growth, strength, and wisdom inherent within each of us. Individuation connects us to the source of our evolving character and potentials. By cooperating with this process we expand our capacities for creativity, enjoyment, and love by tapping the rich sources of intelligence and energy within us.

The Hidden Power in the Shadow

To become people of interior substance means we must discover the essential parts of ourselves that are still unconscious. In the terminology of myths and religion, we must begin a journey to our centers. To learn about and experience the contents of our unconscious helps us experience ourselves more completely as human beings, and "bridges" the separations of our "island" selves with the rest of us. This process usually begins with either meeting or being confronted with some part of our shadows, those suppressed parts of ourselves that don't fit our normal self-images. In our journey through the next few chapters we will explore a number of situations where people meet their shadows. Our shadows often show up in the form of disowned emotions such as anger, physical symptoms like being overweight, interpersonal conflicts, and the reverse sides of the common social virtues we were taught to admire early in our lives.

As we grew up we were taught to evaluate our thoughts, feelings, and behaviors as either good or bad. This way simply ignores the complexity of reality. We may have failed to recognize the value in some of the things we rejected. Or by labeling some things undesirable, we may have been protecting ourselves from the hurtful power of the people whose approval we needed, or from our unknown fears. Most of these decisions were made automatically, unconsciously, without our being aware of what we were doing. As we begin to look inward to see more of what we're made of and who we really are, we're likely to find some very challenging material.

Sometimes our shadows interject themselves straight into our lives. I once knew a woman who was the wife of the minister of a large, well-known church. She came to see me because she had begun shoplifting and found she couldn't stop. While she was telling me her story she was horrified at her behavior: "I could ruin our life," she said. "I can't believe I'm doing this, and I can't stop."

During the time we were getting to know each other I commented that I could imagine how having to always appear nice, appropriately dressed, and even tempered, no matter what the circumstances were, must be frustrating. I likened it to putting one's spontaneity into a closet and locking the door. We wondered together if her individuality was asserting itself through her shadow, or if her anger at feeling imprisoned in a public face needed to be heard more clearly. In a similar vein I wondered if the purpose of this compulsion might be to help her learn to recognize her uniqueness and live in a way that was more creative, clever, and risky. A story that began with feelings of shame and of being out of control and a thief was leading to a transformed perspective of life. As we began to plumb some of the aspects behind the shoplifting, our conversation very quickly moved away from despair and from her berating herself for her actions to the secret joy her thievery and the great risks she was taking were giving her. This was a breakthrough. Keep in mind that shame, though sometimes appropriate, is rarely transforming. By looking for the *meaning* in what she was doing, and understanding how much repressed vitality was being sublimated into living dangerously, her inner integrity began to deepen and very quickly her compulsion began to lift. The more she became aware of how her shadow—her repressed energy and possibilities—was rebelling against her suffocation of life, the easier it was for her to make the choices that would bring increased freedom and opportunities.

Thievery is an archetypal theme. Prometheus stole fire from the gods to bring light to human life. In primitive initiation rites the initiators stole the young men from their mothers to free them in order to become adults. And two thieves were crucified next to Christ, another symbolic connection between thievery and redemption or transformation.

Along these same lines I remember a man in his late fifties who was deeply troubled by his continuous and mortifying fantasies of falling in love with adolescent boys. Filled with guilt and fearful, he assured me he had been married for many years and even had grandchildren. While exploring his life I learned he was feeling much older and trapped than his years or health justified. He hated the idea of retirement but felt he would look foolish starting a new career or approach to life. His wife was excited about the prospect of retiring and looked forward to spending their time traveling. While he recognized that some men would relish this kind of life, he admitted that it held little interest for him. Yet he didn't want to tarnish his wife's dreams, especially when he had no other ideas about what to do.

Images of perversion quickly get our attention but they seldom mean that we're perverted. However, we might wonder in a case like this one what might have happened if the man had not looked into his unconscious for the message it was sending. Might he otherwise, in his desperation and confusion, have felt compelled to act it out? We have seen in Robert Louis Stevenson's thoughtful and dramatic novel *Dr. Jekyll and Mr. Hyde* how a respected physician represses his own dark side until it becomes strong enough as an alter ego to take over his personality. While most situations I have seen have neither been as extreme nor as critical, they can turn out unhappily, or even tragic, because someone refused to listen to his or her shadow.

There was, happily, another way for the man to look at what he honestly saw as a crisis for he had encountered another archetypal theme. For instance, the Greek god Zeus fell in love with the young man Gannymeade and made him immortal as his cupbearer. Old age longs for youth, vitality, and new potentials often pictured as a young person in dreams, myths, and stories. If we aren't growing psychologically and spiritually as we become older, an emotional or physical crisis will develop. Our refused potentials will challenge us. Thomas Mann focused his classic novel *Death in Venice* around this theme, where an older man dies pitifully with images of love for a youth he's seen on a beach in his mind.

Novels like *Death in Venice* and other forms of great art are filled with the dark shadowy aspects of human nature—grotesque figures, angry gods, jealous goddesses, debauchery, murdered saints, and bloody twisted crucifixes. Some of these figures, like the beast in the fairy tale "Beauty and the Beast," are redeemable. Other figures, such as the snake-haired Medusa whose countenance turned men to stone in Greek mythology, are not. Because evil is a reality, we have to deal very thoughtfully and carefully with our shadows and be sure to ask someone competent for help if this material gets too threatening.

If we study many of the classic authors such as Dostoevsky, Tolstoy, Baudelaire, Hubert Sellby, and Sylvia Plath, we discover that they often tell the stories of our society's despised and outcast element. The voices from our shadows, whether illustrated in literature and fairy tales, or emanating from our dreams and symptoms, have something to teach us. We may often find that by giving attention and understanding to the messages from our shadows, they may transform and reveal new potentials for us.

PREPARING FOR CHANGE

The communications from our shadows and even clues as to how we can respond to them are often shown in fairy tales and myths. In one tale a princess may be required to kiss a loathsome frog in order to transform it into a prince. This story shows that in some cases we have to treat an unpleasant aspect of ourselves with love in order to redeem it. In another tale the transformation takes place when the princess angrily slams the hateful frog against the wall. This tale shows that anger can be as transforming as love in the right circumstances. In other examples a beggar may be a god in disguise, a pauper a prince whose throne has been usurped and who has to reconquer his kingdom. Snow White may be the unrecognized values of our hearts that need to take their rightful places in our kingdoms.

The prince who has lost his throne or the girl who has been disenfranchised like Cinderella may represent our potential for richer lives that include new possibilities, inner strength, uniqueness, and integrity. As we continue our journey through these pages you will see examples of these possibilities opening up.

Once you know more about your shadow, how you have hidden potentials both good and evil, you will have a better understanding of how human you are and how many strange, paradoxical things live within you. When you've met and accepted many of the strangers within yourself and dealt honestly with them, it will open your heart and attitudes when you invite *strangers* to your island in the outer world. You will rarely fear them. It's by knowing yourself that you'll find the antidote to hate and alienation both within and without.

Shadows into Substance

In the story language of the unconscious, Ulysses, Ivanhoe, and Robin Hood are, respectively, a king, the son of a king, and a noble knight who have suffered misfortunes. Eventually they triumph and restore a just balance within the domain—their respective homes, or realms, where their true identities will be recognized. Similarly, in a Sumerian myth, Inanna, the queen of heaven, will journey into the underworld to meet her dark sister and return to the light with a new state of strength and understanding. In "Beauty and the Beast," Beauty is sent alone into the house of the Beast and is tempted to break her bargain and desert him. But the entire situation is transformed when she learns to honor loyalty, love, and compassion.

These archetypal stories represent patterns of inner transformation that signify growth and learning. The woman who was shoplifting met her Beast, the longing for her own strength, independence, and vitality that was being rejected and was therefore being expressed in a negative, frightening form. The man who was fantasizing about young men needed a new prince, a renewed sense of spirit and promise in his life. Most of these stories reflect a general identity crisis going on within us. The Ulysses who washed ashore on his homeland and failed to recognize it toward the end of *The Odyssey* was a far different Ulysses from the ambitious, cocky young man who had set sail for Troy two decades earlier.

Beginning the process of developing sacred substance is usually started by a crisis, by encountering some part of our shadows that sets up an inner or outer conflict. The encounters may be emotional difficulties such as anxiety, depression, marital discord; they may be about compulsions or addictions, or physical disorders such as heart troubles, infections, or fatigue. When we determine to treat our *selves* instead of our symptoms, it means we have to take a look into our unconscious if we really want our treatments to bring healing and new life. Crises and illnesses threaten the sense of order and the assumptions we've built up on our little islands. They threaten the secular substance we have built up, however falsely.

My life reached a turning point when I changed careers in my thirties. But this was in fact the fulfillment of a process that had started a couple of years earlier, when I became depressed. Searching myself and my life, with the stormy ups and downs, fears and excitements that attended my explorations, and facing the potential losses of love and security they might lead to, was my version of Ulysses' turbulent voyage through the Mediterranean.

Sometimes my process was difficult and unsettled; at other

times it was exhilarating. And, like any journey undertaken in rough weather, I often felt an impulse to turn back, a desire to seek comfort in the old home of my dreams or in a warm bed of certainty. It would have been easy to return to my old ways and to the symbols of success that I knew would be supported by the people close to me. But somewhere inside of me a voice was saying, "Yes, go back, and you'll suffer a heart attack within a decade." Deep inside I knew that going back wouldn't satisfy me. I later discovered that the mythic patterns supported my feeling. If the mythic searcher refuses the call to adventure he (or she) invites darkness upon himself. In modern life Jung refers to this act as a regressive restoration of the old way of life and appearances in the face of fear—an act that will result in living a hollow life.

Going forward to a new life does mean rejecting the falseness of the old, but the benefits we gain from our old lives are many and valuable and shouldn't be abandoned. Ulysses' ability as a cunning warrior and leader served him well during his ten years of odyssey, just as we learned many things as we formed our identities that we need to hold on to. The choice isn't "out with the old and in with the new." Though I didn't understand it initially, I realize now that my struggle to become successful in business gave me the foundation of confidence, strength, and courage that enabled me to take other risks, face crises, and make additional life changes.

The trust in life and the confidence we build are like a safety net under a trapeze artist; as the artist swings from pole to pole, life to life, the net is there to break a fall. The wonderful thing is that the net is within ourselves. It is our skills and spirit that carry us over to the other pole. That is how we are able to keep growing, moving from one way to another—by taking the best parts with us.

Once the wife of the minister I was working with understood her shoplifting and how much she enjoyed risk and danger, she became more able to risk being herself and face the potential criticism she feared. When the man who had the fantasies convinced himself that it's OK for a man his age to act with the same trust in life as a younger person and to face the future as one full of potential, he was able to come to an understanding with himself and his wife about how he had to live into the rest of his life with his whole heart. And when, at last, Ulysses ends his odyssey, he is a much more complete man of wisdom and maturity than he was as a clever young king and soldier.

Robert Johnson uses the analogy that there is a plan, like the one for a great cathedral or temple, based on the unique potentials within each of us. As years pass the edifice of our lives rises stone by stone if we continue to work and grow. The process takes a lifetime, but as we near the end of our journey and the final blocks go into place, it is only then the magnificent vision of the architect is revealed. We are building our lives and we have to face the challenges and changes that the process of inner growth requires to reap its joy and contentments.

Slaying Dragons

When I was a boy reading the stories of "The Knights of the Round Table" and other adventure tales of knights, ladies, and evildoers, my friends and I were inspired and spent many afternoons playing heroes and villains. In the woods of our backyards we went on many daring excursions, faced serpents with crested heads, and dark and wily villains, and emerged victorious. Knights and dragons are primary themes in our Western heritage. The power of these stories still fascinates; and though they often take new forms such as *Star Wars*, the patterns are the same.

In the Western tradition there are two kinds of dragons that require a heroic effort to overcome. The first one kidnaps maidens, who represent the archetypal symbol of life. The second one collects and hoards gold. In either case the dragon usually stays close to or in a cave, where it guards its booty jealously. The first dragon represents the state of our childhood dependencies that we must overcome in order to win lives of our own, to become adults. The second dragon represents the ways we are bound to the initial identities we develop and the values and conventions of society. These dragons are like forces holding our potentials captive. We must free ourselves of this bondage in order to live as people in society, serving our values rather than compulsively following those of our culture. Slaying dragons becomes a metaphor for how each of us has to free ourselves from childhood dependencies, and from the bonds of our identities and society. We will see a number of examples in the following pages of men and women developing their voices and inner authority.

When I got married in college and later went into business I was doing so to force my way into adulthood. Even though I had little awareness of what I was doing, I was following an archetypal pattern and slaying the dragon of childhood dependency. Later in my thirties when I went through another passage and career change, I was confronting the second dragon—the limits of the identity I had established and the conventional values of our society. Dragons don't die easily. They fight to keep us dependent and tied to them. The struggle is worth it, but there are no easy paths through them.

You may recall that in chapter 1 I discussed how we grow in consciousness. I said that we grow from simple consciousness to complex consciousness, then to individual consciousness and finally to illuminated consciousness. Simple consciousness begins at birth and lasts until late adolescence. It's a period of developing our identities and the skills necessary to live, work, and have relationships in the world and outside of our families. To move from simple to complex consciousness, to become adults, we have to muster the strength to overcome the dragon of dependency. Because our society no longer has effective initiation rites, this quest is as lonely as a knight's.

Complex consciousness is the period of consolidating our identities and using our skills for love and work in adult life. In other words we have established our islands with their rules of order and assumptions about life. To move beyond our adult identities into individual consciousness means we must slay the dragon guarding the gold of our potentials, enter the cave of our unconscious and *begin the search for its contents*.

In individual consciousness we are opening the boundaries of our islands—our previous identities—and freeing ourselves of society's mind-sets in order to live from our hearts rather than impulsively serving the claims of an imposed system. Growing into the area of individual consciousness begins with knowing more about our shadows, the parts of us that have been denied and the families and social systems that caused these denials. Growing into individual consciousness will give us the inner strength and confidence to let go of the familiar beliefs of our culture and to live authentically. It is this process that we will begin to explore in the following pages.

Growth means change, and facing the choice of whether to change or stagnate is one of our greatest challenges. It is hard and scary to shake free of the support of what is known when we can't be sure of what's ahead. There is an understandable fear there will be nothing there, a void, or something alien or disappointing. But as the men and women we will encounter in the following pages show us, there is more. And that more—the recognition and embrace of illuminated consciousness—makes the demands of the journey worthwhile. It's the place we reach when we finally realize our unique personhood and the existence of our greater Self as an image of the divine within us. We sense the purpose and the pattern of our lives and their importance. And we realize that we live in two worlds, our own world and that of the culture outside of us. We live in society without allowing society to dictate how we should live. The journey beginning with individual consciousness takes us on a road that may sometimes feel rutted and bumpy, but it is a straight one. It only asks that we make a serious commitment to honor our inner lives in order not to double back onto the old road, and its ways of living and thinking.

Befriending Our Needs

The wasteland in T. S. Eliot's poem as well as in The Quest for the Holy Grail is a metaphor for our state of being when we're not living our lives from our hearts. When Knight Parsifal, who is seeking the Grail, first encounters the wounded king of the wasteland, he's moved by compassion and wants to ask the monarch why he's suffering. But, having been trained that knights don't ask unnecessary and intrusive questions, he stifles his spontaneity and compassion and at this point his quest fails. It takes him an additional five years of struggle and failure to make his way back to the Grail Castle and to ask the questions that come from his heart rather than follow the rules of decorum for knights. Knowing the right questions reflects the maturity Parsifal has gained through the committed struggles of his quest and begins the healing of the wasteland.

It is a paradox that if we cannot open our hearts to ourselves then we have no foundation for dealing with other people lovingly and compassionately. And, like Parsifal we've been trained not to ask loving and compassionate questions of ourselves, not to question our depressions and heart attacks deeply and lovingly because to do so might upset the value systems we and our society live by. Instead, the system teaches us to go to the refrigerator, buy something, go to the movies or out to eat if we are feeling lonely, anxious, or distressed. But feeling bad and going to the kitchen sets up a cycle that cannot be eased or healed by diet plans, willpower, or medication. Our real needs are deeper than what these palliatives can help. We have to pay better attention to ourselves.

Yes, in spite of our interests in exercise, fitness, and nutrition we still deny many of our bodies' needs. We work out to improve them, but too often we are treating the body like an "it" rather than the seat of our souls. We judge our bodies harshly against media ideals and frequently seem to disassociate from them. We rarely give them enough sleep, rest, and sensual rewards to keep them calm and relaxed, and sooner or later our bodies are going to teach us we're human. Heart attacks, depression, obesity, chronic fatigue, and fibromyalgia are but a few of the ways our bodies do this and insist that attention be paid.

In many of these circumstances we act as if our bodies have betrayed us, when actually they are more often our friends warning us when we are endangering ourselves. For instance our bodies know when we've inadvisably ingested bad or tainted food and reflectively expel what they must. Similarly our bodies issue "warnings" in the form of scares, those small reality episodes that are meant to wake us up to the changes we need to make. And, sometimes our bodies give us important signals about our emotions when we're hungry for love, personal fulfillment, or vitality.

When Janice started crying and couldn't stop, her body had taken over. It quit functioning like a machine that day at school. It's ironic that she would say she despised her body, that she felt it was her enemy because it fell short of what our ideals for women's bodies should be, and yet it was this body that began turning her life around.

I still remember how difficult it was for me as a child to figure out what kind of present to give my father for his birthday or Christmas. I could never figure out anything he needed or wanted and he never voiced a tangible desire. Even when I'd ask him directly he would answer something along the lines of "Whatever you would like to get." The broader emotional undertone of this simple-sounding answer can actually be quite frightening. If someone doesn't want or need anything from us how can we feel important to them? This was a theme that remained throughout my relationship with my father. I thought he loved me but I could never figure out why I was important to him, what value I offered to his life. If we aren't aware of our needs and desires, if we hide them, it makes it very difficult for people to feel close to us for we've positioned ourselves as islands in life.

The fairy tale "The Fisherman's Wife" reminds me of a different danger that can arise when we don't genuinely understand our needs. In this story a poor fisherman who lives with his wife in a humble pigsty is fishing. The day wears on without his having any luck until close to evening he finally hooks a flounder. To his surprise the flounder begins to speak to him. The flounder tells a sad tale of being an enchanted prince. Filled with compassion the fisherman returns him to the sea and goes home empty-handed. At home he relates his adventure to his wife. She becomes upset and urges him to go back to the sea and ask the flounder to grant him a wish. Early the next morning he returns to the sea and asks the fish to grant him a wish, a new cottage, for him and his wife. Home again, he finds that his wish has been granted and his wife is standing in front of a lovely cottage. Enthused, the wife continues pushing her husband to ask for a new favor day after day. They progress from a cottage to a house, a mansion, a castle, and then a marble palace. Finally the disgusted flounder has had enough and returns them to the pigsty. Like the fisherman's wife, if we don't understand our needs we too can get caught on a treadmill of acquiring material possessions that eventually leave us as emotionally or spiritually impoverished as we were when we began our quest.

The hurried pace of our lives discourages us from actively reflecting upon our needs and looking deeper than the material level. When we fail to understand them for ourselves and to share them, we cannot live from our hearts. The point here is that we then live by other people's concepts, calculations, assumptions, or inclinations—right for them but maybe not for us. By probing our own inner lives, we give our relationships a better chance to succeed. Intimacy is about sharing. It is reciprocal. And when we relinquish or lose touch with our hearts' desire, we leave ourselves in danger of being dissatisfied with life without realizing why.

Cultivating our self-awareness frequently helps us discover parts of our lives we're missing. For many years I made the same mistake with my children my father had made with me. Through my inner work I've learned to let them know I want and need things from them that go far beyond obligatory gifts and include their love, value to my life, and the meaning it gives me to be a father. As a result our exchanges of presents have become meaningful rather than obligatory because they symbolize this deeper exchange.

SACRED SELFISHNESS

Not long ago I was asked to give a class on some of the topics we've been discussing at a local church. When I asked the people in the class to think about why it's important to be carefully aware of our needs and what we might be missing if we aren't, they found these questions initially difficult. Maybe they found these questions more troubling because we were in a religious setting. On the one hand our religious institutions generally try to teach us to think of other people and not ourselves. On the other hand our culture teaches us we should think of ourselves on a material level. I then broke the class members into small groups and had them look at these questions, and talk about them for a while. When we all reassembled as one group, sharing our answers, I was pleased by their thoughtful responses:

- *We can't know ourselves if we don't know what we need.*

- *Our real needs can show us what our lives are about.*

- *If we don't know our needs, no one else can really know us.*

- *If we don't know our needs, they are unlikely to get met.*

- *If we don't know our needs, we'll expect other people to know them.*

- *If we don't know our needs, we may become more demanding than we realize.*

- *If we don't know our needs, we'll live like sheep.*

- *Being aware of our needs makes life more personal and real.*

- *If I own my needs, I actually lessen my demands on others because I'm living honestly.*

PREPARING FOR CHANGE

Questioning ourselves in ways like this can help us overcome old cultural mind-sets that keep us from thinking about and figuring out what our needs are, what they're telling us about our lives, and how we need to pay attention to them. If we aren't aware of them they'll be down in our shadows, stirring up our unconscious energy and coming out in ways we don't intend them to. We have all known someone who puts on the facade of being self-sacrificing while actually being controlling and demanding attention. Or, we've found ourselves volunteering or being pressured to serve on some committee or in a campaign and then ending up feeling full of resentments.

A few years ago a woman told me that she tried to ignore her needs because she thought that made it easier to be happy. Walling ourselves off to our needs doesn't make it easier to be happy. Before I figured out that I was repeating my father's patterns of not showing needs, I found myself resentful every year at my birthday about how thoughtless I felt my children were. I'd numbed my needs but not the hurt of feeling alone and unknown to the people closest to me. Our needs, especially our need for love and for people to love, have nothing to do with being selfish or self-indulgent. They have everything to do with being human.

Listening to our hearts, our minds, our bodies, and our unconscious helps us realize our full humanity and its potentials. If we don't, we will be following the machine model of living and creating a wasteland in our souls and relationships. Most of us are brought up to believe that showing our emotions is embarrassing. Learning to hide them almost always means learning not to act on them. To become passionate whether it's from love, desire, suffering, or anger is a call to action and action can upset the sense of order on our islands. Acting on our emotions can sometimes bring shame or the appearance of being naive, out of control, or irrational. Many people in our culture, especially men, have become so used to hiding their emotions they're rarely sure of what they feel.

Robert was one of these men who didn't know what he felt. He thought he felt fine, but his wife and family doctor thought something was troubling him. They also thought he might be more upset about his upcoming fiftieth birthday than he realized. When I met Robert he was affable but there was also a sense of passivity around him that I felt right away. As I asked him a few questions I learned that he suffered from asthma and that it had recently gotten worse. I also concluded that deep down he had a suspicion his wife and doctor might be right in their belief that something was troubling him. But he couldn't figure out what it was.

During this first meeting we talked about his health and about his wife's concern, and he joked, as well, about turning fifty and gaining a little weight. Over the next few sessions we continued to talk casually and during each meeting he would quietly tell me a little more about his life, how good it was and why he couldn't understand why people were worried about him. Nonetheless at the end of each session he would schedule another meeting, as though some instinct was guiding him to do so. I felt that what was trying to emerge in Robert wasn't quite ready to be seen.

After a few sessions I noticed that as soon as Robert left my office I experienced a feeling of sadness, like a weight pushing my spirit down. After reflecting on these feelings for a while I decided to mention them to Robert. I said, "Robert we've gotten to know each other fairly well during the past few weeks and I've developed a lot of respect for you. But I want to tell you that after you leave my office I'm always left with a strong sense of sadness, of heaviness. What do you think about this?" At first Robert looked a little startled. Then, to both our surprise his eyes filled with tears.

Something inside of Robert was waiting until he was sure of the safety of my respect and confident in my ability to accept and understand him. Once feelings come out they're like a gift. To our everyday minds they may appear repugnant and frightening. In fairy tale terms our sadness often seems like a spell cast by an evil witch, and when it's broken beauty and peace return. Our anger may seem like an ugly toad that when transformed can give us a renewed passion for life. And our fear may be an enchanted castle surrounded by a thicket of thorns that holds our abilities captive until they are freed by courage and determination. But folklore reminds us consistently that the things we normally despise are often princes or princesses in disguise. Our emotions and the ways we experience them are never irrational or without purpose. Their logic is not of the mind but of the heart and its values. They're meant to lead us into new directions or understandings of life.

Many of us charge into adulthood with so much other-directed determination—graduate school, internships, job interviews—that we seldom consider our feeling states. Robert had done this and so had I. Today he's a successful stockbroker, but in his mid-twenties he was struggling, trying one job after another and feeling very worried about supporting his young family. When he began selling stocks he worked on commission and has now become a very respected money manager. It turned out that he really is happy today and feels successful but cannot enjoy these feelings because of the burden of depression he is carrying from the past. He needed to go back in time and mourn for the young man with a family who had felt so lost and scared at times, practically in despair and who had worked relentlessly in spite of these feelings. He also needed to grieve for the time lost to work during the early years of his family when he'd wanted to participate with and enjoy his children. Yes, his fiftieth birthday was bringing these feelings to mind, and he invited his wife to join us for a few sessions in order to help him bring this new feeling dimension of himself into their relationship.

Life has its difficult side no matter how well we do. It's often very helpful and comforting to look back and honor our suffering and let it teach us to be more compassionate to ourselves and understanding of other people. Part of this hardship comes from the fact that to grow up or to become somebody we have to make choices. Whether we choose to be married or not, have children or not, work for success or find other rewards in life, or choose one career over another there is a price as well as a reward. Facing this reality and accepting the feelings that originally drove our choices or surrounded them free us to live without regrets.

Childhood wounds also surprise us by recycling themselves every time we move into a new stage of growth. I was devastated when my mother died in my early teens. Within a few years I thought I'd dealt with the experience. But its vibrations come up every time

I go into a new phase of change that affects the way I perceive myself or life. In some ways this early experience left a wound that was slower to heal than I could imagine, living deep within and making it difficult for me to trust life and relationships. But its effects over time have also toughened me, and given me a more refined sensitivity toward suffering. Everyone has something from childhood that recycles. Fifty years later a friend of mine vividly remembers a third grade teacher who shamed him in front of his classmates. A woman I know still recalls the acute loneliness and feelings of inferiority she felt when she was sent to an exclusive boarding school at an early age. She's told me how quickly that old feeling can return if she isn't careful when entering new situations.

Robert, like many of us, constructed a protective wall around his feelings because he was afraid of them. Over this wall he'd put on an illusion of feelings, a "person" of appropriate emotions who he'd come to believe was real. He thought he should feel happy so he put on a cheery act. He bought into the assumption that if we achieve the model of success in our society we should feel happy. But as he became more honest about how he felt he openly expressed his grief about life's difficult times and only acted happy when the feeling was genuine.

Several things indicate when we have walled off our feelings:

- *Their absence.* A lack of feelings, usually a coolness or remoteness, based on the mistaken belief that it's generally better to be nonemotional and objective.

- *Being overly sentimental.* An excess of ungrounded or undifferentiated feelings that come unexpectedly or in outbursts.

- *Having mood states.* Unexplainably going from high to low, or dropping into touchiness, sulkiness, criticism, self-criticism, or vulnerability.

Many of us are more disconnected from ourselves and each other than we realize. Our society is so image-oriented that it's easy to believe we feel something we don't feel. We think we feel good, are having fun, or feel angry because the circumstances make it look like that's how we should feel. And like Robert, we may paper over our feelings in order not to disturb people, or to get their approval. In fact, Robert may have received so much approval for being jovial and good-natured that he learned to admire that quality in himself even though it wasn't genuine.

From Judgment to Acceptance

Understanding the ways in which we form our adult identities, and how we're influenced by the values of society and the traits it structures into our personalities, makes it easier to see how self-alienation is built into our existence. It begins as soon as we leave the womb and are launched into a process of being weighed and measured. Measurement in some form now accompanies almost every aspect of modern life. Ostensibly, measurement is supposed to be for our "own good" to monitor our health, growth, and capacities. Today, as we grow and enter school it tells us how well we're doing, where we fall on the "growth chart," whether we have "potential," and if we're "living up" to that potential from the perspective of society's values. Almost before we realize it the emphasis on measurement is connected to our appearance, our performance, our behavior, and has been internalized into a personal mind-set. As we grow into adulthood everything from our sex lives to our credit ratings is evaluated from this perspective.

We're taught to judge ourselves relentlessly. The author and physician Naomi Remen observes that our vitality is diminished more by judgment than by disease. She goes on to explain that approval is just as damaging as a form of judgment as criticism. While positive judgment initially hurts less than criticism, it triggers a constant striving for more. It makes us uncertain of who we are and of our true value. Approval and disapproval spawn a compulsion to critically evaluate ourselves all the time. For example Judith won't go out for an evening with her husband and friends without spending an hour and a half putting on makeup. Harry can't do enough favors for everyone he tries to become friends with. And Matthew remains quiet and shy, preferring to be seen as a loner rather than to risk being rejected.

In a society that thrives on consumerism, we have become increasingly vulnerable. Advertising takes advantage of our obsession with self-judgment and desire for approval while holding out the promise that if we buy the right clothes, use the right makeup, follow the right diet, have the right appliances, yard tools, vacations, and so on, we can become happy and admired. Even the self-help industry has joined the caravan of marketing with books, tapes, videos, and workshops offering "quick fixes" to what's wrong with our lives rather than challenging us to look deeper into ourselves.

The marketing people are clever and know how to exploit our hopes and fears. Our social engine runs on performance and consumption. But we can face and change ourselves by developing enough self-knowledge to reclaim our lives, take initiative, have a viewpoint, love ourselves, and live in the world without being victimized by it.

After we'd been working together for a few months, Janice was reflecting on how she used to feel standing in front of that magazine rack in the drugstore. It was a pivotal moment for her. She said, "All of those self-improvement articles and advertisements make you feel you aren't good enough. That you're incomplete, inferior, inadequate. And what's supposed to make you feel better? Buying the magazine and buying the products. Now that's self-empowerment for you. Now that I've opened my eyes it seems like our whole culture is geared toward making you hate yourself and believing that buying more is the only thing that can help. It's like 'fix it, charge it.' But all you're really doing is keeping the system going."

PREPARING FOR CHANGE

Janice is right. We're all born with an inner longing to live a meaningful life, to love and be loved. Advertisers have become skilled at redirecting these longings toward consumer goods, trying to convince us that inner needs can be satisfied with external things. They manipulate our needs to keep us off balance, anxious, and fearful of social isolation and loneliness. It is the modern equivalent of tribal banishment.

The system that drives our society promises that life can be good. But if we rely on the values of that system without growing beyond it into our own conscious awareness, all it will deliver is self-alienation.

To know that we are human is to know that life includes loss, darkness, and confusion, as well as magic and beauty. To become a mature, wise person requires that we come to know ourselves deeply and learn to navigate life's waters skillfully. Our growth depends upon our awareness of the reality we're experiencing. In turn, as this awareness grows, it will open us to further growth.

Knowing ourselves more fully, learning how to cultivate our inner resources and love ourselves in a substantial manner heals self-alienation and gives a firm foundation for letting the tides of culture flow around us without threatening us. Additionally, as we work on ourselves we must work on our society so that for future generations the term *culture* will return to its more substantial meaning of supporting enlightenment—the development of intellectual, moral, and artistic potentials—in a manner that can offer guidance to our children and grandchildren.

PART II:
Cultivating Inner Substance

Either you look at the universe as a very poor creation out of which no one can make anything or you look at your own life and your own part in the universe as infinitely rich, full of inexhaustible interest, opening out into the infinite further possibilities for study and contemplation and interest and praise.
—Thomas Merton

CHAPTER 5
Journaling as Inner Exploration

The more faithfully you listen to the voice within you, the better you will hear what is sounding outside. And only he who listens can speak. Is this the starting point of the road towards the union of your two dreams—to be allowed in clarity of mind to mirror life and in purity of heart to mold it?

—Dag Hammarskjöld

In her book *The Right to Create,* Judith Grach writes insightfully, "The unconscious is the raw material of the soul and spirit, it is the source of consciousness and energy." I've found that it's no easy task to explain how our unconscious gives birth to consciousness and how these two aspects of ourselves interrelate as we mature. Whenever I try to explain our personalities and the relationship of our conscious selves, our egos, to the unconscious, I find it helpful to use the island analogy again because this image is so clear and visual. In this description the island is rooted in the earth, which I think of as the collective unconscious, and is surrounded by the sea, which represents the rest of our unconscious.

Freud favored the use of analogy, too, and he used the picture of an iceberg to describe our conscious relationship to our unconscious. He said the tip above the water represents a small amount of consciousness in relationship to the huge mass under the sea representing our unconscious. In this picture it's the part of the iceberg beneath the water that sinks ships. I don't like this analogy because it seems cold, potentially destructive unless avoided, and something that has broken away from its connections. However, it does present a helpful comparison by showing how small our conscious personalities are in relationship to our unconscious.

Growing up and developing enough consciousness to live effectively day-to-day require a tremendous outpouring of energy that usually leaves us separated from our inner worlds or at least from their potential depths and nourishment. While this fact is often unacknowledged we now know that it's true, and understanding the psychology of midlife is essential to mental and physical health and contentment. As we mature toward midlife we experience an urge to reunite with our deeper dimensions in order to bring our outer accomplishments and strengths into relationship with the underlying psychological and spiritual potentials within us. At this point our ingrained, concrete problem-solving approach to life, which has given us many benefits, hinders and sometimes defeats our efforts to understand the parts of ourselves that depend more on mystery, love, imagination, and experience than on rationality. As a culture we seem to be slowly struggling to free ourselves from an attitude that prefers only what we can observe and measure to what we think and feel. Individually we have to become reconnected to our inner lives, and learn to live in the dynamic tension between our outer and inner worlds. The values of the heart and spirit must be recognized and cultivated within us before they can become substantial forces in our outer worlds.

In his extraordinary book *The Road Less Traveled,* Scott Peck points out that when our conscious selves fail to renew their relationships with our unconscious, we become ill or caught in our struggles. We've become like lobsters refusing to outgrow their shells as lobsters have to do at each stage of their development. Our personalities become tighter and tighter until we become sick and emotional or physical symptoms break out. And like most symptoms these represent our personalities' efforts to heal themselves.

For example, a depression may mask a fear of living more authentically. An addiction may hide our inability to confront our pain and become strong enough to be transformed by it. Anxiety, frequently expressed in "activity," may cover the deep feeling that our lives, our stories have no meaning. The Old Testament prophet Jonah ran away because God, or the voice within, wanted him to go somewhere he didn't want to. How many ways do we do the same thing and end up struggling with ourselves?

Dreams are one of the ways our unconscious seeks to guide and heal us. They are so helpful that many psychotherapists gladly receive them as a significant part of their work. However, dream language is confusing and I must admit that there are often dreams I don't understand. Jung mentioned in his autobiography that several of his dreams took him years to figure out. Nevertheless, dreams can provide helpful information about how we are living. They can offer encouragement or can challenge us when we are wrong and don't realize it. They can supply necessary information about ourselves or a situation we're in that we're not aware of, give us direction when we feel lost, or act as pointers to the way we need to go when we're floundering.

During one of my early sessions with Janice she told me she had a dream the previous night she wanted to talk about. Naturally I welcome dreams and invited her to share it with me.

"Well," she began, "When I went to bed last night I was still upset with myself for breaking down in class and humiliating myself. I've been thinking a lot about what happened, obsessing on it you might say, and I got myself so worked up I couldn't sleep. Finally I fell asleep and dreamed I was in a courtroom. I was on trial, sitting next to my attorney. There was no jury, just a judge. The prosecutor brought in a string of witnesses who testified against me. Each time my defense attorney, who looked a lot like me, rose to begin her cross-examination, she simply said instead, 'No questions, your honor.' The judge was a woman around my age who I couldn't recognize. When she asked my attorney to present the case for the defense my lawyer replied, 'The defense rests.' I woke up thinking I was guilty. Guilty of what, I couldn't say. But that's it. I'm always guilty. Always wrong somehow."

When I asked Janice for her thoughts about the dream she replied, "Well, let's see. I suppose it means something about how I judge myself all the time, day in and day out, no defense, just guilty as charged and sentenced to endless torment. I sure hope you know how to help me."

At this point Janice is like most of us, we either cede authority to "experts" believing "they know" what "we" don't, or we want to be told what to do, like through the media with its quick fixes. But that's not the way we come to health or authentic understanding. We have to do the work. Like Dorothy learned in *The Wizard of Oz*, no one can do it for us. The man behind the curtain is . . . just a man. Janice was asking me to give her directions as though her dream was a problem we could solve together, like a puzzle or a car that had taken a wrong turn and needed to get back on the interstate. She had figuratively rolled down her window and asked for directions.

I replied to her comment by saying, "One of the most important things about dreams is they usually help us find the answers within ourselves. I think your dream gives us some important clues as to where to begin. Let's look at it more carefully." As is customary I asked her what she thought and felt about the figures in this dream story, starting with the judge.

"She's my age, she looks competent, and she's supposed to be impartial," Janice responded. "In fact she never pronounced a sentence. The trial didn't end."

"What about the prosecutor?" I asked.

Janice smiled, "She was aggressive, she piled up the evidence."

"And the defense attorney?"

"She was really passive and she looked like me. Does that mean I'm passive in my own defense?"

"Yes, and so were you in the dream. If your attorney isn't doing her job shouldn't you get mad and either fire her or get her aroused on your behalf?"

The meaning of the dream was now becoming clear. I agreed with Janice that it seemed important that she woke up before the trial ended and I wondered if she might be "waking up" now. She also added that she often remained passive when facing a conflict, hoping things would get better on their own, even though she knew deep down they usually don't.

JOURNALING AS INNER EXPLORATION

Almost anyone who has worked with dreams will recognize that Janice's isn't too complicated, but it's helpful and typical of the process that is activated when we try to listen to ourselves. Janice had started working on her problems and soon afterward her unconscious produced a dream that illuminated part of the problem and gave us a road map for continuing her work. It's difficult to imagine anything else that could have happened at this point in her analysis that could have given us this clarity and given her the security that the answers lay within herself. It was apparent her unconscious wanted to assist her and our work together, and did so very skillfully.

Rather than "analyze" the dream I used it and Janice's responses to the figures and interactions in it to help her discover more about herself. The dream gave us two directions to follow as we looked carefully at her life. First she could look for other situations or conflicts, such as ones with her husband, children, friends, co-workers, and extended family members, where she had remained passive and had hoped for the best. Then she could examine the emotions these events stirred up or the emotions she thought should have been aroused when she looked back on the events. And secondly, she could begin to notice how she evaluated herself in or after these situations and how she could put up a better "defense" against judging herself. Finally, I suggested to Janice that she begin to keep a daily journal of the situations that caused her to judge herself and her reflections on these events, and of any new dreams that occurred.

Many of us are passive in our own defense. Too often we tend to wait, or are slow to stand up for ourselves and act. We've been brought up to think that things are best when they run smoothly, that we shouldn't disrupt them with conflict and confrontations. This training double binds us. If we stand up for ourselves and make waves we feel guilty, and if we slowly sell ourselves out we also feel guilty on a deeper level and build up pools of resentment.

It's easy for this process to become so embedded in us that we don't realize how passive we've become, how strongly we judge ourselves, and how little we do in our own defense. Recovering our full awareness of how we're living, and recognizing we have inner allies in our unconscious is a strong first step in reclaiming our lives and moving toward a sense of inner unity.

The Sum of Our Parts

The word *individuation* that Jung used to describe our journey into wholeness comes from the Latin word *individuus*, which means "undivided," "not fragmented," or "whole." Individuation, Jung explains, is "the process by which individual beings are formed and differentiated; in the particular, it is the development of the psychological individual as being distinct from the general collective psychology." This process becomes life at its fullest when it is based on personal awareness. As we learn to read our experiences and understand their depths, our growing self-knowledge is reflected in our choices of values and actions.

One of the great enemies of true personal choice is the strength of our identification with the values of the social character. In far too many situations we've learned not to listen to our creativity or our personal needs and wants in order to adjust to our families and the culture around us. Then it takes a breakdown or a breakthrough of some type to initiate the struggle of building the knowledge of who we really are. One of the most important functions of an analyst or a book like this one is to give you permission to step outside the limits of conventional mind-sets and look carefully at all aspects of your life.

Sometimes we must work hard to give ourselves the freedom to explore the terrain of our total personalities. Our friends, partners, children, and families will often seem to be supporting the dragon voices inside our heads or the goblins around us, as they tell us our dreams aren't "practical" or "responsible." Most of us have had dreams, desires, and fantasies we've never taken seriously or allowed into our active lives. They join the exiled aspects of ourselves we struggle to keep locked in the basement of our personal unconscious. If we want to get to know these parts of ourselves through inner work then we must go beyond simply becoming aware of them, and figure out how to have a conscious relationship with them, how to actively integrate them into our lives.

Relationship means to be connected to something. A conscious relationship means that we're aware of the different features of that connection. We've learned that many human relationships can grow and become enriching as our consciousness of them increases. The more conscious we become in relationship the more we can understand other people, appreciate their complexity, their intentions, and the mystery that lives within them. On the other hand when a relationship is based on an unhealthy connection—such as over-dependence, greed, power, or a lack of awareness—then consciousness may bring it to an end or to a new status. In either case growth requires that we give attention to the relationship and if it's a positive one, respect it and the other party, be open to his or her point of view, and maintain our standpoints as individuals within the relationship. If very much growth is going to occur we must be willing to change and sometimes make bargains and compromises, and yet know ourselves well enough that we don't sell ourselves out during this process. The same general principles hold true for relating to aspects of ourselves, and we'll be looking at various techniques for cultivating these relationships. But first we must learn to know ourselves well enough to become aware and to pay attention to them, to learn how to listen to what they have to say and still be strong enough to maintain our standpoints.

Another analogy I like to use when describing our personalities is to consider them houses with many floors and rooms. The forces we encountered growing up have taught us to live in the attic, leaving the other floors uninhabited and the basement locked. Learning to discover the rest of the house and how to live in it enlarges, strengthens, and opens our identities as well as our potentials. Discovering the rooms in this house and opening the doors are the way we become aware of our unknown parts. Once discovered we must learn how to relate to them, how to convert them into livable space that adds to our personalities.

When we begin opening these doors we may discover desires, feelings, and potentials we've repressed. As we face them we must ask ourselves why we repressed them. In many cases the answer is that our attic consciousness was shaped by forces that didn't acknowledge or know how to deal with these things. For instance the problem isn't that we have hostile, sexual, or creative feelings, but that culture and families foster an identity development that's unwilling to face these feelings and tolerate the pain of dealing with them. We're fortunate that our unconscious—through dreams, fantasies, and reflections—will guide our journey down from the attic a step at a time if we will cooperate with it. During this process our identities are strengthened and expanded enough to face what we will find in the next room.

Living in our attic usually means we've been socialized to get along in a narrow everyday existence. It's who we are in space and time, as our genders, professions, ages, and identities reflect our biographies, our resumes, and how our parents taught us to see ourselves. Claire is a woman I remember who had been raised to live in a small, but secure attic. She was born in the same large southern city that I was, attended a private girl's school and a prominent college for women. Claire fell in love with and married a young man who started his professional career as soon as she graduated. As he became quickly successful she moved into a comfortable life. The turmoil of the 1960s and the women's movement did little to affect the way she thought of herself. Then one day, shortly after her fiftieth birthday, her book group was having a heated discussion over a controversial novel based on a poor, abused woman's rise to wealth and power. As the conversation continued Claire realized that everyone else in the group had strong feelings about the story. It disturbed her to realize that she did not, that she didn't know what she felt or even worse that she wasn't sure she was capable of feeling intensely about anything.

Janice, you may recall, came to see me because she'd been overwhelmed by her feelings of depression. In contrast, Claire came because she was afraid she couldn't feel at all. I remember her initial visit well. My first impression of Claire was of an attractive woman, obviously educated and socially poised. As we talked, however, I was struck by how she would often say something sincerely

JOURNALING AS INNER EXPLORATION

and then apologize for having said it or feel compelled to invalidate it by coming up with its opposite side. She might say something like, "I know my mother was somewhat cold and unfeeling. But, I'm sure she did the best she could under the circumstances and I can't blame her."

Toward the end of the hour Claire told me that while she'd been thinking about herself in the few weeks since the book group, she'd concluded: "I've been so busy pleasing everyone else, keeping harmony in our family and being sensitive to everyone else's needs that I don't even know what kind of music I like, or what I would want to do if I had any spare time. If someone were to hand me a day pass each week to spend any way I wanted, I don't even know what I'd want to do. Volunteer? For what? Take a class? In what? The very idea panics me as much as it appeals to me."

It's fairly easy for us to see the caretaker role Claire was socialized to live. But when we're the ones living in attic roles it isn't always that easy to recognize, especially if our friends and families are living similar roles. However, Claire experienced an opening, a small realization, that made her stop and think about her life. She will do well because once the door opened she began to think about what she was feeling. She could have fearfully closed the door and comforted herself by waving her uneasiness away: "It's silly to get so upset over a book." Once we've made the initial step toward self-discovery, our curiosity can lead us from one door to the next.

Learning to know ourselves can bring vitality, self-acceptance, joy, compassion, healing, and a sense of personal integrity and wholeness. Yet there's no easy path to these results. Our relationships to the parts of ourselves, like any relationship, must be built carefully and intentionally over time. Time and self-knowledge are the foundation for learning to trust ourselves and for figuring out how these inner aspects we discover need to be integrated into our characters and our lives. I'm disturbed when I hear people in the self-help field make simplistic statements that we need to embrace our shadows, our weaknesses, our symptoms, our feelings, or our illnesses. We need to fully understand our shadows or illnesses before we start embracing them. The capacity in my shadow to hurt someone else or myself is certainly something of which I want to be aware. But I don't want to embrace this ability. I may actually want to imprison it. Some emotions, such as the fear of the unknown, also call for a careful awareness. Yet, we may want to overcome these fears rather than accept them. In many cases I've been convinced that it is important to explore our illnesses and what they mean in our lives. But, while some of them must be accepted, others are a call to courage and to marshall the power to fight for our lives. In other words the aspects of our shadows, the strength of our emotions, the knowledge of our weaknesses, and the complexity of our illnesses are calls to get to know ourselves and life more profoundly and then decide how to relate to them. In this way, we can begin the journey to honoring ourselves in the manner I've referred to as sacred selfishness.

Paying Religious Attention Through Journaling

The twentieth-century poet and writer W. H. Auden said in his foreword to *Markings*, the succinctly eloquent journal of Dag Hammarskjöld, the former secretary general of the United Nations, that he couldn't recall another attempt by a professional man of action "to unite in one life, the *via activa* and the *via comtemplativa*." Developing self-awareness requires that we do exactly what Dag Hammarskjöld did. We must learn to unite a life being lived with our efforts to reflect upon that life. But once we become alert to our need to pay careful attention to our actions, thoughts, feelings, and messages from the unconscious, we find this heedfulness a daunting task. It's helpful for us to find a process that can contain our work. Journaling provides one of the best such approaches, a routine that offers both discipline and refreshment.

Committing ourselves to such an approach frees us from our attempts to master ourselves. By mastering ourselves I'm referring to efforts that are usually based on willpower to control our emotions, temperaments, appearances, and actions to fit an ideal. Generally, such ideals are rooted in images supplied by the social character. Knowing ourselves is an effort to emerge from the confusion of images important to society and other people. During the process of individuation we are looking for inner guidelines for putting ourselves and the world into perspective. This point of view is illustrated in the title Dag Hammarskjöld gave his journal. In his native language the word *markings* also means "trail marks" or "guideposts."

If we forsake willpower, the power-oriented approach to dealing with ourselves, we are free to turn to love and desire for motivation. Self-discipline then becomes self-commitment or self-discipleship and is energized by our desire to know and love ourselves and to experience life more fully. Let me give you a brief example of what I mean. If we feel like we're overweight, a feeling that often reflects social values, we may decide to go on a diet. In most cases successful dieting depends on willpower. When we cheat or fail, we feel guilty and weak. A person seeking to know themselves, however, might choose to journal and reflect on what they're feeling whenever they catch themselves wanting to eat. In this way they may learn to understand the meaning of their eating and its place in their lives.

Recently our local newspaper ran an interview with a well-known novelist who said he wrote eight hours a day, seven days a week. As I began to think about what he said it occurred to me that such a person could never sustain this amount of work through willpower alone; this kind of commitment is fueled by passion and desire. Artistic creations don't just leap into being. The creator must have the commitment to carefully becoming proficient in the craftsmanship of his (or her) field or he can't bring his vision into actuality.

We too must be willing to create our lives in a similar manner. Like an artist we must be committed to discovering the visions, the patterns arising within us that can bring order and meaning to our lives, in contrast to the design we attempt to impose on ourselves; Dag Hammarskjöld understood this, too. After reviewing his life through his journals, in the cover letter attached to his writings, which were discovered after his death, he wrote, "These entries provide the only true 'profile' that can be drawn." His statement makes it clear he thought the writings that arose from within him reflected the development and pattern of his life in a way that no biography of external events could show.

Following the examples of some of the great journal writers like Dag Hammarskjöld, Thomas Merton, Anwar Sadat, Anne Morrow Lindbergh, May Sarton, Virginia Woolf, and Julien of Norwich we, too, can begin paying careful attention to our lives by keeping daily journals. Men and women of the highest creative, spiritual, and intellectual caliber—saints, philosophers, historians, artists, and warriors—have found meaning through this process. People have been writing journals about their lives for centuries. Some are simple diaries of events while others become examples of a life's journey through the discovery of its true nature, a transformed view of the world, enhanced wisdom, and the growth of a loving connection to all life.

Thomas Merton, who as a monk chose the contemplative path as a vocation, also led a very active, creative literary life. He left us some remarkable journals that capture the essence of several methods of journal writing. At times he used his journal to capture ongoing daily events as is shown in the following entry:

> *Got back today from being in Washington the weekend with Ed Rice. Maybe I always was bad at picking hotels. Got a very bad one in Washington: the Harrington: not quite so modern or so comfortable as the Olean House. In fact, the Olean House had it all over this great firetrap. Bad rickety joint, people rattling on our doorknob all morning, dark black room on a court from which you couldn't see the sky. Crummy.*

We can also find examples of his dreams in his journals. Below is one of his dreams. In paragraphs preceding the dream he summarized the events that he thought led up to it.

> *Last week I had a dream about planes. It was at Yakutat, one of the small airstrips to which I had been flown in Alaska. There is*

a low ceiling and we are waiting to take off in a small plane. But a large plane, a commercial prop plane, is about to land. It comes down, then I hear it leave again. The way is clear. Why don't we take off now? The other plane is never seen though it lands and takes off nearby.

Merton also used his journal for musings, for letting his imagination play in a lovely manner as the following piece illustrates. If I read this piece quickly it rattles me and seems abrasive. If I read it slowly and allow each image to form in my mind it becomes more fanciful.

Noises:

Outside now it is raining.

Noises of a cocktail shaker at Doublaston, first with a martini being stirred in it, then with something being shaken in it. Generally, sun outside, or late slanting sun through the French windows.

Noise of a toy electric train going around its tracks.

Noise of winding up a clockwork locomotive—slower turn of the key, thickening catch of the spring.

Noise of the cook chopping or pounding things in the kitchen.

Noise of tires singing past the house on the road outside, in winter, in autumn when the road is light and bare and hard.

Noise of a fire, cracking and snapping in the grate, just lit. The sheaves of sparks that rush up the chimney from time to time.

Noise of a dog jumping up inside the door and scratching on it as you come up the steps.

Noise of Pop walking upstairs, beating with his hand on the banister halfway between the beats of his feet on the hollow-sounding wooden steps.

Noises of someone (never me!) shoveling coal into the furnace downstairs, the shovel chunkily bites in under the coal, which smothers its sound: the coal rushing off the shovel into the fire, leaving the shovel ringing slightly, full of a load.

Noise of someone opening up the legs of a card table—a drag and a sudden catch.

Noise of starting the radio: click of the knob, the light comes on, then half a second later, a sudden swell of hum that dies again a little, while the radio settles down to think up a real sound. After that nothing very interesting comes out of the radio, as a rule.

Noise of the cellar door banging shut: never one bang, but a bang and a quarter because of the bounce. Noise of footsteps on the cement steps leading down to the cellar. Noise of dragging ash cans up the cellar steps, step by step, the heavy, muffled bumping, muffled by the weight of the fine pinkish gray ash. All this took place under the window of the room I slept in: that room was Pop's den. It had an office desk and a swivel chair. Noise made by the swivel chair when you turned on it completely. First no noise at all, then a kind of slight, singing protest. (Noise of the drawers opening and shutting.) The protest of the chair comes not from making it turn, but it is uttered by a tough spring as you lean back in the chair and tilt it quite a bit.

Noise of raking leaves, of mowing the grass, of digging with a spade, of raking ground or hoeing. Sweeping the sidewalk and the brick front steps.

Noise of the sprinkler, as it turns scattering whirling threads of water around the air over the front lawn. Twenty or thirty feet away the leaves of the privet hedge move where you would not have suspected water was falling.

And finally let's look at one of his personal reflections, or self-examinations, that's directly related to his growth in self-knowledge:

Identity. I can see now where the work is to be done. I have been coming here into solitude to find myself, and now I must also lose myself: not simply rest in the calm, the peace, the identity that is made up of my experienced relationship with nature in

JOURNALING AS INNER EXPLORATION

solitude. This is healthier than my identity as a writer or a monk, but it is still a false identity, though it has a temporary meaning and validity. It is the cocoon that masks the transition stage between what crawls and what flies.

Journaling for most of us begins with the simple method of recording daily events and the feelings they evoke in us. As we become more at home in this practice it usually grows into musing, reflection, and self-examination—into seeking to know ourselves more completely. When we help it, the practice of journaling matures and we discover things about ourselves that we often knew at some level but were unable to formulate or consciously articulate. The following quotation from Dag Hammarskjöld's journal shows how our reflections can mature beyond the values of everyday life into the realm of spiritual consciousness.

Now you know. When the worries over your work loosen their grip, then this experience of light, warmth, and power. From without—a sustaining element, like air to the glider or water to the swimmer. An intellectual hesitation which demands proofs and logical demonstration prevents me from "believing"—in this, too. Prevents me from expressing and interpreting this reality in intellectual terms. Yet, through me there flashes this vision of a magnetic field in the soul, created in a timeless present by unknown multitudes, living in holy obedience, whose words and actions are a timeless prayer.
—"The Communion of Saints"—and—within it—an eternal life.

Getting away from the everyday world has always been a part of the spiritual life. Monks seclude themselves in monasteries, nuns in nunneries; ascetics seek mountains, caves, and deserts. Seeking retreats to reflect and renew ourselves in privacy from the expectations of daily obligations is an archetypal pattern. Thomas Moore points out that retreats need a concrete physical expression that can take the modest form of a drawer where journals and dreams are kept. A few minutes to write down dreams in the morning and a few for reflections in our journals in either the morning or evening can refresh our souls. But, the key is always *attention*, mindfulness, regularity, and devotion—a commitment to ourselves.

The contents of your journal and dreams must be considered private property and should not be shared. The reason for privacy in our journaling is that it's the way we dialogue with ourselves about our lives. If we're going to grow in our self-understanding and our ability to see reality truthfully, we need to have the freedom to share our darkest secrets, our most fanciful hopes, our inspirations, our disappointments, our frustrations, our unformed speculations, and other aspects of our subjective lives without the fear of being embarrassed about our awkward articulations, more importantly without the judgment, recrimination, or teasing that disclosure sometimes brings. Disclosure immediately activates fear; it may inhibit us, cause us to censor ourselves, or even belittle our subjective lives. We ourselves do that well enough without anyone's help.

Our journals need to be safe places for us to explore spontaneous feelings, thoughts that are still developing, musings, fantasies, and reflections. We grow best when we feel safe—where we're free to express, experiment, and discover who we are in an atmosphere of safety that's grounded in the secure principles of love and self-respect.

I once worked with a woman who could only give herself honestly over to the process of journal keeping after she had made her daughter promise that if she died to come immediately into her mother's house to gather her journals and dispose of them. Only when this woman was assured that no one would ever read her journals could she rest. Some people wonder how long they should keep their journals; I've known people who consider their journals old friends they enjoy revisiting while others feel that once they have worked through the issues in them they belong to a former personality. They want to keep their distance. It's OK to keep them and it's OK to dispose of them. The decision is a personal one, but I'd think about it carefully before deciding to get rid of them because there is value in looking back to see how much you've changed.

Many people use the terms *journal* and *diary* interchangeably, when actually they're different. A diary, like our day-timers and palm pilots, is the recording of the simple daily history of our lives and usually doesn't include many emotional or psychological observations. A journal on the other hand, is meant to say something about who we are today within the context of our lives. It becomes a continuing confrontation with ourselves that leads to new self-understanding as we write and reflect on who we are, what has happened, what we have done, and how we feel.

Author and theologian Sam Keen shares some of his journal entries in his book *To a Dancing God.* The opening paragraph is a good example of how we can question ourselves in order to further our self-understanding:

> *One of the crucial questions: "To what may I give myself?" If I do not ask it with seriousness I end up, at best, a lonely man "fulfilling my potential," concentrating on myself. At worst I descend into despair. The questions of surrender, belonging, self-transcendence, loyalty, ecstasy must be asked. Otherwise I possess myself like a jealously guarded territory. I watch over my boundaries, possessions, energies. I hoard myself. I become a territorial animal.*

In a similar vein, poet and writer May Sarton in her warm, wise journal writings reveals a rich path that leads through self-understanding into serenity as the following passage demonstrates:

> *For weeks and months I have allowed myself to be persuaded into a frustrated pseudo peace to spare the other. But if there is deep love involved, there is deep responsibility toward it. We*

cannot afford not to fight for growth and understanding, even when it is painful, as it is bound to be. The fear of pain and of causing pain is, no doubt, a sin. At any rate, I feel back in myself again, and ready for some weeks of many interruptions, including a commencement address of May 30th.

Our journals become dynamic records of our experiences that we can look at over time and discover some of the truths of our psychological lives.

When we begin to look for the exiled aspects of our lives—our unlived feelings, potentials, and dreams—we can often uncover them by examining the emotional events and images we've recorded. Not too long ago I was listening to Don, a man in his late fifties whose children had humorously described him as a "three-pieced button-down kind of guy." Don took pride in being a poised, carefully thought-out and presented businessman. A few days before seeing me Don had been stuck in traffic and had tuned into a radio station playing rock and roll songs from the 1950s. The first song Don heard was Big Joe Turner singing "Shake, Rattle, and Roll." By the end of the tune Don realized he was practically dancing in his car seat and feeling a rush of energy that completely surprised him.

As Don was writing about this experience in his journal he had a flashback from long ago. He told me, "I saw myself when I was sixteen. I had gone to Panama City, Florida, with several of my friends to spend the summer. My God, what a blowout that was! From a tough prep school to total freedom. There were nights we danced and drank beer into the morning at the pavilion where everyone hung out, and slept on the beach. Those were the days of crew cuts, but I grew 'duck tails' and peroxided my hair just enough until it was a golden bronze. I must've fallen in love every week. When we needed money we 'dead-headed,' worked part-time on the fishing boats for tourists. It's hard for me to believe now that was actually me."

JOURNALING AS INNER EXPLORATION

We talked about this part of Don from his past, which loved being carefree and spontaneous, who was daring and longed for adventure more than respectability. I asked him to describe the young man he saw in his flashback. He replied, "Me, in a pink T-shirt and black jeans, with my blonde hair, dancing with a girl to match. I should feel silly, but I don't." At this point we both laughed and spent the next thirty minutes reminiscing about the fifties rock and roll music that I love as much as Don does.

Then Don began to write about this dancing image of himself in his journal:

> *Ever since I remembered you I can't get you off my mind. I love you, but you haunt me because I am who I am. You hold up a mirror to my serious face. I am too serious. I think too much. But now you're here dancing in my mind. You move my body. But I'm still a careful person, thinking practically, planning tomorrow. I don't know how to live without being careful. I'm rooted up to my neck in work and family obligations. Yet there you are dancing, pushing me, making me think that there may be other lives I want to live. Or maybe I want to live this life differently.*

Paying attention to ourselves and concretely reflecting on our experiences awaken us. Don was experiencing a creative recovery of his potential for living more enthusiastically and freeing himself from his own mind-set about how he should live. Frequently our journaling can lead us to images of the past and our potentials that we have lost or misplaced along the way.

Journaling Suggestions

Author George Sand says that "writing a journal implies that one has ceased to think of the future and decided to live wholly in the present. It is an announcement to fate that you expect nothing more." Even for those of us who don't think of ourselves as "writers" this exercise can become a ritual that provides a powerful place to explore our natures and to prime our creative processes. When a friend of mine began her journey into some midlife changes she began writing daily about the events in her life and how she was experiencing them. As time went on she made several forays into her creative process and into changing her life. During this period she felt her journal became a lifeline that kept her centered and confident of her course.

I've found that examples often help me get started on new and unfamiliar projects. My friend has generously offered to share the opening page of her journal to show us how she began.

> *9/2 I have thought about writing for several days—writing about my thoughts and feelings related to this trip to Washington. I am not sure what has stopped me—fear of expressing myself? Laziness? Discomfort in the process of stopping, taking time to do it. Even now I am having thoughts of stopping. So—to some quick thoughts: I am so very thankful for the friends I have in my life now. It has just dawned on me how many wonderful people are in my life now . . . I feel blessed and very thankful. These are people who are real and have a depth that is quite remarkable. . . .*
>
> *A.M. Carlos Alfonzo exhibit at the Hirshorn. Very powerful. I am brought to tears with his painting* Told—*i.e. "told" that he is HIV+. I feel the power of his agony—is he speaking to me through his painting? I am thankful that I can feel this energy. Am I tapping into another dimension of existence?*
>
> *P.M. Sitting in the Bishop's Garden at the National Cathedral. Roses and fragrant herbs surround me. Bricks and buzzing bees. Water gurgling from a fountain behind me. I feel tears welling up in me and I feel lost. Am I trying too hard? Am I too serious in my quest? I am too intense—I need to lighten up. But how? I am starting to cry. What is the emotion trying to speak? It is the energy of the imprisoned child—the blue-eyed, blond little*

girl trapped within. She is your feminine energy—still so very young and trapped. How can I help her escape? Just open the door and she will walk out. And the keys to the door? Where are they? When you find the keys to your heart, you will also have the keys to this door. But I am afraid of my heart—I am afraid to go near it. But you go near it and don't even know it. You are near your heart every time you feel like crying—those tears are words from your heart. Your fear of crying and your effort at holding back your tears only block your heart's expression. But what is the point of breaking down in a public place and crying? I would feel so self-conscious. You do have to use some discretion—to discriminate, if you will. At the very least, you must acknowledge your tears and talk with them. Ask what they are about—what is your heart trying to tell you? The heart speaks subtly—and unless you are tuned into its language, you will miss a great deal—thus, the tears—your heart's way of getting your attention. Be thankful for your tears, and whenever they appear, know that your heart is speaking to you. Listen. Dialogue. Embrace. And slowly, you will know.

Dinner last night with a woman I met who is also staying at the Preacher's College. In our conversation she told me a joke about a man who regularly prayed to God that he might one day win the lottery jackpot with all of its riches and money. After years of not having his prayers answered, the man made an extra special plea to God who responded in total exasperation. God told the man that it might help if he first bought himself a lottery ticket.

In a few short paragraphs, feelings, musings, and questions have evolved from her reflections and humor has emerged. This lovely piece shows how our journal writing can evolve into a language that is our own. It becomes similar to the silence of meditation because it takes us directly into ourselves. At the same time it is a language of creativity in which we are carefully re-created out of our reflections.

Important Elements in Personal Journal Writing

- Privacy insures trust and provides a space where we can encounter our many aspects truthfully.

- Self-understanding comes from writing down honestly who we are today within the context of our lives.

- Our journals become concrete records over time; studying them can reveal psychological patterns in our lives.

- Examining relationships, feelings, and interactions can be a source for discovering features of ourselves we have denied.

- Including our reflections in our personal journals leads to self-confrontation and to a new consciousness.

In our journals we should include our dreams and our thoughts and responses to them. As we're recording our reflections on the events we've journaled, we can include any new insights, feelings, and other ideas or material that come to mind. It's also a good place to give thought to the feelings and behaviors we had during the day, or to the feelings we didn't get a chance to express.

Writing down a description of each situation where we think we feel a particular emotion can often help us get a better understanding of what's happening. For example, one man I know felt resentment whenever his wife suggested he might need a coat, a hat, an umbrella, or something else when he left the house. He thought she was treating him like a child. As he journaled about these situations he became aware that she might be expressing her care for him and he was "hearing her like a child" whose mother was chiding him. With this insight he was then able to accept and appreciate her love for him.

Journal keeping is both a personal workbook and an intensely personal form of self-expression. Like self-expression itself, there's no right or wrong format. All that matters is that you find a format that works for you, that fits your personality, and that can grow and change with you. Some people I know use elegant notebooks while others use a computer disk. I've always been the most comfortable with the kind of spiral notebooks I used in college.

Normally journaling takes about ten or fifteen minutes a day unless you're exploring something intensely. Then you may take longer, but rarely will you write for more than thirty minutes. People often ask me how they should handle dreams and I advise them to write the dreams down immediately, whether its during the night or first thing in the morning. Spouses, lovers, and other people in your home often have to learn to gracefully allow you some time with yourself before you start the day. In many circumstances, keeping dreams attracts interest and the other people around you might start paying more attention to their own.

Journaling is a particularly good way of reflecting at the end of the day, and many people do it before going to sleep. The time of day or the length of time you devote to journaling, however, can be worked out to fit your own pattern as long as you treat the practice with respect rather than as something you try to conveniently force into your schedule. You may take days off here and there to keep your journaling fresh, and from becoming routine and mechanical. Your inner work has its own inner substance—this is the beginning, where you look for it, where you launch the journey deep within yourself.

Tips for Journal Writing

- Record what is going on or what has happened inside of you as well as outside.

- Make special note of strong emotional reactions during the day.

- Reflect on these reactions, and on the situations and

relationships in which they occurred.

- Record thoughts, ideas, fantasies, and dreams.

- Try to simply reflect on dreams and see what they bring to mind.

- Record events that surround dreams and see if they seem related to you.

- Record drawings, poetry, quotations, and whatever else comes to mind.

- Record your personal fantasies and ambitions for both the present and the future.

In the foreword of her lovely and inspiring book *Gift from the Sea*, Anne Morrow Lindbergh explains how the book began as a journal "in order to think out my own particular pattern of living, my own individual balance of life, work and human relationships." She discovered through her writing, and talking about her writing with other people, that once she looked beneath the surface of life, many men and women in various circumstances and in many forms were "grappling with essentially the same questions." We are all seeking the sense of security that arrives when we have learned to become more intimate with ourselves. Journaling helps us find assurance that the creativity, values, and ideals that arise inside of us are gifts we can nurture and develop. And, when we have found out how to listen to ourselves we are able to act with strength, greet the world with joy, and share our gifts with others.

CHAPTER 6
Dialoguing as Interrelating

It is our lot, if we are honest, to live in duality and paradox. The dialogue of those paradoxical elements is the stuff of life. Surprisingly it is also the surest path toward unity. Our dreams are its stage, its workshop and battleground. And Active Imagination is its superb language.
—Robert A. Johnson

When Albert Einstein was a young man he dreamt he was speeding down a steep mountainside on a sled. He went faster and faster and as he approached the speed of light he noticed the stars above him were refracting light into a spectrum of colors that he'd never seen before. This image impressed him so dramatically that he never forgot it. In later years he maintained that his entire scientific achievement had been the result of meditating on this dream. The dream and his meditations became the basis for his "thought experiments" through which he worked out his theory of relativity.

In Einstein's story we see that the work of the twentieth century's greatest scientist was based not on hard, critical, or even brilliant thought processes, but on dreams and imagination. Einstein's "thought experiments" were *experiments conducted in his imagination.* Our imaginations are the spaces, the fields, where our conscious personalities and the many parts of our unconscious can meet each other, struggle, play, dream, and transform us. We are generally at home valuing the power of imagination in people engaged in fine arts, painting, literature, music, and poetry, but we may be a little surprised to find that the basis of Einstein's scientific theories is the same as the basis of William Blake's poetry. It's this realization that led Robertson Davies to say, "between great poetry and depth psychology [the psychology of the unconscious] there is no division but that determined by the presence, or lack of imagination, for imagination is not dream-spinning but insight." For Einstein his imagination brought insight into the universe. For Blake it gave insight into the soul of human life.

Imagination is the key to creativity. The word *create* comes from the Latin word *creare*, which means "to cause to grow; to bring forth or produce." Julia Cameron, the dynamic author of *The Artist's Way*, says, "Life is energy, pure creative energy. . . . There is an underlying, indwelling creative force infusing all life—including ourselves. . . . When we open ourselves to our creativity, we open ourselves to the creator's creativity within us and our lives." Imagination, the space where our conscious and unconscious minds can come together, is the field that infuses us with creativity and even our images of the divine.

The word *imagination* evokes two kinds of reactions in us. One is to admire it, because we realize that no creative solutions to life's problems large or small can be accomplished without it. We also respect creative people—whether they are artists, scientists, businesspeople, or something else—because they always bring unique expression to what they're doing. But imagination, the space where creativity and transformation prosper, is also a place that arouses fear. The creative person is a risk taker that is initiating or bringing to life an idea, feeling, attitude, concept, theory, plan, or project that may be considered naive, impractical, and even incompetent. When faced with a creative choice versus the path of conventional wisdom we may tell ourselves, "I can't because . . . I'm too old, too broke, have too many obligations, am too shy or afraid." Our fear is often supported by the people near to us because our social character is like a sentry warning us away from

DIALOGUING AS INTERRELATING

anything that isn't practical or realistic or that puts our sense of who we are or should be in question.

If our consciousness is disordered, caught in fear, rage, depression, anxiety, or some other dark state, then our imaginations can end up serving destructive purposes. For example, computer games that focus on the imagination may cause an alienated person to become trapped in an illusion. A depressed person's imagination may work to make his (or her) future seem more hopeless than it is; and an anxious person's may cause him to be unrealistically fearful of the future. In addition, the states we normally refer to as illusions, delusions, and paranoia in the mentally ill show an imagination contaminated by a person's sickness. The term *power of the imagination* emphasizes that it has the strength to affect us either creatively or destructively and therefore we should treat it with respect. If our imaginations become frightening we should seek professional help. However, their creative aspects are essential to help us live and grow in a substantial, fulfilling way. Generally people who are seeking self-knowledge are rarely at risk of being harmed by their imaginations because they are trying to understand themselves in order to live more fully, which is a sign of health and not an avoidance of life's threats and difficulties.

Journaling and paying careful attention to our lives will begin to release our imaginations from their servitude to practicality and their imprisonment by society's mind-sets. Our imaginations are great underused resources as we work toward growth and healing. The more we strengthen them the more they can help us enlarge the boundaries of our personalities. One way we can do this is through a special use of the imagination as a tool for getting to know ourselves developed by Jung. He called it active imagination.

Creating Objective Inner Relationships

Active imagination now covers a wide range of activities in Jungian psychology. The basic purpose of it is to use our imaginations as active fields where we can intentionally discover and come into relationship with aspects of ourselves we don't understand and know little about. Active imagination gives both form and voice to these elements of our personalities that normally aren't heard and it establishes lines of communication with them. It can take place through drawing, painting, writing, sculpting, dancing, and making music. Even when these activities are not interpreted psychologically, the process going on is a creative one and contributes to our growth and transformation as you will see in the upcoming examples.

Active imagination means expressing ourselves in some way and then "actively" listening to ourselves. For instance we are all accustomed to having a dialog with another person—a spouse, lover, friend, parent, child, and so on. When we dialogue, we talk and we listen. Modern communication skills have taught us that listening is an active process in which we must intentionally put aside our need to be understood and listen in a manner that is seeking to understand the other person. If our dialog goes well we may grow as a result of it because we are learning more about the other people and about ourselves in relation to them. If these dialogs continue we will usually become closer to these people, learn to trust them, to feel comfortable in their presence and confident that we may call on them in times of need. In other words while we have grown individually in the process, the strength and dependability of the relationships have also increased. The technique of using written dialogs in active imagination is simple and has the same goal as our other dialogs. We learn to talk with our anger, our envy, our weight, our illness, or what have you. And by setting this process up in a dialog format in our imaginations we can learn to listen to those features of ourselves and understand the parts they play in our lives more clearly.

In my experience, the written dialog is a very helpful tool in getting to know ourselves and seems to be a natural step that evolves from journaling. In his hopeful and heartwarming book *Living Buddha, Living Christ,* the Buddhist monk Thich Nhat Hanh makes it clear that there are three essential elements in a dialog between people or groups of people. He explains that for an effective dialog to take place both parties must be willing to thoroughly listen to each other. Both parties must be open-minded enough to learn from the other person. And, finally, both parties must be willing to change as a result of the dialog. The same guidelines hold true for our inner dialogs. For example if I am dialoguing with my anger I must listen to it. It may be there for a good reason. Someone may be taking advantage of me and I might be trying to hide my anger from myself in order to keep harmony in the situation. Once I've listened to my anger I need to learn from it. I might need to learn to be more aware of how I am being treated and how much I overvalue harmony. Then I might learn how to relate to people trying to take advantage of me in a more forthright manner. This entire process is one of listening, exploring, learning, and growing. At no point does it mean I should blow up or let my anger get out of control. Actually Thich Nhat Hanh says that getting to know ourselves better usually leads to having more compassion for both ourselves and other people, and I agree with him.

As we begin an inner dialog we must be able to keep our minds open and clear while listening to and learning from another part of ourselves. If, for instance, we're dialoguing with our *fear* and trying to identify it more clearly and give it a voice, we must be willing to accept it, question it, listen to it, and require that it listen to and respond to us. Such a dialog should help us understand our fear in a new way, for when really listened to, our fear should affect us in a less dramatic manner. In his delightful book *To a Dancing God*, author Sam Keen explores the problems of remaining human in a busy world by reflecting upon his life. In one of his final chapters he shares a few of the active imaginations that took place during the course of his writing. In the following passage you can see how he addressed, listened to, responded to, and learned from his fear.

OCTOBER 8, 1968. DIALOGUE WITH FEAR

SK: *I wish I could begin by saying, "Damn you, fear. Leave me alone!" but honesty demands that I address you as "Dear fear," for you have been with me most of my life. Now I want to understand why I am attracted to you and did not banish you long ago.*

FEAR: *I am glad you are willing to admit that we are reluctant friends. It has taken me some years to get you to confess that you are a hesitant lover of what you pretend to despise. What a capacity for self-deceit you have, pretending that I was somehow your fated enemy! Or, to be specific, that I was an unconscious legacy from your parents. Such transparent nonsense. If I am your fate, I am at least a fate you have chosen and nurtured. It is not without your consent and satisfaction that we have been together all these years. You might have lived in conversation with love, or courage, or creativity, or desire, or fame. No! You have kept me around. So don't try to disown me.*

SK: *OK you have me. I admit some responsibility for continually talking with you but I certainly do not get satisfaction from your presence. You are like a bad neighbor. I am stuck with you but I wish you would move away.*

FEAR: *You lie easily. The fact is I am a valuable companion and a loyal friend. I don't demand change of you. I am satisfied to keep our relation as it has always been. I do not ask you to venture out into the unknown or act heroically in defining your existence in the carelessness and caprice of the world. All I ask is a token, a ritual, a guarantee that you will not go beyond the limits I have set for your comfort and safety.*

SK: *Ritual or token, hell! You demand the most alive part of me. Your "token" is the whole of my capacity for new experience. You promise security so long as I surrender my autonomy, my critical ability, my reason, my responsibility for reflecting upon and evaluating my own experience. Your price for comfort is giving up growth.*

DIALOGUING AS INTERRELATING

FEAR: *So what if the price is high? If you refuse to acknowledge my authority you will fall into pride and rebellion. I keep the boundaries. I set the limits. Only Adam, Prometheus, and other proud but foolish rebels have the illusion that they are strong enough to define the nature of good and evil for themselves. No man, and least of all you, has the wisdom, the energy, or the time to determine the limits of the possible for himself. Such omnipotent pretense is clearly sinful and stupid.*

SK: *You sound so reasonable and charitable. But, in truth, you wear the face of the Grand Inquisitor. You would refuse me knowledge of my freedom in exchange for comfort, and thus steal my dignity and potency.*

FEAR: *Can you deny that both humility and wisdom are on the side of the Inquisitor? Yes, I speak with the voice of authority. I echo the commands and prohibitions of your parents. But I speak as your past, your tradition. If I limit you to the possibilities which were conceivable to your parents, it is merely to enforce those rules and limits they found necessary to the fullness of life. My voice is conservative. I would have you love what your fathers loved and hate what they hated, for there is wisdom in the experience of the generations which is absent in the individual. I preserve your energies from being dissipated in folly.*

SK: *The limits of the possible change. Human nature is not static. What was psychologically inconceivable to my parents is an open possibility for me, except when you intervene.*

FEAR: *I am glad you spoke about "the limits of the possible." You are aware that Camus used this phrase as a summary of his philosophy of life. Now—can you tell me in all honesty that you are willing to face the uncertainty, the tentativeness, the absolute demand for self-definition in the face of the absurd that was his daily bread and wine? If not, don't pretend that you want me to leave you altogether, because I protect you against this horrible vacuum of the unknown. I give you ground upon which to stand in the swirl. Even if it is sometimes bitter ground, it is a place for your feet. Better fear than anxiety, better a hostile force at the center of your personality than the emptiness which is the promise of death, better pain than chaos. The suffering I cause is only a necessary by-product of enforcing the limits which give you definition and succor.*

SK: *I do not accept your way. Granted, I must have limits or else I would explode into the void of infinite possibility and schizophrenia. However, there is a better way to establish boundaries than you suggest. Decision is the alternative to fear. I can take upon myself the responsibility for deciding, and then the pain of limitation is not imposed but chosen. Maturity rather than fate or fear may determine the shape my life will assume. Your presence is not necessary.*

FEAR: *I will admit this heroic possibility exists. Should you choose to accept full responsibility for your values and decisions, I will leave you. But I will always be waiting for your energies to give out. Few persons manage the heroic style of total responsibility. I doubt that you can abide by this high ideal. At any rate, we are talking in theoretical terms. As of this moment, you are still engaged in dialogue with me. If the time comes when you choose to be fascinated by love, or creativity, or even work, I will leave you alone. For the time being we remain reluctant friends.*

SK: *I accept your conclusion with sadness. Nevertheless, I must say, you begin to bore me. Perhaps tomorrow I will converse with you less, and the day after not at all.*

FEAR: *We shall see.*

DIALOGUING AS INTERRELATING

As Sam's dialog begins we can imagine that his writing and reflections have brought him to a catalytic moment. He has recognized his fear and his ambivalent relationship to it. He sees that while he doesn't like his fear it has been part of him for a long time and he wants to understand his relationship with it better. In an effort to explore his connection to fear he opens the dialog by expressing his thoughts and then listening.

"Fear" answers by pointing out that it has been a "comfortable companion" to Sam because he doesn't demand change. This statement gives Sam a valuable insight into himself as "fear" continues to explain that he protects Sam from taking risks that may lead him into unknown territory or growth beyond the comfortable habits and boundaries of his current life.

This awareness makes Sam angry and he points out to "fear" that such security means the price of comfort is stagnation and it costs him his vitality, uniqueness, and autonomy. "Fear," however, doesn't back down and as Sam continues to listen it says growth beyond the ordinary invites arrogance and a punishing fate. This bit of conventional wisdom uncovers a deeper layer of Sam's concerns with fear, the deeper fear we all encounter when we grow beyond our families' and society's signposts for a good, proper life. We are afraid that people won't understand us, that we may become outcasts or that our actions may cause the ones close to us to react angrily against us. Sam acknowledges the validity of this argument, but also answers by pointing out that it is a trap. Through the benefits of the dialog his insight deepens, another purpose of his fear is discovered, and he is able to successfully respond to it.

In the next stage of the dialog another level of fear emerges, one that we might call "spiritual." It claims to protect Sam from existential failure and spiritual emptiness. "Fear" also indicates that it might give way to love, creativity, or work, but as yet that is only a hypothetical possibility. Sam replies with sadness and with the feeling his interest in fear will fade. But "fear" doesn't seem threatened.

Through the useful tool of dialoguing Sam is able to discover how his fear has protected and limited him, the reasons he has for allowing it to and the price he pays for such protection. By continuing the dialog he discovers the spiritual problems coupled with his fear, and his ability to respond to fear rather than be controlled by it. The ability to become more self-aware and to act in answer to his fear are key goals of dialoguing. The dialog separates Sam from his fear by giving him enough distance from it to develop a new perspective toward it. Instead of being controlled or manipulated by his fear he can begin to deal with it more objectively. By understanding it better he has increased his power to make choices and react realistically to it. Instead of giving simplistic solutions to our problems, dialogs deepen the dimensions of our experiences. They help us learn more about ourselves, and as a result healing our wounds and handling problems becomes growth.

To "know," Thich Nhat Hanh also writes, means to acquire wisdom, insight, and understanding. The dialogs that help us get to know our fear, for instance, bring us to what he calls "interbeing" with it. In this situation we've separated ourselves from our fear so that we can dialogue with it. This step alone, as we've seen, helps us to relate to our fear more objectively and to be less vulnerable to having it control us without our knowing it or being able to do something about it. We can dialogue with almost anything we can imagine—with our emotions such as fear, anger, depression, anxiety, rage, sadness, courage, joy, desire; with physical symptoms such as weight, pain, headaches, diseases like cancer, tight necks, aching backs; with figures we meet in our dreams and fantasies such as men, women, animals, birds, storms, even inanimate objects like cars and houses; or with psychological aspects of ourselves that we may consider our inner critics, children, warriors, lovers, wisdom figures, rebels, and anything else that may represent an attitude or state of mind.

When philosopher Friedrich Nietzsche labeled his depression his "dog" he came into a new kind of relationship with it. Naming something is frequently helpful in dialoguing. Naming increases our differentiation, gives us more distance from our experiences, and a wider choice of reactions. Winston Churchill followed Nietzsche's example and called his recurrent depression his "black dog." The amount of objectivity he gained by naming his experience allowed him to no longer feel victimized by his depression. While he still experienced it, according to British writer and psychiatrist Anthony Storr, even to the point of becoming bedridden at times, he was no longer demoralized by it. When his "black dog" arrived, he acknowledged it and frequently went to bed for a while. But it rarely affected his effectiveness or passion for living for very long. Storr points out that it is people who can't find ways to express and resolve their troubling experiences and conflicts who become paralyzed and neurotic. He goes on to say that it was the courage and spirit that Churchill developed in battling his own despair that gave him the strength to lead Britain with conviction through the hopeless hours of World War II.

In our dialogs we may want to keep our naming simple as Sam Keen did when he called his fear, "fear." Or, we may want to go a step further at times. I know a woman who considered her panic attacks a "black hawk." She opened her dialog with the hawk by asking its name and it replied, "Mariah." She went on to have a very enlightening dialog with Mariah. However, in most of my examples I'll stick to the form Sam Keen used.

Listening to things like our anger, depression, courage, and other parts of ourselves and learning to understand them to a greater degree help us learn to be more compassionate with ourselves and to discern their origins, purposes, and helpful as well as harmful influences in our lives. Self-love is often born from this work toward self-understanding.

Many of the people I meet and work with are interested in physical symptoms and illnesses. But every illness has a psychological component. They affect our emotions, our feelings of safety, identity, and trust in life. This doesn't mean that an illness is caused "psychologically," or that it can be cured psychologically. Our psychology often simply participates in the cause of an illness or our particular vulnerability to one.

In addition, illness often simply requires a change in consciousness. It helps us learn the importance of directing our healing efforts toward the whole person rather than simply trying to cure a symptom. Seen in this way the healing process in its true sense is individuation, a rebirth into one's true and more complete self. This is the whole point of the moving account Reynolds Price gave of his experience of cancer and transformation in his book *A Whole New Life*, which I quoted earlier. A new life, a transformed life, for Reynolds Price included becoming a paraplegic who chose life rather than despair, though not without intense suffering. The transformation left him a hard-nosed realist, yet more compassionate, patient, watchful, and inspired as a writer. Active imagination can be a great aid in healing through helping our processes of transformation.

A short time ago I was working with Roger who has experienced chronic back pain since he was seventeen years old. Doctors have unfortunately been unable to find the source of the problem or do much to ease his pain. Roger has been on numerous medications over the years but because of their side effects, he usually just tries to ignore the pain and carry on. Every couple of years his back pain escalates to the point where he's unable to move and has to miss several days of work. After Roger's most recent attack he decided to try to go to the source of his problem and dialogue with his back pain.

>ROGER: *I'm totally locked up again. I can't move an inch without excruciating pain. If I try to walk (and I hate to even try!) I have to shuffle forward inches at a time. You totally take over my life. What's this about? You've been around for over thirty years now, and I've got to tell you I'm damn tired of you. I don't get it. I'm not a sedentary person. I watch what I eat. I exercise. I don't do anything to abuse you. I don't understand why you have to show up every year or so and totally cripple me. Can you answer me that? What purpose could you possibly serve in my life?*
>
>BACK PAIN: *Well, finally, you've decided to ask me. You've asked all those doctors and specialists and they didn't know. They had their theories but nobody ever came close to the real reason.*

DIALOGUING AS INTERRELATING

I'm the only one that knows the truth. You've waited three decades for this, are you sure you really want to know?
ROGER: *Now you make me wonder if I really do. But I'm tired of you taking over my life and shutting me down. I'm tired of being in so much pain. And most of all, I hate feeling powerless whenever you're around. I don't deserve being treated this way. Yes, I really do want to hear what you have to say.*

BACK PAIN: *OK. Think about it, Roger. Have you ever noticed when I start to bother you? Have you ever kept track of what's going in your life when I show up?*

ROGER: *No, I've never thought to do that.*

BACK PAIN: *Well, maybe you should, because I always show up for a reason. Like whenever you keep doing something that you really don't want to do. Remember when you were seventeen? You started focusing on going into engineering when you went to college, just to please your dad. But you had no desire to be an engineer. I was the one who stepped in and said "No!" And remember that job you had in Washington that you absolutely hated but you took it anyway because of the money? Wasn't I around almost all the time then?*

ROGER: *Oh, you may be right! I never put that together. It never dawned on me that you might actually serve a purpose. You mean you let me know when I start heading in a direction I don't want to go in? All of a sudden that makes perfect sense. It's like you totally throw my body in reverse and I have to stop everything. My whole life becomes one big NO! This is amazing. I never considered that you might actually be looking out for me. This is so much to take in I need to stop now. But I hope we can talk again.*

BACK PAIN: *Certainly.*

This dialog was the beginning of many that Roger had with his pain. To have merely labeled the pain as psychosomatic and treated the symptoms with pain medication or muscle relaxers alone would have robbed Roger of an important piece of self-awareness. He felt the dialog changed his perception of the pain and caused him to experience it as a separate presence within him, "an intelligence, an entity, who was intimately involved with me."

Any kind of serious illness or emotional conflict causes us to lose the "destination and the map" that has been guiding our lives. In another impressive book, *The Wounded Storyteller: Body, Illness and Ethics*, sociologist Arthur Frank searches his and other people's experiences of illness from the standpoint of life as a story. Illness, he says, changes the fundamental assumptions that have given our lives their particular meanings, and leaves us in a state that doesn't immediately make sense. Dr. Frank concludes, "The ill person who turns illness into a story transforms fate into experience: the disease that sets the body apart from others becomes in the story, the common bond of suffering that joins bodies in their shared vulnerability." When we begin journaling about our experiences of symptoms and dialoguing with them, we begin speaking with new voices, telling new stories. Rather than simply being victims we become once again what philosopher Kierkegaard referred to as "the editor of our life." We become healers as well as sufferers.

Laura came to see me to find out why she always felt so depressed. "It's like the postpartum blues came after my children were born and never left," she explained. Considering her twin boys were now in college this was quite a statement. After we got to know each other fairly well I suggested she dialogue with this companion of hers for the last twenty years, but she seemed hesitant.

"How do you talk to something so abstract? It would be like trying to get to know a dark cloud or a fog." Yet despite her hesitancy, Laura was curious enough about my suggestion that she tried it, and the next session brought in the following dialog in the form of a letter:

DIALOGUING AS INTERRELATING

DEAR DEPRESSION,
    I'd like to get to know what you're about. You've been hanging around for years now. Whenever you're around I feel like I've jumped into the ocean wearing my winter coat, and I have to walk around all day never getting to take it off. My energy is always low. Most days I just go from one thing to the next trying to drag myself through the day and handle everything I need to handle.
    Surely this is not how life is supposed to be. Can you tell me why you're here? signed, Laura

DEAR LAURA,
    You've ignored me this long. What makes you think I want to talk now? signed, The "Big D."

DEAR "BIG D.",
    I see your point. Nobody likes being ignored. But you've been invisible to me until now. Forgive me, but I never thought of you as being this real. Now that I know you have a voice I'm ready to talk. Laura

DEAR LAURA,
    I have a voice like you wouldn't believe. And I have to tell you I'm tired of being treated this way. Ignored. Unappreciated. Underrated. And after all I've done for you. "D."

DEAR "D.",
    Please pardon, but what have you done for me? L.

DEAR LAURA,
    How about taking on all your feelings for one thing. When's the last time you felt overwhelmed or angry or really mad? Who do you think carries that around so you don't have to deal with it? "D."

DEAR "D.",
    That's what you do for me? You protect me from my feelings? You may be right. I've noticed that I don't really feel happy or sad or anything anymore. I just walk around in this neutral zone all the time. L.

DEAR LAURA,
    Well I invented the neutral zone. And do you have any idea how exhausted I am? I've been taking this from you for two decades! 'D.'

DEAR "D.",
    I'm sure you are exhausted. But you know what? I'm ready to have my life back now. I don't think this works for either one of us anymore. I want to figure out how we can both get free from this old way of being together. Would you be willing to work with me on this? signed, your friend, Laura

DEAR LAURA,
    A breath of fresh air would be nice. "D."

The end of this dialog seems encouraging. In working with people who have chronic unhappiness, emotional problems, or physical pain, I've realized that frequently their first inclination is to hate themselves or their bodies. In the case of physical pain they see their bodies as enemies and want to disassociate themselves from them. Overcoming this natural human inclination challenges us to see life from a much broader and matter-of-fact point of view. Reynolds Price discovered this actuality when he became a paraplegic and found out he had to be as realistic in his perception of life as a "sawed off shotgun." In these circumstances we have to transform our ideas of who we are and how life should be in order to face the future with promise.

In a few short sentences Laura brought to light that she was disconnected from many of her feelings and they had flowed into the reservoir of her depression. Eventually this container became so heavy that it exhausted her to carry it. At the same time not experiencing her feelings left her cut off from life. When she decided she wanted her life back we saw how the act of writing a dialog began to transform her. And the more she dialogues the more she will benefit as her insights accumulate.

Dialoguing Suggestions

Whether your dialogs take the form of handwritten journal entries or are fed into your computer, the process of writing them is important. Occasionally people will ask if this work can be done mentally, by carrying on an imaginary conversation in one's head, or done orally, speaking perhaps into a tape recorder while they're driving to work. My answer to such questions is always a solid no. Like journaling, the process must be respected. It's an indication that you're becoming assertive enough to value your inner life and to seek the self-understanding that will begin to free you from the pressures of the social character. The form you give to your inner work is a measurement of your reverence for yourself; like the meals you take, you can choose between drive-through or fine dining. Your approach itself begins the healing and initiates a sense of harmony and inner rightness that will be validated by your feelings of increased energy and vitality. To try and force your inner work into a model of living that reflects the causes of your distress, such as being overwhelmed, overhurried, pressured, or overidentified with societal values, simply puts you in a deeper conflict with yourself.

Of course any time we try to make a rule in psychology we immediately discover an exception to it. I work with a physician who has developed an effective series of dialogs that he writes during his coffee breaks at the hospital. He sits at a table writing and people leave him alone because they think he's writing reports. We have to be open to discovering what works best for us.

While the process of dialoguing may quickly come to feel natural, initially it may make us feel silly or self-conscious, or even foolish at first to think of ourselves talking to an abstraction or "talking to ourselves." We've been taught to think so rationally and concretely that we may also doubt the validity of the responses we get. It may take us several dialogs to get over our apprehensions.

Our dialogs are meant to enhance our awareness, to help us get to know and give voice to parts of ourselves we've tried to banish and have feared might make us feel foolish or humiliated. They're not meant to be shared; they're not intended to be oracles or "channels" and are never intended to tell us how to behave. Even if they give strong directions, it's our job to evaluate them and make our own choices.

Jung reported in his autobiography that at one point in his dialogs a feminine figure he was talking to told him he should leave his practice, move to Paris, and become an artist. Reflecting on this he realized this was connected somehow to the satisfaction he was experiencing with some paintings he was doing as part of his efforts to express himself creatively. But he also knew this figure was asking him to do something that would violate his basic commitments to his family and work and that he needed to confront this inner figure with his certainty that becoming an artist wasn't supposed to become his profession.

Sometimes people ask me, "How do I know I'm not making this up?" and "How do I know I'm not controlling the responses?" If you feel similarly, don't become discouraged. Even the most contrived fantasy is still coming out of you and will relate to your inner life. It's like feeling you are singing flat or off-key, when in fact as you learn to relax and become familiar with the process, you'll find your pitch, your rhythm. The purpose of these imaginative dialogs is to help you learn about your unconscious aspects. If something comes into your awareness this way then it must have been living somewhere within you. I've often found that when people feel like they're making their dialogs up what they're really doing is trying to rush the process along in order to make things happen. You need to be patient and to allow your inner relationships time to develop. This is particularly true if you try to get started and nothing seems to come. The imagination, like nature, abhors a vacuum and will respond if you wait patiently, ready to record things when they happen. Your imagination will give you images, people, ideas, and answers to your inquiries. If, however, your imagination seems to fail you for a while, think of it as if your batteries are low and need some time to recharge.

Even so, the important question we must face isn't the authenticity of the dialogs, but what we're *doing* in them and what we'll do *with* them. The secret is to realize that we're dialoguing with real parts of ourselves that have their own autonomy, existence, and power within our personalities. We have to relate to them as if they were people in outer reality, but in greater depth and with complete honesty. Inner work isn't a time for polite equivocation. It requires that we commit ourselves wholeheartedly and with integrity. When we do we will find we naturally get to know ourselves better; our conscious and unconscious minds aren't enemies and aren't in conflict. Our unconscious will usually turn the same face toward us as we turn toward it. The next examples will illustrate how four people approached problem parts of themselves that are common to many of us and carry hidden potentials for living more fully.

Getting to Know Anger

Anger, as I mentioned earlier, is a voice we should listen to, a call to action and a notification we've been intruded upon. As Julia Cameron stated, "Sloth, apathy, and despair are the enemy. Anger is not. Anger is our friend. Not a nice friend. Not a gentle friend, but a loyal friend." And that anger will tell us when we've been betrayed, when we're betraying ourselves, and when we need to act in our own best interests.

But, anger is one of those emotions with which most of us have trouble learning to deal. The values we're taught growing up don't teach us the role of anger in protecting ourselves emotionally or in standing for and achieving worthwhile goals. Or how it helps us develop personalities substantial enough to face its power and energy and use it constructively in our lives. Books tell us all about how to defuse, cope with, and control our anger, but we're still afraid of it. We're taught that it isn't nice, and we learn to repress or overcontrol it until it is in danger of exploding in rage and violence or it turns against us in a destructive form such as illness.

In my practice I've often found that anger is the sign of a person's engagement in life. Many people I've worked with who were angry were touched deeply by the events they were living through and felt strongly about them. Nevertheless when anger serves feelings of extreme frustration, inferiority, neediness, or alienation it can be destructive, violent, and dangerous. Like all powerful human emotions anger can be very beneficial or it can turn demonic—self-awareness is the only factor that determines whether our anger will be beneficial or malevolent. To find the healthy aspects of our anger requires self-knowledge and to use it effectively demands that we thoroughly know and understand what we're doing.

Several years ago I met Jim, a tall, slender man then in his early fifties. Jim had a good job as a government scientist. He came to see me because he was separated from his wife but still loved her and wanted to repair their marriage. While he felt successful and self-confident professionally, he knew there were things that were wrong in his emotional life that he couldn't quite articulate. As Jim's story unfolded I learned he'd been the youngest of three children of educated parents who had remained narrow in their religious viewpoint. They were very sensitive to their family's appearances in the church and community. Following a pattern he'd developed in adolescence, Jim was a perfectionist on the job and in the ways he organized his life, paid his bills, and was always on time in a manner that also belied his rebellious tendencies—smoking and drinking and a certain careless hard living that didn't respect his health. Yet knowing this and aware how much his habits upset his wife, Jim was unable to change.

One day when he was telling me about his journaling and how he was trying to keep track of his anger, he confided that in his exasperation he found himself saying, "Damn it, anger, why are you always following me?" Since he was journaling he automatically

DIALOGUING AS INTERRELATING

wrote down his statement and to his surprise his "anger" answered, "Because I'm sick and tired of you stuffing your feelings and whimping through life trying to please everybody you stumble into."

Jim was curious about this response and I was excited by it. I urged him to build on this reply and to pursue developing this potential relationship with his anger to help him mobilize its energy and plow its meaning back into his life. I suggested to Jim he continue his dialog with his anger and see what else it could tell him. His next dialog went like this:

JIM: *Hello, anger. I'd like to talk some more. I've never really recognized you for what you are. Since I was a kid I've had these bad feelings. Uncomfortable feelings. Like being anxious and stressed and feeling guilty and resentful and full of contempt. I always feel like I'm being dishonest, not really being myself. But I don't know if I even have it in me to be honest about my feelings. Somehow, I think you may be the most honest emotion of all. But I don't seem to ever allow myself to be angry. Did I see too much of you as a child? The anger was never really out in the open. Occasionally there were raised voices which scared me. But I went out and played in the woods after those times and stayed away until the anger went away, or at least until things got back to normal.*

Nobody was ever happy in our house when I was growing up. We were under so much pressure to be proper, with my father being a minister and my mother being a southern housewife. But there was always an undercurrent of unhappiness. I wanted things to be happy like when I went fishing with my dad or when I went off and played with my friends. But you were always there threatening to throw everything upside down. So I learned how to ignore you. Stuff you deep down inside of me like I saw my mother and father do. But I don't like myself when I do this. I'm always in a "bad mood." Sometimes this moodiness seems to take over and I get really confused. I've always felt like

I'm a bad person. And I'm afraid everybody else will see me as a bad person, too, if I let you be around. I don't think I even know how to be angry at this point. All I know how to be is distant and curt and judgmental with my family. I can live with my resentment, anxiety and contempt, even though they never bring me closer to people or make my life more fulfilling. But I don't really see them as the enemy.

ANGER: *I'm amused. You've claimed in the past that you've recognized my presence, but you really have no idea who I am in your life. I've been running the whole show, Jim. I've been in charge of all those feelings you don't like. I'm the captain of a whole ship of emotions and even when you think you run away from me I'm always there. My position is just as secure as it's ever been. You deal me a blow every now and again like when you realize you're angry and you confront me, but most of the time you do nothing to make me feel in danger. To be honest I don't take you very seriously. Face it, I'm running your life. All I have to do is appear and you automatically start beating yourself up. You feel bad, dishonest, moody, unhappy. You even hate yourself. I have more power now than I've ever had.*

JIM: *This is all so confusing. I don't know which emotions are legitimate and which ones aren't. But what I do know is that I want to quit hating myself for not being able to be honest about my emotions and about my life. I'm wondering if there's some way we could work together on this.*

ANGER: *Believe it or not I wish things could be different, too. I would much rather you be spontaneous in expressing your emotions. Wouldn't you like being spontaneous for a change, too? I know you think I'm the enemy but really I could be more of a friend. Don't you think I'd like the opportunity to be directly expressed and recognized and even valued?*

DIALOGUING AS INTERRELATING

JIM: *Well, maybe we're on the same team, then, because I want to learn how to feel good about myself and be free and spontaneous in the way I live. If being able to express you spontaneously and appropriately is the way to live an honest life then I think we should talk again.*

After listening carefully to Jim relate his experience of this dialog, I remarked on how important it seemed that "anger" was willing to have a discussion with him. Drawing on a metaphor I used earlier, this indicated to me that a door was opening to a "room" of his personality. Exploring this room of his anger brought Jim into a new awareness of his emotions and his capacity for enjoying life and having more satisfying relationships. As he continued his dialogs, Jim discovered that "anger" could be both a friend and a teacher that led him into living with more enthusiasm and honesty.

Listening to Our Weight

Being overweight is another one of those thorny situations that reflect a cultural problem that we have to deal with on an individual basis. As a society we judge our health and appearance by strict standards of being thin. Meanwhile we are a food-driven society. We make eating fast, easy, and tempting; we use it as a reward, a pleasure, and as a means of indulging as well as nourishing ourselves. Physicians and psychologists have been trying to help us find a healthy balance in our eating habits for the last fifty years. And for perhaps just as long, our magazine and book racks have been filled with diets of every stripe. Still, our weight problems have persisted in spite of our efforts to control them.

Through years of experience I have learned that when our best efforts fail we need to stop and listen to what life is trying to tell us. I cannot think of a more powerful way to connect with another person, to connect with life or to ourselves than just by listening. Listening requires attention and in the long run how much attention we give to other people usually expresses how much we care for them. Likewise, caring about ourselves must come before we can understand ourselves. It's that simple. But most of us fail to value ourselves or our love enough to know this. I met Richard recently and he turned out to be one of these people.

A hugely talented man, Richard had been an outstandingly successful architect whose residential commissions and commercial projects had taken him all over the world. By the time he was in his fifties he was financially secure, preparing to retire and fulfill his dream of becoming an artist. It was just a few years later when I met him. Richard shared with me that as soon as he started planning his retirement, his health declined. He had already undergone bypass surgery and in spite of trying several diet programs he continued to be forty pounds overweight. Richard was afraid there would be more heart trouble to come and felt paralyzed in his discouragement over this constantly losing battle. His preoccupation with it was taking so much of his energy that he was unable to draw or paint. Understanding his frustration I suggested that he get to know his weight on a personal basis. He started out with the following dialog:

RICHARD: *Hello, weight. I've been thinking about you and wondering if we could talk. We've been together a long time and I would like to know what purpose you really serve in my life.*

WEIGHT: *To be direct, I help you hide, and isolate yourself from the rest of the world. Because of me you get to escape your life. And as long as I'm around you feel like a failure and a slob.*

RICHARD: *That was direct. You must have been wanting to say that for a long time. But why would I want to feel like a failure and a slob all the time? It makes no sense.*

WEIGHT: *You're right, there's no sense in what you do. It's all conflict, a battle. You try not to overeat and overindulge, but you do it anyway. You have no willpower, no will to take control*

DIALOGUING AS INTERRELATING

of your own life because you're so exhausted from the battle. You're forty pounds overweight. You have heart trouble and diabetes. You're depressed and immobilized most of the time. You're always so confused because this conflict batters you around like a ping-pong ball. One minute you want to hide and escape life, the next minute you want to live a full and enriching life without all the excess weight.

RICHARD: *But I'm tired of being this way. What do you suggest? How can we work together?*

WEIGHT: *We can't. You're too invested in all the mental games. You're always labeling yourself and other people without ever seeing the truth. You don't want to know yourself. You don't want a healthy relationship with me. Until you do I don't see what we have to talk about.*

RICHARD: *I think you're wrong. Yes, I know I like to play intellectual games, always trying to figure out what's wrong with everybody else so I won't have to face what's wrong with me. But I really do want to get to know myself. I've even been realizing lately that there's a part of me that likes to play life-and-death games. I think there may even be a part of me that has a death wish and thinks dying would be exciting and a way to get a lot of attention. But I don't think this is a healthy part of me so I want to get this under control. I need your help. Do you think we could work together at this?*

WEIGHT: *Yes, if you'll listen and take action on what you're discovering about yourself. I have very little respect for you when you're playing these mind games, like telling yourself that there's not really a problem. This attitude limits you in everything you do. And the irony is you do have a death wish, but you're not dying. All you're doing is staying sick and suffering. This is a total waste of energy. You need to listen to me and get into real life.*

> RICHARD: *You're right, I think I do need your help. I'm afraid of life and I'm caught in this cycle of trying to escape into food and into the depression. The truth is I don't want to face my own life. As long as I feel like a failure and a slob I don't have to confront and take action on my own potentials. I'm afraid if I do take charge of my life it will change so much I won't even recognize it anymore. I don't like change. But I'm ready to get out of this trap and I would appreciate your help in doing this. I'll be in touch soon.*

Richard's "weight" was very revealing and direct in its response. It disclosed the complexity of Richard's psychology, his previous unconscious flirtation with danger, how much he lives in his head, and his fear of facing his dream—the opportunity to become an artist. The dialog also shows that like the Grail knight, Parsifal, when Richard began to ask the right questions he found help. With this inner help we were quickly able to go deeply into his analytic work. But the main source of help, insight, and support continued to come through his dialogs.

Challenging the Inner Critic

In her inspiring and insightful book on writing, *Bird by Bird,* Anne Lamott says, "Perfectionism is the voice of the oppressor." The pressure of modern life that emphasizes efficiency has taught us since we were little to measure ourselves against other people and strive to improve ourselves. Most of us are very familiar with this oppressor. It's a voice we've internalized, and in psychology we often refer to it as our "inner critic."

Our inner critic didn't just develop when we were young and in school or because our parents were critical. Although our parents often prepare the ground and nourish the growth of our inner critic, our culture supports its growth every day. Our communications industry bathes us in a ceaseless wave of ways we can improve ourselves. The tide of advice on how to look better, feel better, be healthier, parent better, be better lovers, be more effective workers, be more spiritually alive, and so on may often contain helpful information but it is so intense and unrelenting that it begins to make us feel increasingly inadequate. No matter how effective we are at most of what we do, we are continually faced with things we aren't doing and perhaps should be doing.

Suppose I woke up this morning feeling a little blue. While I'm on the treadmill watching the "Today Show" at my fitness center I see an ad for a popular drug that will elevate my mood. Then I wonder if something is really wrong with me. Why am I feeling blue when everyone else around me seems so full of life? The voice of my inner critic is warming up and will soon be in full operation, telling me how unable I am to handle life, until I begin to doubt myself. And self-doubt can start a whole new cycle of self-criticism.

The voice of the inner critic is relentless and shaming. It nitpicks. It causes us to fear mistakes, to be ashamed of them, of ourselves. No matter how successful we become, our inner critic will continue to grade us, to compare us to people more successful than we are. It is the job of the inner critic to find our faults, to find us lacking. It robs us of the enjoyment we've earned and leaves us feeling like impostors when other people praise us. To the inner critic there's always room for improvement. Enough is never enough. Ceaseless, restless, inexorable, it is this inner voice that drives our perfectionism.

Not too long ago I had a good friend, a brilliant teacher who unfortunately and very sadly died suddenly without finishing the book he'd been working on for almost twenty years. He'd become caught in the debilitating loop of perfectionism that keeps us from moving ahead, that keeps us floundering in the details of what we're doing because that voice keeps telling us it isn't good enough—and neither are we. The inner critic disparages, diminishes, ridicules, and condemns our efforts and tries to shame or stifle us. And it always wins.

But, life always surprises us. If we begin to struggle with our inner critic with the same tenacity as Jacob had when he struggled for his life against the dark angel during the night, a new awareness of ourselves and a new personal standpoint can be reached. And a new unity with this most unpleasant part of ourselves can emerge. Constructive criticism can be tough to hear, but it also teaches us, points out new ways to do things, and may even be inspiring. But until we transform our inner critic out of its negative role, we will hear all criticism as threatening.

Dialoguing can help us come to know our inner critic and understand our relationship to it. Once we do, when we can expand our self-knowledge, we can begin to transform ourselves. We may think of the inner critic as the "enemy" but I've been impressed with how often it's willing to be transformed into an *inner companion* that wants to guide and help us when we give it sufficient attention.

Nikki was a puzzle. With her dark good looks, quick mind, and wicked sense of humor I liked her immediately. But as I got to know her better she reminded me of one of those people whose homes are so spotless and "finished" that when you see it, you think your own would never measure up. Then you begin to realize that there are tensions beneath these polished surfaces, and that for all the cordiality and immaculate appearances, your host is perfectionistic and judgmental, and not terribly happy.

Nikki had realized that she was self-critical to the point of being compulsive in the things she did. She felt that she was so hard on herself that she never left room for fun, and she was afraid she was teaching her children to be anxious and unsure of themselves. She worried that in the course of trying to micromanage the details of her life, she'd become very much like her father, judging and criticizing people in ways she'd despised when she was younger. She agreed to try and dialogue with her inner critic.

> NIKKI: *I guess the time has come for me to confront you. I think I've lived with you my whole life, either through my father or myself, and just recently I've decided to give you a name. I'll call you my inner critic. Maybe this is the beginning of the end for you. I sure hope so. I don't like you very much. In fact, I*

hate you and how you make me feel and what you have me do to others. People tell me I can be very sarcastic. They're right. I've learned to judge myself and others very harshly. I cut people to pieces using funny comments. My father wasn't that funny when he did it. But at least I'm funny.

INNER CRITIC: *I can't believe it's taken you so many years to acknowledge my presence. Talk about dense. You've seen me for decades now—in your father, yourself, your sisters and brothers, and you say you despise me but I don't see you doing anything to get me out of here. If I'm so awful why do you still keep me around? Looks like you would have gotten rid of me long ago.*

NIKKI: *I know you've been my enemy, but in a way I think you've also been my ally. That's been a confusing part. I could never measure up to my father or to myself so I used my feelings of inferiority to drive me forward. I kept trying to prove something. My father used to tell me I was stupid so I got a master's degree. He told me I'd never amount to anything so I've made a lot of money just to prove him wrong. In a strange way I owe a lot of my success to you. So you have served a purpose in my life. But you've outlived your usefulness and now you only make me feel hurt. There's no reason for me to keep you around anymore. I'm tired of trying to prove myself to a part of me that will never approve. For years I saw you in my father. It's hard to believe how much he hated me. How could one of the people who's supposed to love me the most hate me and hurt me so much? After living with him I found it hard to believe that anybody could ever love me. Any man who fell in love with me had to be incredibly stupid. I always think men in general are incompetent. I hate them because my father hated me. But I don't like always feeling hurt and critical. Something has to change.*

INNER CRITIC: *Well, I'm glad you noticed what a friend I've been to you, and let me tell you I don't like being shown the* door. *I've asked nothing of you, and this is how you treat me? Haven't I always allowed you to be the same? I let you stay comfortable in your old way of thinking. You know exactly what to expect, there aren't any surprises. I keep you safe. I've kept the fact that your father hated you hidden all these years. Isn't that what a good friend would do?*

NIKKI: *I'm not sure. Maybe I learned you from my father. The part of you that was in him is now in me. Or maybe I used you to protect me from getting hurt. At one time the truth would have been too painful to face, but I think I can face it now. My father hated me, but he hated everybody, because he hated himself. You were a way of life for him. I watched my father criticize employees, my mother, my brothers and sisters, and as a child I thought that was the only way people interacted with others. I didn't know any other way to be. You became a way of life for me, too. And even now that I'm smarter about these things I still find you rearing your ugly head. I'm tired of it.*

INNER CRITIC: *So now I'm ugly? You didn't used to think that. For a long time you didn't even recognize me. You thought you were the mean and ugly one, not me.*

NIKKI: *I think I'm finally beginning to separate myself from you. You are not me, you're just a part of me. A part I don't like very much. And when you're around I can be mean and ugly like when I'm self-critical or critical of someone close to me. Especially when I'm under a lot of stress at work or when I don't think I'm measuring up in some way you're right there in my face. Telling me I'm stupid. That I'll never amount to anything. But I've started to realize that once I'm aware of you then I have a choice. I can stop and think about things, try to decide how I really feel about something instead of just automatically letting you decide how things are. I don't have to let you run my reactions to things. In the past it seemed like you ambushed me. Before I knew it you were there and I had no control over you. I could beat up on myself unmercifully whenever I thought I'd made a mistake. But now I know that whenever I become self-critical, you're present. And maybe I won't be able to stop that mean and ugly part right away from hurting myself or somebody else, but I'm warning you, I've got your number. I'm on to you, and the way you've been running my life isn't OK anymore. Things are going to change.*

Once again you can see how quickly this dialog began revealing some important information that was very helpful to Nikki. And by the end of the exercise she was already feeling some independence and strength in her situation. Nikki realized that her inner critic had also driven her to success. She continued to dialogue with her inner critic for over a year until she felt secure she could count on its support in helping her learn from her mistakes and to be objective and helpful with its criticism.

Talking with an Inner Artist

The American Dream that I like the best is the one that supports the idea that we can continually become more than who we are today. That life is a process of becoming and fulfilling the potentials within us. It took me a long time to realize this process of growth is one of endings and beginnings. No new stage begins without an old one ending. And endings in our personal lives can be difficult. We're often afraid to grow because we aren't sure what may end when we do. What if we outgrow our families, our parents, our partners, our friends, our jobs, or our communities? These are difficult questions to face because true growth means leaving the security of a known way of life. If people love us and are growing themselves, they'll applaud our becoming. It isn't easy to know in advance if that's what they'll do, of course. People who are able to love us that maturely are rare.

Thinking about endings and beginnings, growing and fear reminds me of Lily, a sensitive, intelligent, shy, and intensely creative woman who a few years ago began to wake up to a strong desire to write. Her dreams consistently showed her potentials, an inner artist filling galleries full of paintings and writing dozens of books that were successfully published. In a way this potential overwhelmed her and she often felt blocked when it came to letting the artist part of her life out into the open.

Born into an Irish-American family that had spent generations as working-class people, there was no one in her family who could even begin to understand or support her hunger to express herself. She had already given up a traditional job for two flexible part-time jobs in order to make time for her creative life. But the guilt of being so much more ambitious than her family and her shaky confidence over whether she was doing the "right" thing continued to block her desire to let her creativity be at the heart of her life.

Lily decided to dialogue with her inner artist to see if it had any insights into how she could create a new vision for herself. The following conversation developed out of her journaling:

LILY: *I'd like to speak to the inner artist part of me. I need help in letting you live out into the open.*

INNER ARTIST: *Oh, that would be a great relief to me. I'd be happy to help.*

LILY: *So you're aware that you're blocked?*

INNER ARTIST: *Why yes, of course.*

LILY: *What can I do to get you free?*

INNER ARTIST: *You're doing it.*

LILY: *You mean by talking to you?*

DIALOGUING AS INTERRELATING

INNER ARTIST: *Yes, and by being willing to see what's standing in the way.*

LILY: *What is in the way?*

INNER ARTIST: *Are you sure you want to know?*

LILY: *I'm ready to know. I feel like I'm stuck between the old and the new way of life. I need a fresh way of seeing things. Please speak freely.*

INNER ARTIST: *I think I do represent a whole new life for you, and you're afraid of the new. Writing down your words and being published will set you on fire. You'll have to step out of the comfortable place of the way things have always been and you'll be making a striking statement about who you are—an artist who has a clear knowledge of what she wants to do.*

LILY: *I think you're exactly right. But in a way it makes no sense. Why would I be afraid of something so wonderful?*

INNER ARTIST: *A good writer works in a white heat, crafts their work with unrelenting tenacity and drives through their shyness to read their work in public, do book signings and whatever else is necessary to be heard. Being in touch with me is risky because I am ambitious. Your family is happy with bread and butter and I want champagne and caviar!*

LILY: *Damn! Thanks! I want to ask you something else.*

INNER ARTIST: *Certainly.*

LILY: *Now that I'm very close to getting my first book published—a couple of editors have shown interest—I feel paralyzed. What's that about?*

INNER ARTIST: *Same song, second verse. Fear. You're afraid to admit you have your own voice and want it heard. What if it isn't liked or gets criticized? It seems risky, but what's really risky is* not *doing it. Then your hunger will devour you. Being in touch with me will change everything, Lily, but ah, what a glorious change. You may even have to look into your secret desire to move to Florence.*

LILY: *So fear is what's blocking me? Yes, I can see that now. Fear of the new, of things changing. But despite the fear I know that you need to play a central role in my life. Whenever you're around I feel hopeful and alive. A vitality sweeps through me that makes the fear go away. Like I'm the closest I've ever been to the* real *me. And yes I'm scared, I'm even terrified, because I don't know how to do this. But I want to live my life in a way that makes me feel the passion and aliveness you have to offer me. Thank you for talking to me. Can we talk again?*

INNER ARTIST: *You can count on it.*

After several more dialogs with her inner artist, Lily was able to create a new vision for herself. Her first book was published and was well reviewed. She has quickly finished another. While she still feels blocked in her writing from time to time she's able to quickly return to her inner artist for help. And, she continues to use the encouragement of her inner artist to break through the resistance into her new way of life.

Human growth rests on increasing self-knowledge, and increasing our self-knowledge often seems like making repeated forays into an unknown country. Clarity about our lives comes gradually as the result of enduring turmoil. To have an individual life requires that

DIALOGUING AS INTERRELATING

we deal with the tensions, ambiguities, and tragic dilemmas we face as human beings.

In this quest our unconscious can be a friend if we have the courage to open ourselves to it. We can take the power away from what have previously been the negative forces within us that we didn't know about. By bringing into the light what has been unconscious, unknown, or unchallenged, we begin to understand why it has been so powerful—and by doing so, the power of the negative is neutralized or transformed into new vitality. The purpose of dialoguing is to make the unconscious better known to us, to come to new identity with it, and to bring new awareness into our lives.

CHAPTER 7
Beginning the Search for Personal Substance

We do not grow absolutely, chronologically. We grow sometimes in one dimension, and not in another, unevenly. We grow partially. We are relative. We are mature in one realm, childish in another. The past, present, and future mingle and pull us backward, forward, or fix us in the present. We are made up of layers, cells, constellations.

—Anaïs Nin

"I awakened in fear," Rob said, "shaken to my core. I had dreamed I was in my childhood home, a stone house in the mountains near a lake, surrounded by forest. This house has always been a place of solace in my fantasies, a refuge. During the dream, night was falling and I was in the house with other people. Suddenly I heard loud noises. I ran to the back door and looked out. Men with huge machines and earthmovers were quickly taking down the trees, and bulldozers were clearing the ground as if for new construction. Everything green was disappearing and I was in a panic. I tried to call the police but couldn't get through. I knew the trees would be gone before I could get help and didn't understand how this could be happening."

Dreams are often puzzling. Sometimes they arouse our fear, sometimes our curiosity. Sometimes they are so pleasant we wish we could hit the replay button of our unconscious imagination. But as we rush headlong through our days seeking to maintain a positive attitude, we generally drop them into the trash can of neglect. Something deep within us fears admitting dreams to daylight inspection because their presence reminds us that life isn't exactly what we think it is, that something is going on within us daily that we can't control and have difficulty understanding.

We are more comfortable with the familiar language of our everyday reality, a language that has often reduced proper names to initials or whose meaning is summarized in slang words or slogans. It pictures a concrete rational view of reality that allows us to measure, explain, and maneuver things as much as we like. But it doesn't comprehend the whole spectrum of our potentials just as the sun doesn't embrace the whole span of a day. For a day to be complete, the moon must also have its time just as within ourselves, the poetic and the symbolic must be recognized as part of our wholeness.

Dreams come in the dark when our perception of everyday reality is at rest, in order to add their perspective and make our lives more complete. They may show us, for example, that vitality and comfort are in great jeopardy in our lives, as in Rob's dream, where this message was delivered with alarming urgency.

Or our dreams may encourage us to face a future event, perhaps surgery, a life change, or some other immediate experience, with confidence. Surprisingly, they say all of these things by using a fantastic language, full of extraordinary images and a similar vocabulary. We may find ourselves in a country we've never visited or may meet with someone who is "a friend" we've never actually known. Or we may find ourselves holding an infant that can speak like an adult. We may be held captive by evil people, or we may be able to fly or swim beneath the sea without needing to breathe. Poisonous snakes, huge mountains, monsters, princesses and dragons, wars and floods, lost lovers and forgotten treasures all may turn up in our dream stories.

The symbolic language of dreams comes very close to the language of poetry. There's a poem by Nobel laureate Octavio Paz that captures beautifully the symbolic imagery dreams evoke:

The final shadow may close my eyes,
carry me off from white of day,
unchaining my soul at the hour
of its anxious obsequious desire:

*but it will not leave the memory
of that other shore where once it burned,
for my fire can swim me through the frigid water,
regardless of the strictures of law.*

*A soul which once imprisoned an entire God,
veins that brought fuel to such flames,
marrow that so gloriously burned:*

*they'll leave this body, but not its cares;
ash they'll be, yet still aware;
they will be dust, but dust in love.*

Most of us have become so unaccustomed to poetic language that we may have to read this poem several times, slowly, perhaps even out loud, so we can hear it, see it, and feel it, letting it simmer in our minds, and finally perhaps marvel at it. In his collection of essays on poetry, society, and the revolutionary spirit, *The Other Voice*, Paz observes that modern life has become so pressured and literal that only the voice of poetry can restore balance to our lives and refresh our souls. Similarly, we can think of dreams as giving us rest from life's daily pressures and helping to restore a feeling of healthy equilibrium within ourselves.

I'll never forget the first person I heard say something serious about dreams. She was an old country woman, and when I was a boy I enjoyed sitting on the front porch with her and chatting. When I was in my early teens and trying to face the troubling times after my mother died, it was very comforting to sit and talk with her. She was almost blind and could only see dim forms even in bright light. But she seemed full of the earthy wisdom and an empathy I badly needed. We were talking one Sunday afternoon when I was feeling sad and alone after having another dream about my mother. As this woman stroked my hand she looked at me—but really it seemed she was looking through me or beyond me—and said, "Your dreams will help you, chew on them, then you can become like that tree," and she pointed to a large oak tree with her finger. After a few moments she continued, "It grows up and out for everyone to see, but what you don't see is how it's rooted in the earth. We must have strong roots within us and then we'll keep growing through the storms."

In ancient Greece when people had deep concerns and threatening illnesses they went to either the temple of Apollo or Aesculapius, the father of modern medicine, for healing. They participated in a ritual that included spending the night in the temple and waiting for a dream to outline the path of their healing. References to important dreams are found in Homer's *Odyssey* and Virgil's *Aeneid* and in the works of Plato, Socrates, Cicero, Lucretious, and many other great writers. Even in these early times, thinkers believed that dreams were important paths to knowledge and messages from the divine.

The Talmud tells us, "A dream that has not been interpreted is like a letter that has not been opened." Most of the major events in the Old Testament's famous stories, such as the one about Joseph and his many-colored coat, revolved around dreams. You may remember that Joseph's story began when he was a boy, the favored youngest son of a doting father. One day Joseph dreamed his brothers were bowing down to him. When Joseph told this dream to his family, his jealous brothers became so enraged they threw Joseph into a well and left him to die. Later he was rescued by members of a passing caravan and sold into slavery in Egypt. There he rose to great power by interpreting the pharaoh's dreams and saving Egypt from a famine. His brothers, seeking food during the time of the famine, ended up bowing down to Joseph and fulfilling his earlier dream.

In the Old Testament Book of Daniel, the Babylonian king Nebuchadnezzar had a dream he felt was important to his nation's well-being. But unfortunately he forgot the dream. The anxious king required the prophet Daniel to figure out what the dream had said

BEGINNING THE SEARCH

and then to interpret it. Daniel, with God's help, responded, "This mystery has been revealed to me . . . for this purpose; that the king should learn what it means and that you should understand your innermost thoughts." In another place in the Old Testament, the Book of Numbers, the voice of God emphasized the importance of dreams by saying, "Hear my words: If there is a prophet among you, I the Lord make myself known to him in a vision. I speak with him in a dream."

In the New Testament, the birth of Jesus was announced to Mary's cousin in a dream. The father of Jesus, Joseph, was informed of Jesus' divine origin in a dream, and told to flee to Egypt for safety and when to return through dreams. When Jesus was facing the judgment that led to his crucifixion, Roman governor Pontius Pilate washed his hands of the matter due to a troubling dream of his wife. Early Christian theologians such as Bishop Sybnesius and Tertullian thought dreams were important. The Buddhist and Islamic tradition likewise felt dreams contained enlightened information, instructions, and guidance that aren't available in our waking lives. Buddhist writings describe a number of Buddha's dreams that occurred as he was becoming enlightened. And it was through a dream that his mother, Maya, realized she was carrying a divine child. In a similar manner Mohammed was instructed of his sacred mission through a dream.

With such a history of value you may wonder why so many of us stopped listening to dreams. The rise of scientific thinking and rationalism in the modern world is certainly a contributing factor. Though perhaps the reason is more complex than that because we seem to be forgetting the knowledge and wisdom that humankind struggled to develop over the centuries. David Ehrenfield, a professor of biology at Rutgers University, has said that we're rushing so quickly into new technologies and the latest trends that the knowledge we gained in the past is sinking from our grasp like the legendary lost continent of Atlantis disappeared into the sea. Possibly we've charged so fast into the information age that we've lost touch not only with the wisdom of our heritage, but also with the important knowledge that Freud, Jung, and their followers painstakingly developed in the first half of the twentieth century. As British analyst Anthony Stevens has suggested, in this era we've reduced life to prose and no longer understand poetry.

It could also be that in this information age, unlike in previous premodern ages, we expect to exert more control over our lives. We can predict weather, combat illness, and "find" answers with the click of a mouse. But dreams represent an area of our lives we can control no better than our ancestors did. Our social character emphasizes our need to be able "to take control of our lives." Facing our inner lives may scare us, and our fear of acknowledging things about ourselves we can't control may discourage us from exploring the power and significance of our dreams.

However, the careful work of Jung and others has shown that dreams reflect a purposeful guidance taking place in the life of the dreamer. Our unconscious acts like a hidden teacher, furnishing us through our dreams a series of lessons that are trying to bring a new sense of balance and clarity into our lives. In the long run these lessons are guiding our development along a particular pattern that represents our growth toward wholeness and fulfillment.

Now let's see what Rob's inner teacher may have been trying to help him understand by sending him a dream that awakened him in fear.

Midlife as a New Beginning

A few years ago, Rob, who had the dream I mentioned earlier, came to me with an interesting situation. He was a big man with square shoulders who carried himself with the confidence of someone who'd built his own business. When he began explaining his situation he seemed energetic and interested in the situation he felt trapped in. "I'm scared. I feel vulnerable," he said. "A few weeks ago my best friend fell into a one-night stand with a woman who had been throwing herself at him. Then as soon as they had sex, she went home and described the whole event to her husband. Now he's threatened my friend. His wife and kids are devastated, and his life is wrecked. I'm not really unhappy," he continued, "but I feel like something is missing in my life. I could see myself making the same silly mistake my friend did. I don't dream and plan for the future anymore, I don't feel very much enthusiasm about anything, and now I'm afraid of what I might fall into to fill this void."

Years ago while Rob was starting his business with his wife, Tina, his life had been very exciting. They had lived cheaply, but it didn't matter because they were working and dreaming of their future together. As his business grew they had three children, a boy and two girls. After the children became school age, Tina began her own career as a freelance writer although she also still handled most of Rob's advertising copy.

Rob had decided early in his life that he wanted to be successful and he figured out how to play the game to get there. In fact, he mastered it. Initially he worked for a large company after college and quickly discovered he disliked working for someone else and being bound by the framework of a corporate structure. However, he stuck it out for several years in order to learn enough about the business to help him feel confident that he had the knowledge and connections to strike out on his own. By the time I met Rob, he'd done a fine job of developing what I've called secular substance, a place of esteem and value in society.

Like most of us, Rob had to focus intently on building his life in early adulthood in order to achieve his ambitions. In other words he had to narrow his awareness of what life is about, identify with collective values of success at work and at home, and become respected in his business and community from a conventional point of view.

What had caught Rob by surprise was the erroneous general belief that few major changes are expected of us once we reach adulthood. This notion promotes that we pilot our own planes into a social airspace, and once we reach cruising altitude, we switch our lives onto autopilot. Oh yes, Rob had heard of midlife crises but in his mind they were storms and turbulence that happened to other people. Rob, like so many of us cocooned in the safety of our secular substance, did not understand that life is an evolving process from beginning to end and that many of the changes we have to make in adulthood come just when we think we have life figured out. Rob was facing a midlife transition just as necessary for his growth as the struggle for identity likely was during his adolescence. In other words, we never stop growing.

Rob's dream signified the tumultuous inner landscape that he and most of us confront when it's time for us to let go of old identities, values, and views of success that have developed and served us since childhood. Letting go of them doesn't mean abandoning them, however. It means they have to leave the center stage and become part of a much larger personality that's being born.

In Rob's dreams the bulldozers that were clearing the woods away from him in his childhood home were preparing the ground for new construction. Perhaps losing the trees and the sanctity of a childhood home required that he paid a price in giving up some of his nostalgia for the old ways that comforted him, or it could have represented a kind of loss of innocence that meant his growth had to be intentional and he couldn't just rely on nature. However, Rob was upset in the dream because powerful forces were at work and he wasn't in control of them. And, he couldn't reach the police who might have been able to enforce the conventional social values on which he previously depended.

In order to make his midlife transition, Rob had to find the courage to face deeper needs and discover the answers to them within himself. He had to face the fragility of his self-esteem and how much of it depended on his being successful and earning recognition, and how he often used this recognition and the financial rewards that came with his position as substitutes for feeling loved. Of course, he had previously hidden these needs even from himself, but they had often fueled his potency and potential as a businessman, while keeping him emotionally childlike, in the incessant way he competed with friends, made demands of his children, and related to women, including Tina, by either idealizing or denigrating them.

If we have found ourselves in a similar situation in our own lives, this is the point where we discover there really is a hole in this game we've mastered—and if we learn something about the psychology of this transition then our discovery should become *freeing* rather than threatening. This is a good thing—and a good time in our lives. That's the joy of it. And, because we have the gift of living longer today, we have the ability to live lives not of regret, but lives that allow us to use this work and wisdom in the world of careers and relationships. Who am I really? is a question that can't only be answered, but maybe for the first time in history for large numbers of people actually *lived*.

Yet, we all know transformation and a renewed future don't come without a price, without work and commitment. Rob wasn't afraid of working, however, because he'd learned from building his business that while such a process can be scary and difficult at times, it can also be exciting and rewarding. As Rob and I continued talking and the surface issues were replaced by the more substantive thoughts and feelings he had been avoiding, his mood darkened. He sat back in his chair and quietly told me how difficult his success had been at times, how it had forced him to do some things he wasn't proud of or to rationalize doing things he wouldn't have normally done—how he had lost much of his lightness.

I knew I had to look for a way to hear and understand Rob's darker actions without judging him. I listened carefully to his experiences as he told me how at one time when his business was in financial trouble he'd overbilled several large companies and how he'd gone for months not paying invoices, claiming they were lost, asking for proof of delivery of the merchandise on the invoices, anything to drag out the time before paying them. He also felt he'd been cold and had rationalized decisions he knew had hurt people as he tried to move ahead. In the large firm he worked for after college, his boss had mentored him generously and invested a lot in Rob's training and felt betrayed when Rob left and went out on his own. He'd disciplined employees at times, cut their pay when business was difficult, and been slow to give raises on occasion without considering the personal circumstances in their lives. In addition, he believed some of his loyal employees had felt hurt during the early years of his business because he'd demanded a great deal from them without giving them much recognition for how valuable they were.

More than that, he was aware of the pained look in his children's eyes when he had missed some of their important moments in sports and school. "Hypocritically," he said, "I rationalized that I was doing all of this work for them, for their college and the family's future. The truth is I was doing most of it for me. I need to be successful and I love it."

Rob reacted first to these honest revelations by feeling pain and guilt—pain that beneath the surface, he was greedy and self-centered, a bad person. Whenever we confront the hard truths about ourselves we normally prefer to deny, we naturally take it on ourselves. We feel low, unworthy, horrible, but in fact none of these realities mean that we are bad people. Rather we are good people encountering our own realities, our shadows—in Rob's case, the negative aspects of himself that he hid beneath his good social face and didn't allow into the way he saw himself.

It is crucial to accept our encounters with our shadows because doing so educates us about ourselves. For example, Rob realized his darker characteristics. He also saw how determined he'd been to be successful and that a force was driving him that was stronger than he'd recognized. New insights like Rob's are important for all of us because they ground the way we see ourselves and engender a true sense of humility. If Rob accepts the existence of the aspects of himself he doesn't like, that there is a part of him that can be desperate, cold, power oriented, and deceitful, this awareness will balance and strengthen his personality. Then Rob's actions and productivity will take on a different character. A good person who understands the power of his (or her) dark side is more human, more secure in his person, and paradoxically therefore more open to compassion, joy, and love. Facing the negative parts of ourselves is the first step on the path to developing the sacred substance that comes from knowing ourselves. And only then can we truly understand the value of sacred versus sickly selfishness.

There was still a deep level of the shadow Rob needed to explore. As a child he had felt loved by his parents but never safe and emotionally secure. They had taught him the "reality" of this world as they saw it, which they perceived as a vicious place. In order to prepare Rob for it, they were demanding and critical. Rob's father, a middle-level federal employee who made a bureaucrat's living, complained for years about how unrecognized he was, how stupid his bosses were, and how prejudiced they were against him for his ability to "see through them." As a result of this indoctrination, Rob closed off parts of himself early in his childhood. One of these areas was his need to feel loved, understood, and appreciated for who he was. This closure hampered his ability to be open to intimacy later in his life, to let himself be fully known by the people important to him. Deep within himself, beneath the confidence he'd earned by becoming successful, he still had trouble trusting life and other people—he had a lurking suspicion that something bad might happen or that the people he trusted and loved would ultimately let him down or betray him.

Revisiting the Past

The poet Rilke, with his classic insight into the nature of life, notes that we all go into adulthood unprepared. The deepest part of Rob's work to understand his shadow carried him far back into the origins of his personal history. The journey back into the past seems like a detour to many of us. Frequently people get impatient with reexamining their childhoods—with reopening old sores and wounds—and want to get on with solving their problems. Nevertheless looking back is essential for any change or growth in consciousness to be lasting. Every time we look back into our histories with new awareness, the better able we are to understand how the old hurts, angers, successes, failures, ideals, and ideas of appropriate behaviors and feelings continue to pattern our lives. The better we understand our pasts, the more freedom we have for making choices for the future.

Rob had to reexamine his childhood and his parents' attitudes to learn that deep inside of himself, he saw the world as a hostile place. He was surprised to discover how much this perspective permeated his life, how he guarded himself even with his friends and wife, rarely letting them see the feelings that showed his vulnerability. Worse, he saw that he was passing this fear onto his children. By closing himself off in this way, he was losing many of the comforts and pleasures of family, friendship, and intimacy.

The transformation of Rob brings to mind a similar situation I had when I began working with Mary Ann. A middle-aged woman, she gave an impression of being so "nice" that I felt somewhat disheveled in her presence. If I had been sixteen I would have felt tongue-tied and dirty, like Huckleberry Finn in the parlor of Tom Sawyer's Aunt Polly. I soon realized that being "nice" was the script Mary Ann lived by no matter what happened. Her commitment to being nice was as strong as steel. She came to see me at the suggestion of a friend after having had a cancer scare.

When I asked Mary Ann to tell me a bit about the story of her life, she replied, "Oh, I had a decent childhood. We don't need to go back to that. My parents did the best they could and I don't see any point in getting mad at them." Of course I hadn't said anything about getting mad at her parents. I'd simply asked to hear part of her story. Clearly Mary Ann learned the script (always be "nice") as she grew up, which she still rigidly lived by even though her parents were both dead. Reexamining our relationships with our parents is intended to help us become aware of, understand, and change old patterns of living. That is to say that growing up, we may have adopted patterns of behavior that are harmful, unhealthy, or don't reflect who we are. And therefore part of our task at midlife is to become aware of these patterns so we can change them. It's easier to say than to do, but it's not impossible. We have to reclaim the emotional integrity we had to sacrifice in order to fit in, to adjust to school and our parents' values, ideas, and even quirks. Adapting in our youth meant we had to learn how to deny our real feelings because in many cases we couldn't control them or they would get us in trouble or bring disappointment. We need to resurrect our childhood feelings at midlife—the anger, joy, sadness, disappointment, hope, and the others we learned to renounce—so we can open ourselves to the full experience of life that our adult personalities have become strong enough to deal with.

BEGINNING THE SEARCH

I can remember one man I worked with whose mother never allowed him to question or talk back to her without giving him a severe rebuke. Even though in adulthood he was educated and became a respected securities analyst, he went through several marriages and affairs until he could work through his deep anger at his mother and learn to relate to women without being caught between fear and resentment.

Lily, who dialogued with her inner artist in the last chapter, felt like an adopted child in her family. Being a sensitive, intelligent, ambitious person, she was forced to hide herself in introversion and shyness as a child to avoid ridicule. She needed to go back through childhood as part of her inner work and learn to revise how she saw herself and the promise of her life. She needed to show herself she was lovable, and a talented, ambitious person, a person she hadn't been able to recognize before.

To some extent or another we all need to revisit our childhoods, reflect upon them and examine how we learned to think and feel as we do, to see ourselves and other people in general. In unraveling and deciphering the patterns acquired, it is often helpful to consider questions like the following ones, mull them over, and perhaps write about them in our journals:

- *Which emotions were you raised to think were good and bad?*

- *Which behaviors, values, and appearances were rewarded or discouraged?*

- *What did you learn your self-esteem depended on?*

- *Did you learn the world was a supportive or hostile place?*

- *Do you believe people are basically generous or out for themselves?*

Questions like these help us understand the forces that control us today. And, reflecting on such questions are important throughout our growth. Every time we reach a new level of consciousness, we will probably have to let go of something we learned early in life.

Our unwillingness to look back, define, and rework the problems that keep us from genuinely getting on with our lives simply reflects our social character with its emphasis on productivity, busyness, and practicality. The irony is this very desire to "get on with our lives"—unless we stop and do the work we need to do, we will remain stuck without realizing it and make "getting on" a meaningless concept.

Recently I met a woman who'd just left a pressured job in publishing to start a spiritual retreat center in our area. Her plan was to have a center where people could come to seminars on various spiritual and self-help topics focusing on feminine wisdom—a wonderful idea! But when she finally came to talk with me she was close to despair. She still believed in her vision, but she realized, after several key employees had resigned, she was living in the same driven manner she'd been living in before. Her career change seemed dramatically different on the surface, but since she hadn't made the necessary inner changes, the real patterns of her life had not changed. Our changes need to reach deep within us in order to strengthen and nourish our roots and unless they do, our development won't have access to the nourishment needed to sustain it.

Obstacles to Feeling Deeply

If we take the attitude of not paying careful attention to our lives, we block our own chances to grow. We let our activities begin to strangle us like ivy slowly covering a tree. Growth and self-understanding depend upon learning to comprehend our pasts and the patterns of living we've developed.

Stop and think for a minute about the tendrils you believe society wraps around you that are obstacles to getting to know yourself.

Compare your answers to the following list and see what you can add to it:

- *Peer pressure*
- *Work ethic*
- *Television*
- *Advertising*
- *Goal-oriented mind-set*
- *Hurried mentality*
- *Materialism*
- *Herd mentality*
- *Lack of alone time*
- *Self-expectations*
- *Lack of role models*
- *Shame and guilt*

If we look at our lives closely it can get a little scary. Let us consider, for example, how we might spend a hypothetical weekend. Many of us come home tired from a long week on Friday evening, grab a bite, and flop down in front of the television. On Saturday we buy the groceries, go to the hardware store or the mall, mow the lawn, do the laundry, clean the house, make a deposit at the bank, take the children to soccer games, play racquetball, wash the car, play golf or tennis, and go out to a movie or have friends over in the evening. On Sunday some of us go to church, then to our parents or in-laws for lunch; we watch a ball game, finish mowing the lawn, and perhaps take a walk. Before we know it the six o'clock news is on. By the time we've finished supper, put the kids to bed, reviewed our schedule for the week, and made a couple of phone calls, it's time for bed again. We're almost as tired on Sunday night as we were on Friday night.

If this is the way you live then you're part of the "normal" pattern in our society. A pattern that leaves little time for introspection, reflection. It is the modern way of avoiding the confrontation with the big, fundamental mystery of what life's about and what death has to teach us. In other words, we go through life with the mistaken assumption that everything important is known and obvious. I'm afraid of this pattern of living because I know how easy it is to get bound up in it—to be caught up in the necessary and neutral pleasures and obligations that make life "real." But it is a reality that sets us up for burnout. Its symptoms are the sparks of illness, unnecessarily difficult midlife crises, or something worse. We become conflagrations waiting to happen.

I recall listening to the story of a couple who were entangled in a serious struggle. The wife was furious because her husband had been spending a lot of time with a female colleague. His response was, "I don't find her that attractive. I just need someone to talk to. You always seem to be too busy. When I try to say something you don't even stop what you're doing—folding the laundry, wiping down the counters, writing out lists. I feel like I'm another item to deal with on your 'To Do' list. I feel like I'm interrupting you." This pair are letting life run them instead of backing off from their own routines, taking a look at what's going on, and then intentionally acting in a manner that is based not only on their needs and values, but also on things that bring pleasure, intimacy, and joy. Frequently we've become so caught in our programs of daily living we have to pause and restart our relationship with ourselves by listening to our dreams, looking at our lives, and asking ourselves how we really feel about how we are living. It shouldn't come as a surprise to hear that the more important we consider our relationships to ourselves to be, the more valuable our other relationships will become.

The conflict between desires and duties is frequently a stumbling block that seems to hinder our progress. I've often experienced situations where I was committed to a course of action I didn't like and may have even despised. It may have been as simple as taking statistics, a course I disliked intensely in college. Or it may have been something more serious such as working in difficult surroundings, at a job I didn't like because I needed the money, or having to take care of a parent or someone else who was terribly sick or bitter and abusive. My professional training was long and slow because I didn't want my children to feel impoverished since I was returning to school; therefore I worked for almost the entire time I attended graduate school. We all have to do things at times we don't like because our values or circumstances require it. But if we face the truth about what we're doing, why we're doing it, and the values behind it, what we're doing will not be self-destructive in the long run. What I did was a conscious sacrifice. It wasn't the ideal for me or my family. It was a compromise, but because it was conscious it enhanced my self-respect rather than leaving me regretful or bitter.

The stress of modern life and the corresponding lack of time we have, the responsibility of families, the preoccupation of business and careers, and, of course, the values of the social character we've identified with are corroding the quality of our lives, devaluing our relationships with loved ones, and dishonoring the true meaning and potential we're capable of living up to. In an insightful lecture delivered at Queens University entitled "The Deadliest of the Sins," writer Robertson Davies remarked, "There is only one kind of failure in the art of life itself. This failure one does well to fear." It is something that comes when we reach a point where we're so busy and preoccupied that, without realizing it, we no longer feel anything deeply, and when this happens nothing is really important anymore. When we die to feelings, we also die to pain, joy, and enthusiasm. Life is too valuable to allow ourselves to become the victims of this slow killer.

The Meaning in Feelings

The social character of our culture teaches us how to relate to life on a literal, functional basis. In contrast to this "getting the job done" approach, we must also realize that our feelings provide the ambiance and frequently the meaning that make the "doing" worthwhile. Feelings, the engagement of our hearts, make our tasks and our relationships personal, valuable, and fulfilling. When I had three children at home, a functional approach to the evening was to get everyone fed, on to homework, and into bed. To make our lives more personal and relational we tried to eat supper together, without television, in order to have conversations as a family, and then to all work together cleaning up afterward. We soon discovered that in our efforts to bring feelings into our evenings, we were opening ourselves to the frustrations of arguments and disagreements as well as the pleasures of being together. However, whether we are in families, relationships, or are single, real satisfaction comes from leaning in to the feelings revealed in the life experience, and accepting the bumps and growing pains that accompany it.

This same idea holds true for relating to ourselves and our interior lives. Feelings are what give meaning to how we experience and value these connections. It's also important to remember that just as in all successful relationships, we must be grounded in a sense of who we are, in what we call our *ego,* the Latin word for "I," the center of our conscious awareness; and to relate to the inner parts of ourselves we must consider these parts, as we have seen, as separate entities like: my fear, my inner critic, my headache, my inner artist, or something else. At first appearance this perspective may seem like we are willfully fragmenting ourselves; but in fact what we are doing is differentiating our various attributes so that we can relate to them consciously and bring ourselves into a state of more conscious unity, like a tree trunk holds its branches.

Working with our inner characteristics follows the same relational principles we use when interacting with people in the outer world. In his highly personal and poetic style, writer Sam Keen introduces the inner dialogs he shared in *To a Dancing God* by saying they're records of what takes place between the "voting members of the commonwealth that is Sam Keen." Like him I agree that the "citizens" within us should have their say, even the ones who shout in anger, are defiant, plead, or shrink back in vulnerability, or who are, as Keen would say, the lost and the hostile, the grateful and the joyful. He continues wisely, "No government refrains from repressing some of its citizens when they appear too seditious.... There are voices in me I would like to banish in order to keep the peace." The better we know and listen to ourselves, Keen reminds us, the more we can live with clarity, a feeling of empowerment, and joy.

Relating to Ourselves: A Four-Step Process

"Seek first to understand, then to be understood" has become a well-known dictum in the field of human relations. The same principle holds true as a guideline for the inner relationships that take place between our egos and the other members of our inner commonwealths. There are four helpful steps in this process: *paying attention, listening, questioning,* and *reflecting.* In order for the four steps to work we must each have a substantial ego, a clear grounded sense of who we are, defined boundaries, and a personal value structure we understand. Of course having a substantial ego doesn't mean having a rigid one. We want to be able to grow and evolve as we get to know ourselves better in order to experience life more fully. And if we're dealing with a problem that threatens to be too big , it's best to ask a trusted friend or professional to back us up. I've often found outside help valuable when I'm trying to get a better perspective on my inner or outer conflicts.

By reading this book you've taken the first step in this process, which is the decision to get involved or to *pay attention* to what you're experiencing. The more attention you pay to your life the more you realize that everything—your thoughts, feelings, dreams, fantasies, events in your outer life, and physical or emotional symptoms—is important and warrants your time and attention.

When Rob came to see me, he'd decided to pay attention to his boredom and try to understand it. He made the time to see me, to look at his life and try to figure out what was going on. If he'd read a book like this one, Rob could have decided to take the time to think about his life, and journal to explore his feelings about the day or about his boredom. If he'd read about dialoguing he could have tried that as well. But Rob was looking for someone who could help him get started in an effective way. As far as he was concerned he came to me in the same way he would've gone to an investment advisor if he'd wanted his money to grow and didn't know how to begin.

Involvement normally leads to the point where listening is necessary. However, listening, whether it's to another person or to an inner part of ourselves, sounds easier than it actually is. Unfortunately most of us are taught to rush in and fix things before we've learned to really understand them. Few of us are trained to listen openly to other people or ourselves. Listening openly means cultivating the ability to put aside our points of view in order to try and fully understand the point of view of the other party. What if, for instance, the other party is criticizing or attacking us? Or what if one of the defiant, angry, or hostile "inner citizens" are criticizing or attacking us in a dialog we're having with it? How far do we go in trying to understand, while at the same time protecting ourselves from being hurt? Maintaining mutual respect is essential in any effort to dialogue, but we may often find that dialoguing with inner citizens is challenging.

Recently John, a friend who is an excellent technical writer, related his story about dialoguing to me. John also loves to read and he decided he'd like to try to write a novel. Approaching fiction writing in the same way he approached technical writing, he figured out the "format" he believed most successful novelists used and thought he could easily flesh out a story around it. After writing a few chapters he found himself completely blocked. After a few frustrating attempts to go on he decided to stop and dialogue with his inner artist. She (as it turned out, his inner artist referred to herself as "she") responded to him angrily, saying, "You are shallow, stubborn, and arrogant!" At first John became angry in response, threw his pencil down and stopped the dialog. Later, after cooling off, he took a walk and thought about the situation. He concluded that since he was blocked he must be in some sort of inner conflict and that perhaps he needed to try the dialog again and listen to what his inner artist might want to make known. He began by saying. "OK, I want to hear what you have to say, but can we please not get into name calling?" She responded, "Yes. If you want to write a novel you're going to have to open up, to use some feeling and creativity, and let me help you. You can't write a novel the same way you write a technical manual."

At this point John stopped trying to write his novel and spent more time dialoguing with his inner artist and reflecting in his journal about what makes for good technical writing and the qualities in a good novel. He decided the clarity of thinking and expression that were his best qualities in technical writing would make his novel cold and cerebral. A novel needed more than what had been his

BEGINNING THE SEARCH

most dependable strengths, and if he pursues it he'll have to expand himself in some new ways.

John went on to the next step in trying to understand himself, *questioning*. The best place to begin questioning is with our immediate circumstances. What's really going on in our personal worlds? Who else is involved? How do our external situations affect us? When John felt blocked, a process important to him had stopped. Then he questioned what was going on and listened to his inner artist, asking for her guidance in seeking out his feelings and creativity. Once again I'd like to emphasize the qualities of respect and gentleness. Questioning John's inner artist didn't mean examining her like a district attorney. We should approach our inner citizens whenever possible with a genuine sense of curiosity, and a desire to discover how perspectives other than our own can be different and yet enriching.

When we are blocked, frustrated, or want to understand ourselves better, we may need to get "out" of our familiar surroundings for a short time or even a longer retreat. John's walk helped him recover his ability to pay attention. We can take a bath, ride a bike, listen to music, bake bread, or whatever helps us recover a feeling of being centered. Then we can return to the process of seeking to understand ourselves instead of being consumed with trying to solve our "problems." This reminds me of Rilke's lovely and wise advice to a young poet, which I find so much comfort in—advice that's completely opposite to the rational, functional approach to life: "I would like to beg you, dear Sir, as well as I can, to have patience with everything unresolved in your heart and to try to love *the questions themselves* as if they were locked rooms or books written in a foreign language. Don't search for the answers. . . . Live the questions now. Perhaps then, someday in the future, you will gradually, without even noticing it, live your way into the answer." Living into the answers shifts our concerns from our problems to our growth and allows us to evolve and change naturally, based on the strength of our inner roots.

Following the first three steps of attention, listening, and questioning generally leads us into an attitude of *reflection*. In fact if we're using a process like journaling to pay attention to our lives, we are also reflecting upon them. Listening and questioning will prompt further reflection as well as give us new opportunities for dialoguing. Ah, well enough, but *when?* We are like heat-seeking missiles locking on opportunities, not for contemplation but activity. We are afraid of being alone because it puts us in the company of the very unhappiness we don't want to acknowledge.

The irony is, as many have discovered, that it's only by risking loneliness, embarking on the journey inward, and paying careful attention to life that we discover a hidden teacher within us who cares a great deal about us. As Nikki, the woman I mentioned earlier who felt she was so hard on herself she never had any fun, continued her dialogues with her inner critic and reflected upon them, what she'd termed her inner critic—the symbol of the painful attacks of self-criticism and self-depreciation she'dexperienced —began to change and what had seemed destructive transformed into an ally in rebuilding her life. The turning point began when she asked the following question:

NIKKI: *I know you have driven me to some successes that I actually am happy about now. But, can't I get these some other way?*

INNER CRITIC: *Yes, I could help you if you would let me. But first you will have to get more ambitious and figure out what you want to achieve.*

John, who wanted to write a novel, also experienced his inner artist as a teacher and guide. During his reflections he reached a point where he wasn't sure whether he wanted to write a novel just to prove he could do it or if he wanted to grow into a new career as a novelist. Through his dialogs and reflections he decided that while he wanted to stretch himself and develop his feeling and creative abilities, he didn't actually want to change professions. He still enjoyed technical writing.

BEGINNING THE SEARCH

Consciousness as Relationship

Using the word *consciousness* in any discussion can be confusing because it's a word used to mean so many things. In the morning my cat is conscious of me as I'm moving around the kitchen preparing her food. I'm conscious when I'm not asleep. As Jung defines it, consciousness is the perception of a relationship between a subject (my ego) and something else that's either outside of me or part of my inner world.

When we examine the roots of the word, we find that it comes from the Latin *con,* which means "with," and *scio,* which means "to know." Consciousness is "knowing with" and this makes it a relational activity. To use the terms of Hebrew scholar Martin Buber, consciousness requires an "I" and a "thou," two distinct entities capable of having a relationship. Becoming conscious in the Jungian sense doesn't come easy. It requires a committed effort to know ourselves, but this effort rewards us with a sense of energy, assurance, and peace. Becoming more conscious helps us feel more unified within and more capable of love.

The ancient mystical traditions of the East and West considered our everyday state of consciousness as an illusion, a state of "waking sleep." This state, which I call *complex consciousness,* isn't one of being unconscious as if we were actually asleep. It's a state of having limited awareness, of being trapped in the social attitude created by our history and the social character of our culture. To begin awakening to higher consciousness is to begin the process of discrimination of things into twos so they can become an "I" and a "thou." It's an interesting paradox that we have to first *separate,* then *relate to* in order to contribute to our feeling of wholeness. But without this process we have no way of being aware of feeling whole.

If, for example, I don't become aware of myself as an individual, I remain part of the herd mentality. But once I become aware of myself as an individual I can then relate to the nature of our culture's social character and live effectively in it without losing myself to it. When I mentioned Churchill and his depression earlier I told you about his ability to separate from it, and to call it his "black dog." Before he made his discrimination he *was* his depression, and whenever it came it dominated him and his life. Once he'd separated from it and became an "I" and his black dog a "thou," his perception changed and he was able to relate to his depression in a more objective manner. This detachment helped him live with it without being victimized by it and allowing the depression to control his entire life.

I remember Erin, who'd just taken a job with a major hotel chain as a sales representative. Erin loved her job except for one thing. At times she had to speak to groups of travel agents and convention planners, explaining the hotel's advantages or services, or give a group an enthusiastic welcome to the hotel, explain the facilities and mention some interesting activities in the city. Erin was terrified of public speaking. Her hands would shake, her voice would quiver; she would lose her place, feel faint and extremely embarrassed that she wasn't projecting the enthusiasm she believed was part of her job, that she really felt but couldn't express.

Erin tried separating herself from her fear and even dialoguing with it, but her efforts did not work. I asked her to close her eyes, take a few relaxing breaths, and tell me what image, what mental picture, came to mind that could represent her fear. After a few moments she answered, "A large dark raven."

I suggested that she begin dialoguing with the raven by visualizing it and then writing the dialogs. I asked her to approach it courteously, simply trying to get to know it by asking its name and if it was willing to talk with her. The raven responded that his name was Fred, that he'd be willing to get to know her, but slowly because ravens don't trust humans. So began a very careful, respectful, and constructive exchange.

If we're having trouble with dialoguing, adding an imaginary image is often helpful, but it needs to come from our imaginations and not be forced or we won't be respecting the "legitimacy" of what we're dialoguing with. We won't be allowing it to be a "thou."

Later Erin told me that this beginning changed how she experienced her fear. She said that before the active imagination exercise, she felt helplessly caught like an actress in a drama, and soon after it, part of her was free, sitting in the audience watching the drama. This separation helped her to feel calm and hopeful.

Most of the dialogs I've shared with you show that *knowing with* means going a step further. We must seek to know the particular aspects of ourselves and allow them to know us. If I'm dialoguing with my weight, I must listen to it and also tell it how it makes me feel. As an "I-thou" relationship develops, we both must be willing to change and allow this willingness to bring us to a state of *interbeing*. The more I follow this process, the more self-awareness I build. I can now depend on my weight to keep me well informed about how balanced my life is. My body often seems to understand whether I'm overfocused in an area, working too hard, or not recognizing particular feelings. In many ways my body seems to know what's affecting my soul before my mind does. And at the same time, I feel more whole, like the different parts of me know each other and are working together. I find this work very exciting. The assurance of being centered and feeling authentic is the result of how well we know ourselves and relate to ourselves.

Dialogs aren't the only way we can create a conscious relationship with ourselves. Paying attention to our lives and reflecting on them, journaling, exploring dreams, and expressing ourselves through drawing, painting, music, sculpting, and dance can act as mirrors for seeing our experiences and aspects of our personalities more objectively.

Becoming more conscious means changing the rules by which we live and the beliefs we've maintained. It means actively listening to our inner lives, taking the time and effort to relate to ourselves. While it may temporarily cause us to feel alone or threaten a few immediate relationships, it's actually the path to having more creative and fulfilling relationships—with the people in our lives and with ourselves as well. Learning to know ourselves is a step out of fear into love. As we continue exploring ways of cultivating our inner substance in the next chapter, we will look into dreams more carefully.

CHAPTER 8
Befriending Our Dreams

During the day, our souls gather their . . . impressions of us, how our lives feel. . . . Our spirits collect these impressions, keep them together, like wisps of smoke in a bag. Then, when we're asleep, our brains open up these bags of smoke . . . and take a look.
—Marsha Norman

Catherine, the heroine in Emily Bronte's passionate classic *Wuthering Heights,* says, "I've dreamed in my life dreams that have stayed with me ever after, and changed my ideas: they've gone through and through me, like wine through water, and altered the color of my mind." Dreams, we know, speak to us in the "other voice," the voice of poetry and symbolism, the voice that puzzles us because it isn't the recognizable, familiar voice of our rational, literal selves. If we are seeking to know ourselves then we must be willing to listen to our dreams, to see how *knowing with* this other voice can teach us about ourselves and help us live more completely.

Befriending a dream means letting it simmer in our minds, listening to its poetry, looking at its images and reflecting on them. Befriending a dream means allowing ourselves to feel its moods, the dramatic energy of its scenes, and the intensity or lightness of its characters and story line. Befriending is a kind, personal way of explaining how to relate to our dreams. It is a gentle process summarizing how we pay attention, listen, question, and reflect upon dreams. Growing familiar with our dreams in this manner is an honest route toward understanding our inner worlds.

In his profound book *Insearch: Psychology and Religion,* James Hillman tells us the messages in our dreams show how our inner worlds are seeking to become known and befriend us. He says we need to wonder, "Who lives in me? What inscapes are mine? What is recurrent and therefore what keeps coming back to reside in me? These are the animals and people, places and concerns, that want me to pay attention to them, to become friendly and familiar with them. They want to be known as a friend would. They want to be cared for and cared about. This familiarity after some time produces in one a sense of at-homeness and at-oneness with an inner family which is nothing else than kinship and community within oneself."

Dreams as friends are our allies and the advocates of our living with awareness and integrity. Sometimes they speak to us in straight-forward ways as I experienced not too long ago in a short dream that stood out clearly. When the dream opened I was in the examining room of a doctor's office. In the room with me was a white-coated physician who had just given me a physical exam. I felt pleased because I knew that I ate well, exercised regularly, and was in good physical condition. To my surprise the doctor said, "You're going to be sick." I was so startled by his pronouncement that I woke up. Within a couple of days I came down with a particularly rugged virus that was coursing through our community at the time, followed by the secondary complications of a bacterial infection that eventually became pneumonia. In retrospect, I imagine my friend was trying to help me prepare for experiencing something that was already underway in my body.

We generally think it's rare for dreams to be direct and explicit, but there are many of these exceptions. Musicians, for example, whether they're popular composers like Billy Joel or classical composers such as Mozart, Beethoven, or Wagner, have acknow-ledged that the inspiration for their music and often the specific sounds come to them in their dreams. Thomas Edison disclosed that an image of his dead brother came to him in a dream with instructions for designing the electric lightbulb. Simply paying attention and listening to dreams bring their meanings within our grasp.

Other dreams speak to us in a more subtle manner. Recently I dreamed I was attending an elegant dinner party with close friends. As the dream opened we were entering an exquisite Oriental-style restaurant, one whose nationality I couldn't determine. A courtly, refined maitre d' showed us into the dining area, where waiters in formal white jackets helped us take our seats at tables of golden bamboo covered with white linen tablecloths. My friends and I were dressed in dark suits, though they weren't people I know in real life. The conversation was warm, cordial, and humorous. Accompanying us was a woman I'd known as a little girl when I was an adolescent. In the dream she was the same age as the rest of us and very charming and attractive. The food was beautifully arranged on a large side table, and the aroma was wonderful.

It was a lovely dream, but with no direct message. In fact it was more of a sensual statement than a clear message or a story. The dream seemed to invite me to enjoy its mood and images, and I've savored them many times in my spare moments. I've let this dream "simmer" in my imagination, remembering the smells, the elegance, the courtesy and style of the waiters, the warmth and charm of the room, and the quiet pleasure of being with friends.

As I've mulled over the dream I realize that everything in it was new, exotic, colorful, and inviting. In a sense even the woman was new. I've wondered what she might represent, perhaps some part of me that has been dormant for years. But my intuition has been to enjoy this dream and delight in the pleasure it offered me rather than to try to formally interpret it. While I was reflecting on it one evening an old saying came to mind: No matter how exciting growth and change may be, we often find that there's a long hallway between leaving a comfortable, old state of being and arriving in a new one. Suddenly I understood the dream's purpose because I was in the midst of struggling through a major change in my writing style that often left me frustrated and disappointed. The dream reassured me that I wasn't alone in that hallway. I was with friends, inner friends.

Poetically speaking, dreams are like friends. One friend may give us directions, another one may provide comfort and companionship or fun. But good friends do more than that; they also confront us, show us where we're getting in trouble, and get angry with us when we don't listen to them or show them the respect they deserve. Frequently our dream friends communicate with us in story form with a beginning that sets the context for the story, a middle that shows how the story develops, and an end that brings a resolution or a release.

When a dream comes in story form, we need to listen to it as a story and see its action as a dramatization of the story. Where and how it begins orient our perspective. Whether we're in our childhood homes, in a bathroom, on a battlefield, in our marriage beds, or floating down a river sets up very different kinds of stories. The people in the dream are the characters in the story, and we should pay careful attention to them—who they are, what they're doing, and how they fit into the story line. And whether we're observers or participants in the action is an important point to note and reflect upon. Then, of course, we need to look at how the plot develops and whether it includes a problem or crisis that leads to a climax, reaches a solution, and then ends; or if it simply trails off or ends by awakening us.

I remember a brief, but helpful dream story that came to a man seeing me a few years ago. Jack was middle-aged and had been struggling with depression and marital conflicts for several years. Jack dreamed that he was strolling down the street with his wife one evening. As they walked they left the well-lit, comfortable neighborhood they lived in and became lost in what appeared to be a ghetto undergoing urban renewal. The streets became darker and they walked faster but couldn't find their way out. The buildings were old and ramshackle, but seemed to be in the process of being remodeled. Jack was becoming frightened. Suddenly a large, brutish-looking man ran out of an alley and began furiously smashing the windows of the remodeled buildings with a large iron bar. Jack awoke terrified.

When we're looking at dreams like this one, we need to keep in mind they have a purpose, they want to lead us into new realizations or offer us a fresh point of view on how we're dealing with life. In Jack's case, his dream has a clear opening scene with him and his wife, and as it unfolds you quickly sense the story building. It seems that dreams like this one want to push their way into consciousness and press us into action.

As he initially reflected on it, Jack thought the dream was talking about his marriage and how it was progressing into darker areas. He also wondered if it had always been impoverished and if he was trying to renew its "facade" because he thought it was the "right thing to do" rather than it being something in which he had invested his heart. However, the challenge of the dream was in trying to understand the large, angry man. After thinking about it for a while Jack remarked, "This man scares me. I suppose part of the message of this dream is that I have to wake up to this part of myself and figure out how I am going to get to know him."

While Jack's line of thinking about the dream made sense, I cautioned him to continue letting it "simmer" in his mind, reflecting on it, musing over it, and writing in his journal about it. As he continued this process he discovered that the dream generated deeply felt thoughts and memories related to his marriage and to how as a child he'd been taught to deal with conflict. This work helped him feel his situation more intensely and orient himself more clearly. The results of his efforts helped Jack act with increased certainty and experience less distress.

Another guideline to remember about dreams is they frequently have many different meanings. If we try too hard to boil them down, to reduce and extract from them one clear interpretation, we may lose some important information. For example, you might be able to see other meanings in Jack's dream than the ones he saw. Thomas Moore compares a dream to a Monet landscape and says it may "mean" something different to each of the various people contemplating it. In a similar manner Jack's dream may evoke different reactions in him every time he considers it. The meaning to Jack of this one dream may evolve for years as he reflects upon it from different perspectives. You can imagine that every time Jack thinks about his marriage in terms of the dream, he'll see it differently. And the more he considers this brutish man in himself, wonders who he is and how he can know him better, Jack will in fact be changed. In actuality, the more Jack reflects upon this angry man, the more his former view of himself as an easygoing guy who doesn't get angry will begin to soften and shift. Befriending the dream will alter the "color" of how he sees himself.

Dreams as Friends

True friendship is both an art and a craft. Friendships may often seem to begin easily, but their nature is delicate at first, growth is slow and is easily checked or diverted. For friendships to become strong they need to be nurtured, cultivated, and appreciated. Few of us are born with a natural gift for cultivating friendships. They take time, caring, and mutual respect. And the busyness that devours our lives makes enriching our friendships difficult. But once a friendship has become strong, it's very sturdy and reliable. A real friend can tell us things we don't want to tell ourselves and yet we're always comforted to know there's someone out there we can lean on.

Some years ago writer Sophie Loeb said, "A friend is one who withholds judgment no matter how long you have his unanswered letter." These characteristics of friendships explain why befriending the dream is an idea that makes immediate sense to most of us. It's much more comforting to feel that our inner lives are friendly toward us even if they're provoking us with dramatic images or confronting our preferred opinions.

In therapy it's tempting for both the therapist and the patient to translate dreams into their favorite theories, perspectives, or rationalizations. In many of these situations, dream interpretations are used to dredge up childhood conflicts; or to gain information, power, or energy from our unconscious to help us pursue our goals. Yet these approaches are actually hostile to our unconscious. They go against the grain of friendships for nothing damages a friendship more than trying to exploit it. Unfortunately, modern therapies are often influenced by the social character of our times, which emphasizes solving problems in order to become more functional, rather than honoring our inner lives so that we can become more whole as human beings. When the fruits of friendship and the cultivation of our inner lives and wisdom aren't valued, therapy can actually work against our healing and growth and contribute to devaluing life.

The beauty of befriending dreams is that it doesn't require special knowledge and training. It simply asks that we *listen* to what they have to say to us and appreciate their importance. Though while the notion of befriending dreams is appealing, and the logic of allowing them to reveal themselves slowly makes sense, this process can be difficult to live out. Keeping in mind the same four-step process we used in relating to ourselves may make the craft of cultivating our relationship with our dreams easier.

Paying Attention

Paying attention to our dream lives involves several activities. To begin with it's beneficial if we can create favorable conditions for receiving our dreams. An overextended schedule, exhaustion, poor sleeping habits, and the general habit of just being too busy can distract us from the quality time we commit to our dreams, or for that matter to any friendship. Making an effort to create an attitude of interest and receptivity by trying to have a good night's sleep and waking up gently very likely will invite a response from our unconscious.

The second way of paying attention to dreams is to write them down as soon as we wake up. It's better not to put them off till morning if we remember them in the middle of the night, or to wait until after we've had coffee and are dressed. Time and experience have proven that until this friendship is firmly established, no matter how often we go over a dream in our minds, we can lose it in a moment if we haven't written it down. Research proves we dream every night. If we don't remember their contents it usually means we're overtired, anxious, or haven't been interested in or have some other trouble keeping us from concentrating on our inner lives. Having a pencil and paper available nearby and writing dreams down quickly is a helpful ritual that stimulates our memory of them. When we wake up and don't remember a dream, lying quietly and focusing on what we have been thinking since we awakened can be helpful. Perhaps a thought or an image, a mood, an impression about ourselves in some past action, or thinking about the future will come to mind. Recalling a random thought, image, or impression and writing it down can revive or recall another, jump-starting a train of thinking that can lead to reconstructing a dream.

I've often awakened in the morning and been surprised by the number of dreams I wrote down during the night with no memory of even writing them. At other times, when I only recall a brief scene, I've discovered that writing it down carefully may help the entire dream return to memory. A short time ago I remembered the image of a brown bear from a dream. As I was writing a detailed description of the bear, the dream story began returning and eventually covered three pages.

And now we come to the third important aspect of paying attention to a dream, which is to write it down with all the detail you can. Writing it down carefully helps you to see or feel the full development of the dream. In the beginning of Jack's dream, he was strolling with his wife. As the dream progressed they became lost and were walking faster. The change of tempo says more than if Jack had simply reported, "I was walking with my wife." Describing the moods, people, animals, landscapes, and actions in lively ways helps you reimagine the dream as a story that you can experience again.

In his delightful and wise book *The Star Thrower,* anthropologist Loren Eisley shares a dream in a manner that pulls us directly into it:

> The dream was of a great blurred bearlike shape emerging from the snow against the window. It pounded on the glass and beckoned importunately toward the forest. I caught the urgency of a message as uncouth and indecipherable as the shape of its huge bearer in the snow. In the immense terror of my dream I struggled against the import of that message as I struggled also to resist the impatient pounding of the frost-enveloped beast at the window.

BEFRIENDING OUR DREAMS

> *Suddenly I lifted the telephone beside my bed, and through the receiver came a message as cryptic as the message from the snow, but far more miraculous in origin. For I knew intuitively, in the still snowfall of my dream, that the voice I heard, a long way off, was my own voice in childhood. Pure and sweet, incredibly refined and beautiful beyond the things of earth, yet somehow inexorable and not to be stayed, the voice was already terminating its messages. "I am sorry to have troubled you," the clear faint syllables of the child persisted. They seemed to come across a thinning wire that lengthened far away into the years of my past. "I am sorry, I am sorry to have troubled you at all." The voice faded before I could speak. I was awake now, trembling in the cold.*

As I read this dream I feel like I do when I read a good poem—left with a sense of wonder. Most of us have to relearn how to express ourselves in such a complete manner.

Julia Cameron, in *The Right to Write,* offers useful advice in this direction by urging us to become what she calls "bad writers." By this phrase she means letting everything be expressed even if we think we're describing feelings and events in tabloid terms, where beauties are breathtaking, villains hideous, victims helpless, and murders grizzly. We've been so schooled to censor our feelings, especially in writing, we tend to automatically censor ourselves, putting down "just the facts." When we do this we can end up losing the poetry and flavor of our dreams, like someone who stops digging in a hollow tree a few inches before reaching the honey.

Listening

Listening to the dream includes writing it down as completely as we remember it and including its colorful aspects. However, we must keep in mind that listening to a dream is similar to what we do when we *really* want someone to listen to us: We want them to put their agendas, their censoring mind-sets, and their "plans" to answer us aside. This is why I like to tell people that while writing the dream down, they should suspend the temptation to interpret it. Likewise, if we're thinking of dream theories and interpretations or problems in our lives, we can't be fully listening to the dream and we're in danger of forcing it into a framework we already have in mind. I once heard someone say that we don't need to kill the bird in order to study it, it's much better to let it sing; and the same is true with dreams.

A second aspect of listening to dreams is also made possible by writing them down—sooner or later we'll have collections of them we can review as dream series. These series are like ongoing conversations with our unconscious, the structure that supports our lives. At one point Jack reviewed his dreams over a period of several months. He first read over them to get a feeling of their different emotional contents. Then he made a list of the main characters and their positive and negative attributes, a list of the places where the dreams took place, and a summary of their story lines and outcomes. He discovered that many of the dreams seemed to fit in the series like chapters in a larger story and his feelings in them appeared like nuances of color in a large painting. This activity can be fun as well as offering important insights into how we're growing and changing, and how some of our dearly held attitudes and beliefs are being consigned to the past.

Questioning

The questions we ask ourselves about our dreams can fall into as many areas as we can imagine. Just as examining a painting reveals its details and beauty, questioning a dream opens up the view of specific scenarios and leaves us wondering where is this place, who are these people, what are they like, why do they keep appearing? We may ask ourselves why this animal, this landscape, this concern, or this dream is appearing in our lives at this particular moment. The unconscious is trying to tell us where our energy is, and where it's going, in the plot or story line of the dream. With this in mind, how the dream is developing and concluding become important questions.

It was helpful to Jack to ask himself how being in a well-lit, upper middle-class neighborhood with his wife led him into a scary ghetto inhabited by a powerful, angry man. "Is my relationship with my wife what I think it is?" he asked himself. "What does this changing inner landscape mean?" and—most crucial—"Who is this angry man within me?"

Reflecting

Reflecting on our dreams can be like selecting new clothes. We have to try them on and if they seem to fit, we take them. Then we have to wear them for awhile and move around in them until they feel comfortable. Similarly, we may mull over a dream's images and moods and consider the questions we've asked and the answers that come to mind as we're trying to figure out how the dream "fits." Finally the dream's components may become part of our lives and change our habitual way of seeing things, especially ourselves. In other words each little bit of new understanding we gain is something we integrate in a manner that expands our awareness.

If we think about Jack again we might imagine that the better he comes to know the hulking, angry man in his dream, the more he may become aware of his own anger and strength, and the structure of old values that kept these aspects of himself in an emotionally impoverished section of his unconscious. As I came to know him better—more important, as Jack came to know *himself*—this became clearly true. Thinking about the dream increased Jack's capacity to be more forceful in searching out his real needs and values. New strength and more authentic values fastened new self-responsibility and integrity in the ways he approached his marriage and his life in general.

Inner Darkness

Dark dreams are no strangers to any of us. When Shakespeare has Richard III cry out in the following verse, most of us have an idea what he is talking about:

Oh, has past a miserable night,
So full of feareful dreams, of ugly sights.
That as I am a Christian faithful man,
I would not spend another such night
Though 'twere to buy a world of happy daies:
So full of dismal terror was the time.

When more powerful scary dreams disturb our nights with strong images what can we do with them? Should we try to forget them, or tell ourselves they aren't important? And, if they have meaning, why are they attacking us so fiercely? People often ask me if we should try to befriend frightening dreams and "really weird" dreams. The answer is a *qualified* yes and we need to look at several kinds of frightening dreams to see why.

One kind of dream that can be scary and very stressful is what we commonly refer to as an *anxiety* dream. The purpose of these dreams is to alert us to some kind of danger in the outer or inner world. They warn, prepare, and motivate us or inform us we aren't taking something seriously enough. Anxiety dreams may also tell us when we're living in a "fool's paradise" or are too relaxed toward an issue to which we should be giving more attention. For instance a busy woman physician once came to see me because she'd dreamed her husband had been unfaithful to her. In the dream she was shattered as she would have been in real life. While she was telling me about her marriage, she explained how dependable and thoughtful her husband had always been and how completely she trusted him. The more she spoke, the more she realized how full her schedule had become and that she'd slipped into taking her husband for granted. Later, when she talked with him, she discovered he was indeed growing dissatisfied with how impersonal their marriage seemed. Her dream, as an inner friend, was trying to wake her up to an important problem developing in her life.

Other anxiety dreams may be about the same kind of situations that make us anxious in everyday life. If we fail to prepare for an important meeting or event, figuring we'll be able to "cram" or "wing it," we may find ourselves dreaming we're back in school unprepared for an exam. In many examination dreams we may not be prepared, cannot find the classroom, or have to face some old, dreaded teacher. These dreams may be metaphors for some other test we're facing such as standing up to a boss, confronting a partner, or making a career choice. Dreams may also be trying to show how we evaluate ourselves in stressful situations, how we fail to have the confidence our past accomplishments should have given us. In addition, they may be metaphors for transitions in our lives or growth that we're reluctant to acknowledge. Major life changes such as marriage, divorce, moving, midlife transitions, children leaving home, and retirement frequently fall into this category.

If anxiety dreams are frequent they may be trying to show us we've developed or are living in a mind-set of anxiety and self-criticism that leaves us continuously vulnerable to situations that threaten our self-esteem. Sean, a successful man in his early fifties, had a recurring dream of not being able to find the classroom for a college exam. In every dream this was the last exam he needed to pass in order to graduate. At first he didn't write the dream down and tried to forget it. But then he decided to pay attention to the dream and write about it every time he had it. Sean also responded to the dream by writing, "I don't really have to worry about this exam. I have graduated from college, have a family, and am successful."

Eventually Sean realized how insecure he'd felt in college. He'd gone to a very competitive school and felt inferior to other students during his entire time there because his family had not been wealthy and he didn't have the expensive private school preparations his fraternity brothers did, nor the money for their kind of social life. In spite of his achievements in college and later, this basic sense of anxiety continued to live on beneath his everyday awareness. But attention is a major step toward healing. One morning Sean awakened in excitement. He realized that his dream had repeated with a new twist. As he was about to panic because he couldn't find the classroom, he said to himself in the dream, "Wait a minute. You don't have to take this exam, you've already graduated." Befriending these kinds of dreams can be useful but if they continue repeating themselves or become more upsetting, you may want to ask a professional who is experienced in dreamwork to help you try to figure out their messages.

The first dreams many of us can remember are the nightmares common to early childhood. During this time of life these dreams are primarily developmental as the child is seeking to gain some control over the powerful feelings in his or her personality. Children feel small and afraid. The bogeyman under the bed and the monster in the closet show the defenselessness children experience in a big world. Nightmares full of lions, tigers, and dinosaurs also reflect the vulnerability they experience in the face of their own strong emotions and needs, particularly the ones they have to learn to control in order to feel approval, love, and safety. In most cases, unless these dreams become severe and continuous, they're part of the natural struggle to develop and grow. For adults, however, a dream where we feel helpless in the presence of great danger, and experience overwhelming fear with little or no chance to escape, must be handled carefully. Even though Jack was afraid in the ghetto and woke up terrified, his dream was a mild form of nightmare meant to wake him up to how he was living. We know this because the threat in the dream wasn't directed at him and wasn't threatening his survival with no possible avenues of escape.

Pursuit dreams are a common form of nightmare and a primitive state of fear. It's important in such dreams to pay careful attention to what's pursuing us in the dream. It may be a storm, an animal, a person, or a group of people. Occasionally I've heard people say, "If you turn around and face your pursuer, it will stop and turn into a friend." This advice, though well intentioned, may also be naive. I remember a woman who came to see me concerned about a recurring nightmare. In the dream she was in a dark movie theater and a murderer with a large knife was pursuing her. No one in the audience would respond to her cries for help or come to her aid as she ran desperately up and down the aisles. All of the exits were locked and the murderer was gaining on her. After relating the dream to me she said that a friend had told her to imagine simply stopping and facing the murderer. She continued, "I just couldn't do that. It was too scary."

I supported her sense that this was the wrong thing to do. I trust our feelings and intuitions in these cases more than I trust easy solutions and shallow responses. The inner threat to this woman's personality was real and when a dream's message is too threatening, it needs to be examined in a place that will make the dreamer feel *safe*. A therapist's or analyst's office is often like a room where the bomb squad goes to detonate a bomb. It's safe. There's expert help and whatever's frightening can be left right there, knowing we can always come back and work on it when we want to. Sometimes, of course, we can create these safe places on our own, though we have to be careful we aren't fooling ourselves, replacing safety for honesty. Remember that dreams were once taken to holy men and healers for the same reasons; many of us take them today to mental health professionals, for safety and interpretations. It's sound thinking not to underestimate the power of our inner worlds if we feel threatened by them.

For example, another woman I worked with had a severe and devastating inner critic. She continually dreamed that she and her children were being hunted down by Nazis who wanted to torture and exterminate them. In dream after dream she fled through destroyed houses, villages, and forests looking for basements and caves to hide in. We did nothing in her analysis to confront the Nazis. This would've been too much for her to take on. Instead, we worked for a long time to strengthen her personality and self-esteem until we could approach the problem from a different direction, by beginning a dialog with her inner critic. This course turned out to be helpful and profoundly liberating.

Another kind of frightening dream is one that involves physical danger. Very commonly, this type of dream concerns some aspect of "falling," then waking up before landing. When we awaken during a certain part of a dream or before its conclusion, the act of "waking up" seems to be part of the dream's purpose. Jung once told the story of a doctor who refused to allow his arrogant, intellectual approach to life be questioned. One night the doctor dreamed of falling off a cliff. He brushed off any attempts to get him to take the dream seriously or to acknowledge it might have some meaning. A few months later while hiking in the Swiss mountains, he accidentally stepped off of a cliff and was killed. Jung concluded that the doctor's stubborn refusal to value his inner life transformed the dream from a helpful message about how his attitudes needed to change into a prophesy of how they could literally destroy him. Falling due to a lack of awareness or wisdom is an archetypal theme and it's important to listen to these warnings.

Mythology also offers suggestions for thinking further about what the theme of falling might mean in our dreams. The story of Icarus, for instance, has become a classic example of the fate we invite on ourselves when in our pretensions we fly too high. As the story begins, the great craftsman and inventor Daedalus has grown tired of his life on Crete, and wants to leave. However, King Minos, who is angry at Daedalus, refuses to let him go. In order to escape, Daedalus designs feathered wings held together with beeswax that he and his son Icarus can use to fly away. In his youthful arrogance and exuberance Icarus ignores his father's warning not to fly too high or too low. Icarus soars higher and higher until the sun melts his wings and he plunges downward into the sea. Falling is a way of bringing us down to earth when we see ourselves unrealistically, stay too much in our heads, or assume unwarranted or naive perspectives on life.

A young woman came to me not too long ago with a dream of falling. She and her husband were getting divorced and they were particularly proud they weren't fighting and were going to remain friends. In her dream she and her husband were in an elevator going to their attorney's office. Suddenly the elevator dropped downward, floor after floor. Miraculously they weren't hurt, but when the door opened they found themselves deep in the earth, groping around in the dark. When we began talking about the dream, the fantasy of having a friendly divorce began to drop away. She realized that deep inside she was wounded, and as she explored beneath the surface, there were feelings of grief and failure about the marriage ending and anger that her husband could let it conclude so easily. These feelings needed to be recognized and worked through before she could truly be divorced. Her dream is not surprising, considering how difficult it can be to face deep emotions and conflict. While it always seems easier to avoid them, bury them, or clean them up by slapping them down with a smile, pleasantries, or even indifference, they will gain on and eventually overtake us. This is what we call depression.

Alarming dreams are unpleasant events. But they offer valuable opportunities for learning and growth. They may draw our attention to potentially threatening situations and to important inner or outer work we are ignoring or failing to confront. Understanding these dreams may become an urgent necessity in helping us to grow and deal with the threats in our lives.

Dreams may appear frightening especially when their language is poetic, alien to the ways we've learned to process information. And we don't feel safe when things are going on within us that we don't understand. But with attention and practice, it isn't that difficult to become at home with this other voice in our lives and fluent in its own varied and rich vocabulary.

Recently a man told me that he dreamed two tornadoes were chasing him and his wife across a plain. In the nick of time they dove into a storm shelter. Then he explained, "My wife and I had a date to balance our checkbook together the next evening. We were planning to meet with our accountant to prepare our taxes and this is always a stressful time for us. After the dream I concluded I'd better try to be very calm and sensitive or I would be facing an emotional storm." In another situation a man going through a particularly bleak period in his midlife transition dreamed he was alone in a lush jungle. In the dream he was struggling to make his way through the dense vegetation toward the ocean. He could hear large animals stalking him through the brush getting closer and closer. Soon he was feeling desperate, but then, to his amazement, an old mentor from his first job stepped out from behind a tree and handed him a machine gun. Then he awakened with a great sense of relief and empowerment. Dream stories are rarely like the other stories we read or watch on television and in the movies. They always describe something about our personal situations at the present time and offer new perspectives, information we need to be aware of, or even solutions to problems. But the more attention we give them, the more comfortable we become in listening to them—and the more adept we become at understanding their language.

The Purpose of Dreams

Befriending dreams is the foundation of Jungian dreamwork, though learning this skill is something we can do without a lot of formal training. In brief, Jung discovered that dreams have several important functions in our personalities and keeping the functions in mind can greatly enhance our self-understanding when we're working with them. After his extensive research on dreams, Jung concluded that they generally *compensate or complete our conscious attitudes and perspectives.* By this he meant they present the other side of the picture. They show the side of reality we filter out due to the habits, attitudes, and perspectives we have adopted in our development. For example, Jack's old but crumbling value structure kept him from realizing how much of his strength and anger was repressed. It even hindered his capacity to see that this old structure was failing. In addition, when we're being active during the day, our consciousness selectively focuses on what is necessary to accomplish the tasks of the moment or our most accessible desires and goals. Our everyday consciousness puts aside or represses things we don't have the time or inclination to immediately process into full awareness, which may include how the events of our lives—personal and even public events—are affecting us emotionally or impacting us psychologically. If these contents are important enough, our dreams will return them to our attention.

A few years ago, Tony came to me with a surprising story. A faculty member at a local university, he had just accepted what he described as the ideal job. Following an evening of celebration with his wife and family, he had a troubling dream. He shared his dream the next day with an associate in the psychology department. His colleague looked disturbed when he heard the dream and suggested to him that he talk with me about it.

The first time we sat down together, Tony briefly described his decision to take the new job, but was more anxious to tell me the dream. He said, "I dreamed I was in California near a large city. A huge disaster was taking place. There were earthquakes, fires, and floods. People were streaming out of the city, fleeing. I was standing on top of a large hill some distance away where I could see everything." Tony paused for a moment and then asked, "What do you think it means? Do you think I'm making a mistake by taking the job?"

I explained to Tony that dreams often help us understand life better and that with the dream as a background I wanted to hear more about the decision he'd celebrated earlier in the evening before the dream. Tony revealed he and his wife, Theresa, had four children. This town had been their home for fifteen years, and they loved the mountains in the area. They had a nice, big house close to the national forest and enjoyed hiking and camping as a family. Their family had developed a close circle of friends and felt a strong sense of community with them. At the university Tony had a tenured position as a full professor and considered himself a well-liked and influential member of the faculty. He'd been a major influence in the growth of his department and felt an intense loyalty to the program they'd developed. Tony also believed that his family was as happy and generally as well grounded as a family could expect to be.

Tony's description of his life left me wondering what kind of job could have tempted him to leave. When I asked him this question he explained, "A phenomenally attractive position." The job was at a well-known midwestern university where he would occupy an endowed chair and be the director of a prestigious research institution. Tony said, "It looks great, it sounds great, and my friends and colleagues think it's a dream come true. But since I had the dream my enthusiasm is wavering."

"Tell me how you made the decision to accept the offer," I said. "Oh, I discussed it thoroughly with Theresa," he replied. "And she was as thrilled as I was. It's a no-lose situation. More money, more prestige, we can send our children to private schools, and there's no telling where I could go from there. I might even become a dean or provost someday."

"The dream makes me wonder about a few things," I responded. "In it you have a clear standpoint to see what's going on. Could it be that your point of view in making this decision isn't as clear as you think it is?"

"Well, I suppose that's possible. What do you mean?"

"Perhaps we should consider your feelings behind this decision more carefully. Earthquakes, fires, and floods remind me of deep disturbances or strong emotions. Could something be bothering you about your current job that you aren't allowing into the picture?"

Then a surprising thing happened. Tony's mood became somber and he began to express irritation toward his department chairman. The department was in the process of restructuring its curriculum and Tony was worried that a course he'd designed might be discontinued. He was proud of this course and thought it contained some of his best academic thinking up to this point in his career. As we were talking Tony realized he felt hurt, unappreciated, and angry with his chairman. "I haven't realized how deeply I feel about this, how upset I am," he said. "I haven't talked about any of this with Theresa. I'm sure there's a part of me that wanted to say, 'Well, if you don't appreciate me I'll show you. I've got a better job than even yours!' That doesn't sound very admirable does it?"

While it may not have sounded admirable, it certainly sounded very human and Tony began to become more relaxed as he shared these feelings. Then I asked him to tell me the dream again, slowly, giving us both a chance to let it sink in a bit further.

"What comes to mind when you think of California?" I asked him.

"Sun, fun, glamour, money, show business. The high cost of living, earthquakes," he answered.

"Can you imagine how any of these characteristics may relate to your decision to accept the job?"

"Well," he began very quietly, "I think my decision was based on ego needs. Maybe because my ego was hurt and I was angry. But I was, *am* very proud of being offered this job. It symbolizes affirmation, prestige, success, and even power both in influence and my ability to make a difference in my field. These are very tempting things. I know my family would have to give up a lot but they would get a much higher standard of living in return."

"I don't believe those reasons are necessarily wrong, unless they influence us to the exclusion of other values," I responded. "But it seems like you may not have looked deeply enough into what leaving your friends, community, and the mountains you enjoy could mean on a more personal level."

"Perhaps I'd better rethink this, talk more with Theresa and the kids. Maybe I'll even talk with my chairman and just put what I'm feeling on the table. We've known each other for a long time and I would feel better if I did that."

"What happens if you change your mind?" I asked.

Tony smiled and said, "I'm sure it's not too late to reverse things if it comes to that."

As our visit was closing I explained to Tony my thoughts that the dream wasn't saying to take the job or not take the job. It was trying to show him that in making his decision, his conscious perspective had ignored a number of serious questions that would be helpful to consider carefully. By calling Tony's attention to the feelings he was denying as well as his family's emotional connection to our area, the dream was working in a *compensatory* way. As you can see in this example, compensatory dreams help us balance our perceptions and attitudes by showing us what we have left out. With more complete information we are able to act with better clarity.

Generally the decisions we have to make about our lives aren't simply ones of right or wrong. Their outcomes depend on how complete our awareness is when we make the decisions, and how this awareness affects the way we carry out the decisions. Tony went on to have serious conversations with his department chairman and family. To his surprise, his department chairman was warm and open. He intended to keep Tony's course intact even if Tony left. But, he told Tony very frankly, he believed Tony was too energetic and gifted to stay where he was. He assured Tony that as much as he would like to have Tony stay, he thought that in a few more years he would become bored and that a new opportunity might help his professional growth. He surprised Tony further by saying he'd watched him in departmental and university subcommittee meetings and thought he had a talent for administration.

When Tony spoke to his wife and family, he told them about his discussion with me and his chairman. He said that after he'd thought about it, he agreed he needed to stretch himself further professionally and that he was more ambitious than he had realized. Theresa surprised him by saying she'd also been thinking that as the kids got older, she might like to be in a place that offered more stimulation and enrichment for her than our small town did. They all realized that while living here they enjoyed rich family times, but these experiences would soon change anyway as the children began leaving for college. What they all agreed upon, however, was that in moving they should try to honor their family and community values. A bigger house, private schools, and more affluence wasn't nearly as important to them as finding a new home that offered opportunities for family enjoyment, friends, and community involvement. They decided to visit the new town and university as a family and to look the place over from this perspective. Rather than make a move based on the exuberance of their status and material gains, they were going to make it in a more balanced, thoughtful manner that respected their deep, personal values.

BEFRIENDING OUR DREAMS

Many people search their dreams in an effort to find clues that will help them make significant life decisions. However, the compensatory aspect of dreams means they help us more often by giving feedback on committed decisions we've already made. Tony's dream could have reminded him and his family of values they'd ignored that would have made his move a mistake. In this case he would have needed to find a creative way to reverse himself and stay. Generally our dreams aren't oracles helping us foretell the future. They're friends whose perspective aids us in seeing the things we've ignored in our decision-making process. Tony had made the decision and enthusiastically accepted the new job when his unconscious sent him the dream that made him reexamine his decision. With the help of the dream, Tony and his family were able to make the same choice but with a deeper understanding of the reasons and values that needed to be considered in order for the move to truly enhance their lives.

Tony figured out another aspect of his dream that he told me about later, one that showed what could happen when the right decision is made for the wrong reasons, or in his case the wrong values. As Tony mulled over the different images in the dream—the earthquakes, storms, people fleeing the city—he began to understand them clearly as signs of instability and symbolic emotional upheaval. Theresa imagined the people fleeing the city were people forced to flee from a source of life and opportunity. As Tony thought about himself as an observer in the dream, he felt that if he'd not paid attention to what he was seeing and had not tried to discover the meaning of the dream, he might have ended up like one of the crowd who were at the mercy of events.

In other words, dreams may also have what Jung called a *prospective* function. The prospective characteristic of dreams can show us in symbolic form the kind of emotional mess we can get into when we act without enough information to really know what we're doing. The "absolutely, phenomenally attractive" new position for Tony could have turned out to be a hurtful event for him and his family if they had moved without understanding the full complexity of what they were doing. The prospective quality of dreams can be very valuable because it leads us through increased awareness to reconsider what we're doing or to become more open to new directions and attitudes.

By paying attention to the dream, listening to it, and reflecting upon it, Tony was led into a process that reawakened parts of himself, renewed his sense of values, and enlivened his love of life. He was already a successful person in his profession, family, and community, a man of substance in the world in the manner I've described as *secular substance*. Tony had succeeded in developing an effective adult personality that could function and fulfill social tasks in the world of work and relationships. In psychological terms, he'd reached the level of complex consciousness and done well in it.

The dream, and the experience it led him into, took Tony away from what society generally considers the definitions of success and helped him look more closely into his inner experience and essence. This process began his journey into individual consciousness, the level of maturity where our inner lives become more important, and how we live and understand our outer lives becomes an expression of *our* values rather than society's. Beginning this process puts us on the path of growing into *sacred substance*. This is the course we take when we're seeking the inner awareness that enables us to know and live from our essential natures. Dreams and the other aspects of our unconscious are there like internal lighthouses, helping us to navigate the dark, open seas of life.

CHAPTER 9
Facing the Dark and Finding Life

If we arrange our life according to that principle which counsels us that we must always hold to the difficult, then that which now still seems to us the most alien will become what we most trust and find most faithful.
—Rainer Maria Rilke

"It was as though somebody I hated spoke from my mouth before I could silence him," said a character from a Graham Greene novel. Have you ever had a similar experience or thought? "I don't know what came over me." "I just wasn't myself." These experiences happen when something unknown within us takes over, something we don't officially recognize as a part of ourselves—surprises, little gremlins, we think, who frequently embarrass us. In other words our shadows come to the surface and are revealed. But if we begin to watch these slips closely, especially around midlife, we may find that some of them are trying to move us into new ways of living. Recently a friend of mine had one of these encounters with his shadow. When as a volunteer he was asked to run for president of our local arts alliance, he spontaneously stood up and said, "I'll do it!" Later he admitted to me, "I don't know what happened." He's a quiet, team-playing sort, someone who had previously shunned any kind of public or leadership role. "But all of a sudden," he continued, "I knew I wanted to do it and I would do a good job."

Some time later I was just as surprised at another meeting when a second friend was asked to chair an important committee and declined. "No, I don't think so" was his immediate reply. Normally this friend relishes leadership roles. "No?" I whispered to him. Looking a little sheepish, he shrugged his shoulders and whispered back, "I surprised myself. But it felt good." In a brief moment, without their realizing what was happening, the shadow had stepped into these two people's lives and changed, at least on that occasion, their habitual way of doing things.

Generally when we talk and read about the shadow, we think of its being our darker side, and therefore dangerous. Perhaps it is because we repress so much of our energy into it. But it also becomes easy to forget how much of our *positive* potential it contains. The process of becoming our own person *begins* with finding out about this shadow, for that is the only way we can learn about the molds that shaped our development. Both of my friends were thrust into new states of mind and behaviors by what appeared to be a simple slip of the tongue. But actually these slips are deceptively powerful and potentially life-changing if we pay enough attention to them. They represent new potentials trying to emerge into the sunlight of our everyday lives and new growth trying to take place in our personalities. They are important and like dreams are our friends if we choose to see them as such; and at midlife and beyond, they become even more so. They represent the potentials we've denied and pushed away.

We build our shadows as we build our identities. They're like two sides of the same coin. Every time we identify with a value such as "It's good to be active and efficient," we reject its opposite—it's as if we've said, "It's bad to be lazy and lackadaisical." Eventually our identities are based on collections of such identifications and they define who we believe we are.

Until we begin to understand the things we've denied, whenever we say the word "I," we are referring to the identifications we have made and are ignoring our capacity to be the opposite of them. For instance, if I think of myself as active and efficient, I am ignoring my capacity to be lethargic and indifferent and the ways that I actually am lazy and lackadaisical. In addition, a person might say:

FACING THE DARK

I am a man, an American, a husband, a teacher. I am active, dynamic, tolerant, competent, romantic; I love nature, enjoy sports, and so on. From an objective point of view, our identifications represent only one way of looking at things—a point of view that was shaped by the forces that influenced our development and temperament. If I choose to be introverted, I reject extroversion. If I'm literal minded, I reject intuition. If I base my decisions on logic, I reject emotions. Each decision becomes a foundation stone in building our identities because these decisions determine how we'll relate to the world, gather information, and make choices.

When we identify with something such as "I am tolerant" or "I am open-minded, fair, and honest," we've identified with values that will form our character structures. As a result of these identifications, everything that's opposite to these becomes something we don't want to be. In other words we don't want to discover how bigoted, prejudiced, inequitable, and crooked we can be. So we repress these capacities into our shadows. The shadow is a frightening reality because any serious encounter with it can threaten who we think we are, how we feel about ourselves, and the value structures we live by.

For instance, if I like to see myself as a friendly, level-headed guy that people can depend on, the experience of an explosive surge of anger will scare me. It threatens my self-image and I'll quickly seek to avoid situations where this may happen. Fear is never far away from any experience that evokes our shadows. For example, if something happens to me that can make me really angry, it forces me to exert a lot of energy trying to stay in control. If I fail, I will feel embarrassed and ashamed—and I'll be reminded once again that I don't have the mastery of my own personality I like to think I have.

Just as small children imagine they can make themselves invisible by covering their eyes with their hands, many adults imagine they can get rid of what they don't like in themselves by not looking at it. You know what I mean. It's that impulse or tendency we all to some degree share that can range from avoidance and procrastination to the little fibs we tell ourselves, or others, to avoid hurt, feelings, criticism, or rejection. Many of these fibs, however, are told primarily to ourselves so that we will continue to feel good about who we are and how we're handling things. Unfortunately the illusion of *not seeing* our unpleasant characteristics is rapidly expanded to include *not having* them, and this progression leads to seeing these displeasing qualities in other people. In the jargon of psychology we've *projected* them. Projection means attributing the features in ourselves that we've disowned onto someone else. Projection makes me think of Martha, a woman who was mad at the world. However, she denied her anger and talked about how afraid she was of her husband's temper. She had projected her anger and her fear of its power onto her husband. Or in another situation, Barry, a young man who had been brought up to be afraid of women and as a result was always acquiescent and kind to them, wondered why women were always so mean to "nice guys."

On a larger scale, our society, which wants us to be successfully adapted, productive members, teaches us not to do things that may be disruptive to the status quo, the values of our social character. Therefore we are taught to repress our powerful emotions rather than to handle them with skill and understanding. Psychologist and author Kathleen Brehony says in *Awakening at Midlife,* "Very few families teach the healthy expression of anger, for example. We don't say, 'It's okay to be angry but it's not okay to hit.' Instead we say, 'How can you behave like that to your little sister? You're bad. Go to your room.'"

Yet at a later stage, if we don't recover the power to use our emotions on our own behalfs, we'll become the victims of them. Martha may actually provoke her husband into a destructive rage at some point or her anger may also begin to fester in her unconscious until it becomes an illness. Closing our eyes to these emotions doesn't mean they've disappeared, just as holding them in has its effects. If Barry continues placating women, his resentment toward them will build until it becomes a corrosive rage that can sour his life, spoil his relationships, and threaten his health. Reclaiming the emotional power we have repressed into our shadows and learning how using it skillfully can strengthen our personalities lead to better health and more honest relationships.

FACING THE DARK

Our shadows are our most paradoxical aspects. While they seem to be the containers of the dark forces that can threaten the foundation we've built our lives on, they are also the containers of some of our best potentials for achieving balanced, more dynamic, and fulfilling lives. The very anger we were taught to fear and deny, and came to fear and deny even more when we glimpsed its smoldering presence, is like buried gold. If we can learn to safely mine and refine it, we'll be rewarded with new energy, passion, and strength.

Shadow qualities may first appear as a surprise as my two friends discovered when unlikely words sprung from their mouths. Or they may appear as a wound or embarrassment when we feel overly sensitive or resentful, misjudge someone's intentions, or become tongue-tied or uncharacteristically shy. Like dreams, with proper attention these situations can often be transformed into a helpful new awareness that improves our lives. But the *process* of refining qualities from our shadows will cost us something. We may have to lose some of our innocence or experience a feeling of shame. By innocence I mean our naive views of life, the ones that believe the values of our society and families are the true values that provide a meaningful life, that we are who we think we are, that the world is like we have been brought up to see it and we can make (and have made) choices that direct and control our lives. Frequently a loss of innocence means a loss of self-esteem because we realize we are less knowledgeable, well intentioned, virtuous, or competent than we thought we were. And a loss of self-esteem can lead to feelings of shame. I lost some of my innocence and felt some shame as well when I realized I was treating my children as impersonally as my father had treated me, something I'd vowed repeatedly I'd never do. Ellie, a friend of mine who owns her own business, lost a large piece of innocence when she discovered her oldest and most trusted employee had been stealing from her for years. And Rusty, a man in his late thirties who worked with me a few years ago, was appalled when he figured out that he'd been using his moodiness to manipulate his wife.

But the new awareness I gained through my experience caused me to become a more caring father and to enjoy fatherhood more completely. Ellie became a more mature businesswoman, who paid better attention to the actual nature and performance of her employees; and Rusty became more self-responsible and interested in his growth and healing. Shame and a loss of innocence are important parts of the human journey, and we find them repeatedly preceding experiences of transformation and redemption in the teaching stories of the past. In the ancient Greek tale *The Twelve Labors of Heracles*, Heracles' mythical journey of development begins when in a rage he murders his wife and helpless children. The twelve labors he must complete range from killing a lion, an act of bravery, to cleaning the Augean stables, which have accumulated the manure of three thousand oxen for thirty years, a humiliating task that he accomplishes with strength and intelligence. The labors culminate in a confrontation with death as Heracles overcomes Cerberus, the three-headed dog guarding the underworld, where Heracles encounters several famous ghosts.

The twelve labors, also known as "challenges," which is another meaning of the Greek word that translates as labors, actually have a collective dual purpose. The first is to purify Heracles from his past. The priestess who prescribes his labors also acknowledges his rebirth into a new identity by giving him the name Heracles. Before that his name was Alcides. The second goal of these tasks is to help Heracles attain immortality, which in mythological terms symbolizes full personal authenticity. Jung frequently used this story and its labors to illustrate how hard we must work to overcome the conditioning of our pasts, realize our true identities, and then develop our previously hidden strengths and abilities in order to become unique.

For many years I was troubled by the "slaughter of the innocents" in the Christmas story, the part where King Herod has all of the sons born in Bethlehem during the Christmas period murdered as he attempts to eliminate the Christ child. It took me a long time to realize that if we consider the Christmas story from a psychological standpoint, as a metaphor, symbolizing the birth of the spirit or new life within us, we also need to recognize that such a change requires a sacrifice, a loss of innocence.

Rilke beautifully sums up the paradoxes within our shadows by saying, "Perhaps all the dragons of our lives are princesses who are only waiting to see us once, beautiful and brave. Perhaps everything terrible is in its deepest being something that needs our love." In the next pages I'd like to invite you to join me in looking at how our shadows hold our potentials while reflecting many of the paradoxes we live in, and how they help us challenge ourselves to new growth and meaning.

Respecting the Objectionable

The journey into wholeness means we have to learn to respect the *other* voice that speaks within us. It means to pay attention to our emotions, thoughts, dreams, and fantasies even when they're unpleasant and objectionable. At midlife, the time when we're challenged to grow beyond the ordinary state of adulthood that I've labeled complex consciousness, our psyches invite us to meet our inner devils and angels. The invitations come in symbolic form through slips of the tongue, through new or unusually intense feelings, and through our dreams and reflections. It takes courage to begin admitting there are parts of ourselves that are strangers and yet with whom in some odd way we feel a kinship.

Appreciating the attraction and the fear our shadows arouse in us reminds me of a captivating Hans Christian Andersen fairy tale called, coincidentally enough, "The Shadow." In many ways the story's symbolism is simple and direct. It opens with a young man who has traveled to a tropical country to become a writer. He is described as a scholar from the colder region of the north. In story language it isn't hard to imagine that the narrator is presenting him as a man who needs to warm up his nature and learn to experience some of the power of passion and suffering pictured so well in the life and art of southern Europe.

One evening after he has been there a while, the scholar is sitting in the dim lamplight of his room when he begins to notice his shadow on the wall. He sees that in the dim light it's longer than he is, that it moves when he does, and that he can affect its shape by how he stands in the light. His fascination with his shadow grows and becomes kind of a nightly ritual. Then one night he's awakened from a deep sleep by a radiant light, and for a brief moment he catches sight of a beautiful young woman in the window of the house across the street. He jumps from bed and creeps to his own window, but as he is looking the radiance fades away and the night is dark again. The next morning when he awakens he discovers his shadow is gone.

But the young scholar is not dismayed. He returns to his own land and concentrates on writing books about the good, the true, and the beautiful. By this point in the story we can begin to see the lesson that is unfolding. The beautiful young woman, a symbol of life in folklore according to Joseph Campbell, has tried to wake the scholar up, to help him desire to seek and experience life in its many dimensions. But by remaining idealistic, the scholar has separated himself from his capacity to be courageous, passionate, and ambitious—the powers of the heart that could cause him to fully engage in life with blood, sweat, tears, and laughter. These capacities have been repressed into his "shadow" and live separately from him, we can assume, in his unconscious and outside of his awareness. Many years later, however, he hears a knock on his door and discovers his old shadow has returned. It is obvious that his shadow has become a man of substance; it is dressed as a person who is rich and powerful. When the scholar asks the shadow why he left him, the shadow replies that it was for the beautiful woman who'd been across the street. The shadow explains that he met her, explored the many rooms of the house, and learned everything there was to know about life. Then the shadow tells the scholar that he has to say good-bye. Before leaving he gives the scholar his card and lets him know where he can be found. Of course the scholar never goes to visit him.

As the lesson of the story continues we see that the shadow is making an effort to contact the scholar. Our shadows often knock on the doors of our awareness as you saw in my opening examples in this chapter. When we have become closed and rigid, we repress even more of ourselves and our shadows grow in proportion to how much we cut ourselves off from life's experiences and vitality. Like many of us, the scholar doesn't want to risk change or having to reevaluate the principles he lives by, and therefore he doesn't make any effort to pursue his relationship with the shadow.

Two themes now seem to be coming into perspective in the story. The first is of separation, which the scholar, though fascinated with his shadow, is quite comfortable staying apart from. It often seems more comfortable to keep a safe distance from life rather than to risk the tumultuous effects it can have on us when we become passionately involved in it. The second theme is how life seems attracted to the shadow, which becomes enriched by it; and this theme continues.

As time passes, the scholar, now a writer, continues to focus on the good, the true, and the beautiful, but his books don't sell and he comes to remark, "No one seems to care about it. I am quite in despair and take it to heart very much." Soon it seems that everything is going wrong for him and after a prolonged illness, people begin to say to him, "You really look like a shadow." This curious reversal of destiny sounds very much like the despair that overtakes us at midlife if we haven't had the courage to grow beyond the molds of our youth. Almost without our knowing it, the substance can quietly leak out of our lives.

At last the shadow returns to visit the scholar again and it appears even more wealthy and powerful than before. It is even about to marry the princess of their kingdom. Then a strange thing happens. The shadow feels sorry for the scholar and hires him to become his shadow. Thus the shadow becomes the master and the scholar the shadow. While the shadow offers to reward the scholar with a rich, comfortable life, the scholar is envious of his success and seeks to expose him to the princess. In self-defense the clever shadow convinces the princess the scholar is mad and they have him imprisoned. The story ends with the scholar's execution.

This story leaves us on a sad note. It teaches us that when we refuse the opportunity to meet our devils and our angels, we not only rob our lives of their rich potentials, we actually endanger them. When too much of our unlived lives are held repressed within us, they can eventually coalesce and become more powerful than we are, just as happened with the unhappy scholar's shadow or when Mr. Hyde took over the life of Dr. Jekyll in the story by Robert Louis Stevenson. While the scholar's life dried up, the shadow's flourished—it became healthy, substantial, and beloved by the king's daughter. When we lose ourselves, we may become physically ill, depressed, lost in an addiction, or simply on the way to a bitter old age. Each time we uncover and assimilate a piece of the shadow, it strengthens and broadens our personalities in preparation for living more energetically and meeting the future with confidence.

Reclaiming ourselves means recognizing and accepting the parts of us that we shunted into our unconscious. It means realizing our duality: that we're capable of fear and courage, generosity and selfishness, vulnerability and strength, love, and the desire for power. None of these things cancels the other out. When we reclaim the ones we've banished, it does more, much more than bring balance to our personalities. It makes us more complex, more complete, and thus in more control of deeper, fuller, more satisfying lives. It offers us a full range of power in our responses to life. We don't live in an either/or world. Our fear may give birth to courage, our vulnerability to strength, our despair to creativity, our denial to integrity, and our drivenness to love.

From the way I've described the shadow it should be clear that it's usually the opposite of the "public face," the persona we like to believe is the way people see us. If we remember that dreams are trying to reveal us to ourselves then we shouldn't be surprised to discover that at midlife, when it's time for us to look inside of ourselves, our shadows will show up through interesting and sometimes disturbing images.

Thinking of appearances and opposites brings to mind the first time I met Margaret. I was immediately impressed when I saw her. As a forty-four-year-old graphic artist she presented herself with poise and professionalism. During our initial conversation she was self-assured, articulate, and showed a good sense of humor, especially when describing the plate-spinning balancing acts that define our family lives today. While we were talking I noticed she referred to her age several times, almost as if time was running out. She was married and her children were in high school. I wondered what unlived desire might be pushing her.

Margaret belonged to an association for businesswomen. At one of their luncheons the speaker had addressed several topics concerning midlife changes. During the discussion period the group focused on the many issues common to midlife. While listening, Margaret realized that she'd been experiencing a growing feeling of restlessness for over a year, and decided she wanted to find out more about herself. It was with this simple goal that she came to see me. "I want to find out what's making me feel restless," she said, "and I want to figure out what living an authentic life really means."

We spent a few hours getting to know each other and helping me to get a broad picture of the landscape of her life. During that time I asked Margaret if she ever dreamed and she answered, "Yes, but I have trouble remembering them."

Then one morning she came in and told me she had remembered a dream. In the dream she was in a foreign city, perhaps London, and had decided to go shopping. In the next scene she found herself walking in an area that was full of smart shops and attractive people. While she was strolling down the street she noticed a rather large woman approaching her. At first the woman appeared old and dirty and Margaret thought she might be a homeless person looking for a handout. As the woman got closer, Margaret saw she was dressed like a gypsy, not garishly, but in colorful old-fashioned clothes that had become worn and faded. She was wearing a wide-brim, rumpled velvet hat with several bright feathers in it.

The woman's face was so intense and her eyes so dark, it frightened Margaret. The woman began gesturing strongly as if she had something urgent and important to say. "But," Margaret continued, "she was speaking in some foreign language that I couldn't understand. I was so stunned by her confrontation that I just stood there. She wasn't begging but she wanted something. Suddenly I felt time was running out and I hurried across the street. Feeling guilty I looked back and I could see her standing there, her back to me, shoulders drooping, arms hanging limply at her sides. On her back was a sign that read, 'I am the way!'"

Most dreams are about ourselves and reflect the stories and images particular to the patterns of life we're living out. For instance, figures that are the same gender as we are represent aspects of our personalities that, like the gypsy woman in this dream, we consider part of our shadows. In other words the dream is trying to reveal something to us we don't normally identify with or want to see as part of ourselves.

While we were talking about the dream, Margaret admitted it frightened her and yet she was drawn to it. The strong image of the woman and the curious sign on her back kept returning to her mind. I was also struck by these images and as I was thinking about the dream, I wondered why London was the setting for it. When I asked Margaret if London had any special significance for her, she told me that she'd taken a year out of college to study art there and then for several years had struggled with whether to become an artist or marry and pursue a career. "I did the adult thing I guess, and made the practical decision to start my career," she explained. London, as it turned out, had several meanings for her. It represented a road not taken earlier in her life and yet was still a path that called to her and that she hoped to take in the future.

We also considered the costume of the gypsy woman, colorful but faded. And the velvet hat, once striking but now rumpled though its feathers were still bright and alive. All-in-all this woman was a figure that still suggested life, intensity, and a sense of something beyond the ordinary. Of course this woman frightened Margaret in the dream. She was on a fashionable street being approached by a formidable person who was everything but fashionable. Margaret didn't know what the woman wanted and couldn't communicate with her. Margaret fled fearing the woman might make a scene and embarrass her.

At this point Margaret and I began to muse about what it might mean if this woman was picturing some kind of energy in Margaret, perhaps her desire to be an artist, or to live more intensely, or to risk freeing herself from the careful rules and values she'd identified with to become successful, competent, and to have such an impressive appearance. Such musing can be exhilarating, but like the woman in the dream it can also be frightening. This kind of gypsy energy can make us feel ashamed and vulnerable in the face of our own value judgments.

Margaret's dream is rich in the potential substance that can be mined from her shadow. The more she can reflect on it, journal about it, and perhaps even try to dialogue with the gypsy woman, the more of herself she may be able to reclaim. As poetic figures, gypsies have been with us for centuries, symbolizing a life of earthly vitality, risk, and sensuality outside of ordinary social values. And this particular gypsy is certainly seeking recognition. We will return to Margaret's powerful dream later.

There are other kinds of dreams that show the characteristics of our shadows. They bring us face-to-face with some of the more everyday, but still important, aspects of ourselves that need our conscious attention to straighten out or reclaim. For example, Christina, who was in her early thirties, told me that she would often dream of being in a car with her mother. In every dream, the car was Christina's and her mother was driving. When I asked Christina to tell me the qualities she liked the least about her mother, it became apparent she had some strong feelings of anger and resentment. Christina said her mother had been anxious and demanding—qualities that made her appear needy and dependent—almost as long as she could remember.

Listing these qualities isn't difficult, but the next step becomes more challenging. When we remember that dreams are usually about ourselves, we then have to ask what the dream is picturing in our personalities that *we aren't aware of.* The question for Christina to reflect on is how *she* might be anxious, needy, and dependent without realizing it, and how these feelings may drive and control her life. While she was reflecting on this dream, Christina was courageous enough to ask her husband if he saw any of these characteristics of her mother in her. While her husband was kind and tactful in his answers, Christina was shocked to learn that not only did he see them, he felt helpless in trying to deal with these aspects of her personality and their harmful impact on their marriage.

Situations like this one may make us agree with Jung's observation that facing our shadows is a Herculean task—a mission that is both profound and transforming. It's hard, tough, humiliating work. We may need the support and safety of a therapist's office, a close friend, or a kind and loving partner. But it was also helpful for Christina to understand these were shadow qualities that were structured into her personality early on—and now that she had some emotional distance from them, her range of behavioral choices increased and they could no longer define her. Dreams acting as a radar screen for our minds can help us see the course of these characteristics and then like an air traffic controller, we can prevent collisions.

Christina discovered this work had another dimension as well. Once she had a better perspective on these negative energies within herself, they were no longer so glaring in her mother. Her work freed her to see some of her mother's positive qualities, like her quick sense of humor and her loyalty to the family. Christina learned that once we spot the channel markers that will lead us through the shoals and shifting currents, we can gain the pleasure of sailing on the open sea. Her work also shows how important it is to become *aware* of our shadow qualities, to *confront* and seek to *understand* them, and to try to *refine* and *integrate* them into our lives and personalities. This one piece of work was immensely gratifying to Christina. She ended up feeling better about herself, more satisfied with her marriage, and able to have a more fulfilling relationship with her mother.

FACING THE DARK

Exploring the Shadow Land

Once we begin to realize how much our identities are shaped by outside forces, it's easier to see how childhood becomes a series of losses—personal losses of will, spirit, and essence. It is frequently a paradox that when we grow, we also lose part of ourselves. For example, as I mentioned earlier, we aren't taught how to be angry; we're taught to "behave yourself," which teaches us to misjudge and condemn the feelings we're experiencing. In order to fit in we have to sit quietly at the dinner table, or sit docilely at our desks in school to keep from being sent to the principal's office. Consequently, we learn to be still, quiet, and afraid to act. In the childhood pictures we draw, we're taught the grass has to be colored green and the sky blue, and it must all be carefully done within the lines. We learn to follow instructions, moderate our expressions of love, hide our fear, and be ashamed of our tears. What's more we learn to adopt the will, desires, and values superimposed by the social patterns around us; to be competitive, constantly evaluating ourselves; to seek rewards, satisfaction, and even self-esteem by doing well and being affirmed by other people in respect to these same standards. The end result of all this is an adult life based on self-gratifying needs, or what I've called sickly selfishness. When instead what serves us most is to step outside of the social structure to cultivate a life of substance or sacred selfishness.

Growing up means embracing the life of the outer world and finding a place in it. Once we've basically accomplished this task, usually around midlife, it makes sense to consider that if we're to mature into our full possibilities, we must reverse our course and learn more about our inner worlds. From this time on our growth will have to come from inside ourselves so that our true qualities and feelings can be recognized and lived. Embracing life at this point is a choice, and if we make that choice, it begins with an exploration of our shadows.

Dreams

There are several useful methods for exploring the territory where our shadows reside. The first method, as we've seen, is by looking at the figures in our *dreams* who share the same sex as we do. When our dreams include familiar figures, known figures like our mothers, it usually means some old wounds and unconscious feelings need tending to, healing, and understanding.

Let me give you an example of another dream, of a professional man in his early forties. Tim dreamed he was home in bed with his wife when a large man in jeans and a T-shirt started breaking down the door. The man looked rough and strong, but also had a large beer belly. Tim said that in the dream he was scared and knew he had to get up to defend them. However, he couldn't move because his wife was lying on top of him and seemed oblivious to the danger. You might imagine that Tim may have been socialized to disown his masculine power and was easily smothered by his wife's criticism and/or by his own unconscious passivity. But whatever Tim's dream turns out to mean, exploring his early life and the conclusions he drew about himself will be an important part of reclaiming his sense of personal empowerment.

Christina's and Tim's dreams occurred in the everyday landscape of their lives and include figures well known to them. Margaret's dream of the gypsy woman in London reflects a foreign landscape and a shadow figure that are more removed from her daily experiences. Dreams like this one come from a deeper level within us and call for a more profound exploration into the conclusions we've drawn about who we are and how we should live.

Normally I befriend a dream, as I've explained earlier, by giving it attention, listening to it, questioning it, and reflecting upon it. When a shadow figure is involved like Christina's mother or Tim's intruder, I also like to list all of the negative associations I have for the figure and then all of the positive ones. I asked Christina to tell me what she didn't like about her mother and then what she enjoyed about her, and suggested to Tim that he make a list of his

FACING THE DARK

associations, too. These connections often help open the door to understanding these figures.

Personal Reflections

A second method for exploring the territory of the shadow is through *personal reflection.* Writing these reflections in our journals gives us a safe place to pursue them to their conclusions and keep a record of them. I think it's useful to pay careful attention to the particulars of our days in order to isolate events that make us feel anxious or uncomfortable.

Roberta, a manager of the leasing section of a large real estate firm, told me that when she looked over her journal after the first week she was surprised to see how many times she was frightened by the grumpy attitude of her boss. Roberta knew she did her job well and that her boss was pleased with her work. Yet when confronted with an authority figure's bad mood, she immediately felt afraid. This awareness led Roberta to try and pinpoint other similar situations or incidents in her life. She was soon able to list a number of times when her anxiety threatened her self-esteem. Roberta then began to review her life and early experiences with fear and soon remembered how afraid she'd been as a child of her big, tough-looking stepfather and how carefully she had always behaved around him. When she looked back on him through her now grown-up eyes, she realized he'd never harmed or threatened her. It was his strong, quiet persona and his moods that had amplified the insecurity she already felt as a stepdaughter. Awareness of the source of her fear and the automatic response it had become enabled Roberta to reclaim her usual equilibrium and self-esteem. She was even able to have a talk with her boss about how his moods affected the office staff.

It's also helpful to notice when we make other people feel uncomfortable without intending to. Along this line I remember how Nate discovered he was intimidating the employees in his framing shop without realizing it. One day when he thought he was explaining how to set up a new display to one of his young employees, he noticed a stricken look on her face. That night when he was writing in his journal he remembered her look. The more he thought about it, the more it seemed to haunt him. When he went to work the next day he asked the young woman why she had looked that way, and whether he had said something that offended her. He explained that he thought he'd been talking in a casual, easygoing manner. She responded, "Well it must have been your casual voice of command, because you were explaining things in such detail you were making me feel pretty stupid in front of everyone else." Nate was astonished for he hadn't meant to intimidate or insult her. As he thought about it, however, he believed she might be right. He realized that he could drop into an impersonal "let's get the job done" attitude and push people pretty hard.

Another way of exploring our shadows is to look for how we feel when our opinions or favorite beliefs are challenged. For example when I was growing up in the south in the forties and early fifties, most people were staunch Democrats. They would become very angry at neighbors who voted Republican no matter who the candidate was. A conviction that isn't based on moral or ethical principles is usually the result of an indoctrination, and it is just this kind of social and family pressure that pushes our ability to think or feel for ourselves into our shadows.

A friend of mine who is an elementary school principal recently told me what a difficult time he has getting parents to let their children do their homework without the parents' help. The parents generally answer him by saying their children have too much homework, and that they won't do well in school if they don't finish it, and (I'm sure you know what's coming) if they don't have good grades they won't get into a good college. My friend's response is that it's more important for the children to learn to struggle with their work, face the consequences if they don't do it, and talk to the teacher if they're having difficulty with getting it done. This teaches them to become self-responsible. While I agree with my friend, I also understand the fear of failure that clouds our culture and the conviction it engenders that there are no second chances. This is part of our societal shadow, the dark side of the social character.

In our reflections it's helpful to remember that any experience of the shadow results in uncommonly strong feelings. Strong resentment, intense anger, repugnance, contempt, revulsion, and loathing live close to shadow territory. So do the more positive feelings of deference, intense admiration, and adoration. These feelings can lead us to understand that many common statements we make or hear are revealing parts of our shadows. Often, they carry hidden messages that can help us learn more about ourselves. Consider the following statements, which might identify our shadows by exposing our exaggerated feelings about other people:

- *She's got to be in charge of everything.*

- *I wish I could speak as well as he does.*

- *I just can't believe she did that.*

- *He's disgusting.*

- *Her book was awesome.*

These next statements may reveal our shadows speaking in a language of exaggerated anger or resentment about other people's faults:

- *He never gets to work on time.*

- *Look how fat she's gotten.*

- *His kids are out of control.*

- *I can't stand her hypocritical attitude.*

In the following expressions we can single out our shadows by paying attention to the feedback they inspire in other people that show we are exasperating them or making them feel belittled:

- *Don't you think it's time to let go of that?*

- *It's the third time you've forgotten our anniversary.*

- *You don't call when you're late.*

Sometimes our shadows appear through slips of the tongue and in accidental or compulsive acts:

- *Oops, I didn't really say that did I?*

- *I'm so sorry. I didn't mean to spill that.*

- *Oh dear, I didn't hurt you did I?*

- *I knew I shouldn't have gone there.*

And in many cases our shadows may become evident by the satisfaction we get from other people's failings:

- *She finally got what she deserved.*

- *That should take him down a notch.*

- *I told him he should be more careful.*

- *I knew she was courting disaster.*

Projections

A third method for exploring our shadows and coaxing them into the light is to study our *projections*. Earlier I said that a projection is when we see some feature of ourselves that we've disowned in someone else. When the contents of our shadows remain unconscious we'll see them all around us in other people. Cathy, for example, resents her wealthy sister-in-law, who she considers arrogant and a person who enjoys showing her affluence. "At our family Thanksgiving dinner," Cathy told me, "she hardly spoke to anyone and her son refused to play with the other children." In addition, she continued, she usually wears expensive, tailored clothes while everyone else dresses more comfortably. Perhaps, Cathy's sister-in-law is slightly arrogant, enjoys her prosperous lifestyle, and feels a bit put off by the rest of the family's careless approach to how they look and behave. Generally there has to be a small hook of truth to elicit our projection. In most cases that's why we project something onto one person and not onto another one. However, the amount of arrogance Cathy sees because of her projection is probably greater than the reality.

In psychological terms this process is known as a *defense mechanism*, and it works to protect us from having painful realizations about ourselves. It allows Cathy to be arrogant, to remain safely unconscious of it, and to keep her ideal image of herself intact. Cathy can be resentful of her sister-in-law, treat her coldly or with hostility, and justify her own behavior by claiming, "She's treating me arrogantly." In our daily lives we see projection-based antagonisms going on all the time between family members, friends, colleagues, and even strangers. In a larger context, this same mechanism also works between ideological or political groups like religious conservatives and gays, or between pro-life and pro-choice advocates, between militia groups and the government, and between nations that have long learned to demonize each other.

While this defense works as a psychological process, it's also very destructive. It distorts reality, alienates us from each other, and frequently leads to conflicts. When Soviet President Mikhail Gorbachev told President Ronald Reagan that by agreeing to declare a détente with the United States he would be performing the greatest disservice possible to the United States by removing our enemy, he knew exactly what this statement implied. To not have an enemy onto whom we could project our darkness left it all right here for us to have to deal with in our politics, institutions, businesses, and city streets.

Projections are a natural, unavoidable process and are not a pathological problem that needs to be cured. We can't stop them, control them, or predict what they will fall on. But we can learn to see them as a great way to learn more about ourselves; like a periscope that can see around corners and over barriers, they can help us discover things about ourselves that are usually walled off. Yet, if we fail to spot them they can get us into conflict after conflict.

We often find ourselves putting some of our larger shadow projections onto our partners. For years Joe had been angry and resentful at his wife for how much money she spent and how she maintained their checkbook. Every month when he sat down to pay the bills, their relationship became tense and stormy. In fact Joe had never been all that good with numbers himself. Furthermore when he was a teenager his father had gone bankrupt and Joe had felt badly embarrassed in front of his friends and classmates. When his wife finally became exhausted by his outbursts of temper and his anxiety over how much money she spent, she insisted they see a marriage counselor. Then in a safe atmosphere she quietly reminded him about the many things he'd purchased that weren't in their budget. She told Joe she would help him both with the budget and his fear, but that when he was upset he drove her away by projecting all of the blame for his anxiety on her, and the more she resented him the more she wanted to spend.

The development of self-knowledge and understanding of how projections happen is the way we reverse these interactions. Catching ourselves when we are about to project is very much like discerning our shadow qualities. First we must learn to recognize the signs. Remember I said that intense emotional responses like strong resentment, rage, repugnance, contempt, loathing, and even more positive feelings like deference, intense admiration, and adoration often indicate when we are dealing with our shadows. When these responses are directed toward a person they usually mean that we've projected a piece of our shadows onto them. As this happens we need to begin questioning ourselves, journaling about our experiences, and trying to figure out what this situation can tell us about ourselves. Like journaling and befriending our dreams, getting acquainted with our shadows and figuring out what our projections mean call for slowing down, paying attention to life's details and to what we're feeling, and giving ourselves the space to feel safe to do our inner work.

Advantages of Having the Courage to Uncover Our Shadows

- We open ourselves to our humanity, which brings us a natural feeling of being grounded in life and open to it.

- By understanding ourselves we increase our feelings of completeness, personal power, and energy.

- We regain our awareness of our true potentials, especially those the social character has taught us to deny.

- We refuse to lend our participation to emotionally charged conflicts.

The Dance of Virtues and Vices

We've seen that forming our identities causes us to split ourselves into two parts: identity and shadow. Because of this split we often find ourselves in confusing inner and outer conflicts; sometimes we find we're our own worst enemies when trying to pursue certain goals. There's no way around it; to become a person of substance in the world we must have a guiding sense of what's right and what's wrong. We must have virtues we can identify with in order to form ethics and character. Yet as we form our characters we're also forming shadows that will bring us into conflict with other people and ourselves. But, *we are only trapped in this position if we refuse to grow in self-awareness.* If we choose the path of individuation and seek to grow beyond the mind-sets and indoctrinations of our pasts, we can rediscover and reconnect with the unknown parts of ourselves, and this reunification will give us an increased feeling of being at home in ourselves.

In her lovely book of healing stories, *Kitchen Table Wisdom*, Rachel Naomi Remen shares an encounter she had with famous psychotherapist Carl Rogers during her medical training. Carl Rogers, one of the twentieth century's greatest healers, based his work totally on respecting people, giving them his full attention and listening to them with great care. But Rachel Naomi Remen discovered there was something more powerful than knowledge and technique in the room when Carl Rogers was there. It was his *presence*. Before he began his clinical demonstration, Rogers said to the medical students, "Before every session I take a moment to remember my humanity.... There is no experience that this man has that I cannot share with him, no fear that I cannot understand, no suffering that I cannot care about, because I too am human. No matter how deep his wound, he does not need to be ashamed in front of me. I too am vulnerable. And because of this, *I am enough.* Whatever his story, he no longer needs to be alone with it. This is what will allow his healing to begin."

Carl Rogers was a man who'd come to terms with his shadow, who let it remind him that we're all human while it also reminded him that we possess, no matter what our state in most cases, unseen, unimagined potential.

Over the centuries our culture has evolved a set of virtues that we consider outstanding and a list of vices we regard as destructive to our general welfare. Our cardinal virtues are commonly thought to be humility, generosity, temperance, love, moderation, patience, and industry. The corresponding list of vices is pride, covetousness, lust, envy, gluttony, anger, and sloth. Several years ago when I was speaking to a group of spiritual directors I began to wonder what it really feels like when we are taught to identify with a virtue like humility and thereby repress its opposite, pride, into our shadows.

For instance, if I do a good job of being humble will I secretly become proud of how virtuous I am? Might I even become arrogant and critical of people who are less humble than I am?

Of course teaching virtues is intended to help us grow into responsible adults. But if we learn this lesson too rigidly we will end up splitting ourselves because we will polarize our feelings of responsibility and freedom. Acting virtuously or responsibly is supposed to make us feel good, superior, and worthy of respect and admiration. Acting irresponsibly becomes a vice and makes us feel ashamed, unworthy, and bad.

However, as I reflected on my life experiences it didn't take long for me to realize that my efforts to be good backfired sometimes or caught me in traps. Whenever I tried to be intentionally self-effacing, I found I was fairly successful. But then I would often feel proud of how good I'd been, which made me feel like a hypocrite because of my growing arrogance. I also learned early in my life that the self-effacing courtesy of some people gave them an excellent cover for manipulative and aggressive activities. Very quickly I realized how connected these two opposite things are and when we split them and repress the vice, it gains a life and energy of its own.

Nevertheless, virtues remain important as signposts in our development and as guides for getting along with each other. But recognizing the dance between virtues and vices, between the "good" person we have been taught to be and the "bad" person we have learned to repress, can help us become more alive, human, and less critical of ourselves and other people. If we polarize ourselves we may end up defeated by life like the scholar was who stuck to the good, the true, and the beautiful—or rather his very restricted idea of the good, the true, and the beautiful—in the fairy tale.

Once I began my midlife transition and explored my shadow carefully, I arrived at some interesting conclusions. The more honestly and authentically I tried to live, the more I was accused of being arrogant. Then I realized that living honestly brought me into conflict with some of the conventional models I had internalized. Actually people were accusing me of being arrogant for not doing what *they* wanted me to or for not living the way *they* thought I should. Sometimes I even became confused myself and wondered if I was putting my self-interests ahead of the needs of my family.

From this struggle I learned that I needed a system of ethics and morality to act as a container for my efforts to both grow and live responsibly. The idea of living an authentic life is not as simple as just doing whatever comes to mind. I had to learn to struggle between the contradictory aspects of conventional morality and the moral duty I believe I have to grow as a person. Without that struggle there's no true inner growth. To avoid the struggle is like trying to refine gold without fire.

The next thing I discovered was that the more I learned about my shadow, the more humble I became without making any efforts to be self-effacing. Like Carl Rogers, I realized how all of the aspects of being human were within my reach. What humbled me, however, was learning how often I had acted in ways I hadn't intended to and how many things I'd done I was ashamed of and hadn't admitted to myself previously.

Carl Rogers, whom I'd met, had a very earthy, substantial presence. It came from his great self-awareness and the balance he kept between himself and his shadow. Self-knowledge brings humility. It also brings the awareness that there's a proper time to be arrogant and proud. In his memoirs about his friend Ernest Hemingway, A. E. Hotchner observed that it was Hemingway's pride that goaded him into writing his Pulitzer Prize–winning novel *The Old Man and the Sea,* following the heartbreaking failure of his previous novel.

Psychological maturity reveals that every virtue can have an unseen negative effect. Humility can make us passive, compliant, and it can cause us to build up an unconscious volcano of resentment or even pride in our "virtuous" behavior. On the other hand, a vice, like pride, can have a positive effect, urging us to reach beyond what we think are our abilities, to respect ourselves and even save us from despair as it did Hemingway.

The more we learn to work with our shadow material, the more our efforts will help us rediscover and enjoy a fuller share of our humanity. As we understand ourselves better we gain confidence, strength, and energy; we regain the potentials we pushed aside earlier and uncover new ones.

CHAPTER 10
Sacred Selfishness—
Learning to Love Ourselves

I have always tried to understand "love your neighbor as yourself" because it seems so easy for us to treat ourselves harshly and with neglect. I believe the search for peace and joy begins with truly loving ourselves.
—Massimilla M. Harris

Nikos Kazantzakis's grand novel *Zorba the Greek* begins with a young bookish writer traveling south to the island of Crete. On the last segment of his voyage he spots someone who is his opposite—the grizzled, robust man of action Alexis Zorba—and is immediately fascinated by him. Up to this point the story is similar to Andersen's fairy tale "The Shadow," where the young scholar travels south and becomes interested in his shadow. But in the warmer climate the young man in the fairy tale loses his shadow in a manner that eventually leads him to despair and finally destruction. The outcome of Kazantzakis's story is just the opposite.

Zorba refers to the bookish young man who he has convinced to hire him as "boss," and it becomes apparent that Boss is the narrator of the story. Boss and Zorba are clearly two completely different kinds of men. Boss is shy and retiring, a man of books, while Zorba is a strong, earthy man educated by experience. We can see this story as an allegory, where Zorba represents the qualities Boss has repressed into his shadow. When we meet someone who personifies helpful aspects of our shadows, we usually find that person fascinating and yet suspicious and intimidating. Interestingly, however, Boss overcomes his doubts and accepts his attraction to Zorba and pursues his friendship. As the book unfolds it becomes the story of a friendship that grows into love instead of a story of estrangement like we saw in the fairy tale. The journey of Boss and Zorba's developing friendship is a long one, beautifully written and also made into one of those rare films that actually brings a great novel to life. Even though Zorba is moody, sometimes intimidating, and not always easy to understand or get along with, he initiates Boss in the experience of being fully alive. He teaches him to plunge wholeheartedly into living, to experience love, to accept suffering, to take risks, and to laugh at failure. He explains that "life is trouble" and that women must be loved.

Zorba teaches Boss everything the shadow could have taught the scholar in Andersen's fairy tale if they hadn't become separated. In his final bit of advice, Zorba tells Boss he needs a "little madness" to help him cut the string that binds him to his conventional attitudes. As the story approaches its end, Zorba looks at Boss and says, "I've never loved another man as much as I have you." And then Boss asks Zorba to teach him to dance before they part. In the book, Zorba looks at Boss when they've finished dancing and says, "Now that you, my boy, can dance as well and have learnt my language what shan't we be able to tell each other!"

"Love is difficult," the poet Rilke explains in contrast to the sentimental way we like to think of it. We prefer to believe that love brings happiness, ease, companionship, or at least security. And, if love is present there should be no explosions, sharp edges, or potholes in its course. But this perspective trivializes love, makes it shallow and frivolous because we know life isn't like that and so love can't be that way either. And yet we're always trying to make it light and easy, something that anyone can do without developing the strength, commitment, and character required by what Rilke described as "the most difficult of all our tasks."

LEARNING TO LOVE OURSELVES

Love was demanding for Boss and Zorba. There were many times when Boss was skeptical of Zorba and he felt he was being taken advantage of. Zorba, too, had his moments of frustration with Boss's timid attitude and the distance from life he maintained. The growth of their friendship was a journey of getting to know, accepting, and learning from each other. The same pattern holds just as true when we are trying to learn how to love ourselves in a significant way. Cultivating self-love is also an odyssey with moments of difficulty and of joy. It's an excursion into knowing ourselves, learning to accept and deal with what we discover and how to relate to the new members of our "commonwealth," and struggling with our fear of allowing in a little madness to set us free.

Loving ourselves means recognizing how bound we are to practicality and convention like Boss, who nearly wept when he said, "As a child I had been full of mad impulses, superhuman desires, I was not content with the world. Gradually as time went by, I grew calmer. I set limits, separated the possible from the impossible, the human from the divine, I held my kite tightly, so that it should not escape." Boss, like all of us, learned to limit his imagination and the desires of his heart. The shadow qualities that Zorba pictures—his living from the heart—frees us from these bonds and opens us once again to joy. Years later when Boss reflects on his experiences with Zorba, he concludes that Zorba's purpose in his life was to create joy.

I often get the feeling that self-love is a taboo in our society, something we think of as forbidden, profane, or dangerous. We associate it with excess: We can't have just a little of it, or just enough either. It's all out, like shopping sprees and outlandish vacations. It's a misunderstood term that reflects how little we know about love. Self-love is the firm foundation that determines how strongly we can give love and receive love. Without it our structures of relationship will crumble under the pressure of the smallest storm. Self-love is neither selfish nor narcissistic. I have defined selfishness in its negative sense as being sickly, egotistic, and self-centered, a hunger for power and affirmation that uses others for self-serving ends. Narcissism is also like selfishness in its negative form. It is self-infatuation, an obsession that actually reflects an inability to love oneself or anyone else.

I've also defined *sacred selfishness* as a second kind of selfishness that represents the opposite pole of how we usually think of selfishness. Sacred selfishness means making the commitment to become people of *substance,* people who are filled with gold, who aren't hollow or filled with lead. It's a commitment to building the footings that will support our growing capacity to give and receive love. Sacred selfishness leads to what Emerson referred to as "character—a reserve force which acts directly by presence, and without means." We can see this kind of substance developing in Boss through Zorba's instruction. He taught Boss compassion by tenderly caring for a dying old woman who had grand illusions; cunning in the way he tricked a religious order into letting them use the monastery's land; courage in accepting the love of a beautiful widow and in recognizing his desire for her; ambition in the scheme he developed for harvesting the timber on Boss's land; to face death when the old lady died and when the widow was murdered; and finally to laugh when their plans for success failed. In each situation Boss learned to open and change himself and to engage in life in a new, more active way.

Growth is what life is about. And we must realize that when we're beginners in any new phase or activity, especially in something as difficult as the art of self-love; we must be willing to learn step-by-step, experience-by-experience. Otherwise it's too easy to fall into the popular way of thinking that there should be an easy answer, or that self-love can be a change in attitude rather than a journey. All too often we try to make ourselves think love should be easy, even exhilarating, because we've lost our ability to see that our dedication to a great work is rewarding no matter how challenging. Inner work is noble work and I've compared it to constructing a great cathedral or temple, a work that begins with building a solid foundation, and continues as we patiently add piece after piece. At the same time it has an ambitious design in mind, a purpose that combines work and beauty, and in this way it reaches beyond ourselves toward the heavens. Learning about love is also a great work, and inner work performed in the spirit of individuation is an expression of love.

Thinking about life and love as great works reminds me of a story told by Rachel Naomi Remen. The story begins with three stonecutters being interviewed about building a cathedral in the fourteenth century. When the first stonecutter is asked what he's doing, he replies with bitterness that he's cutting stones into blocks, a foot by a foot by three-quarters of a foot. With a defeated look he complains he'll follow this tedious path for the rest of his life. The second stonecutter, who is performing the same work, answers with more warmth. He tells the interviewer he's earning a nice living for his family, which provides them food, clothes, and a loving home. The third stonecutter, however, responds to the interviewer's question with pride and exaltation that he's participating in the building of a great cathedral that will welcome people for a thousand years. Whether we have the vision to see that we're contributing to a great work often defines the spirit of our lives and whether we live them with a sense of joy and purpose.

Learning to know and dance with our shadows as Boss did with Zorba's help, leads us to the place where we can relate to what Carl Rogers said, "There is no experience that I have had that I cannot share with myself, no fear I cannot understand, no suffering that I cannot care about, because I am human." And yet, in a radically achievement-oriented, bottom-line society, it shouldn't be difficult to understand why we find it hard to have a deep sense of love for ourselves, to have compassion, to suffer with and accept our wounded parts, and to deal with our failures and transgressions with mercy, kindness, and forgiveness.

Many of us have personal secrets that fill us with an inner feeling of shame or inadequacy. We may be blaming ourselves for early failures, missed opportunities, choices made in youthful ignorance or desperation; for abuse we experienced, an unwanted pregnancy, a period of promiscuity, a failed marriage, or some dishonest or cruel act. Out of fear we've learned to bottle up these events as secrets and push them deep into our unconscious. It may take so much energy to keep them there that we dare not risk putting much intensity into the rest of our lives. Such secrets deter our growth and may block it completely. But when it comes to loving ourselves it's worthwhile to remember that birth comes out of darkness. And in the ancient tradition of the alchemists, darkness was a necessary condition for purification and transformation. The secrets we've held in darkness need to be brought into the light so we can begin distilling them through our hearts until compassion can turn them into gold.

Larry was a man who had carried a devastating secret from childhood to midlife. When he was six years old, a group of older boys, one of whom was his next-door neighbor and baby-sitter, sexually abused and humiliated him. Then they terrorized him into silence. As a result of this experience he learned to live in fear. The more tightly he held his secret, the more he began to fear life in general. He became continually anxious, hypervigilant, a perfectionist who feared making any kind of mistake and being "found out." After blaming himself for being too cowardly to tell his parents, he, like many of us, eventually came to blame himself for the incident. One day when he was feeling particularly hopeless he broke down and told his wife the secret. She urged him to see me. Once the pressure was released, he was in time able to stop blaming himself and to begin feeling love and compassion for that small boy within himself who'd been so betrayed and brutalized. This is the gold that comes out of darkness—the complete alchemical transformation that happens when our secrets are processed in a healing manner. Slowly, Larry became more self-confident, less worried about mistakes, and able to stop seeing the world as a completely hostile place.

Glen was another person with a secret she'd held tightly for years. She had grown up in a troubled home where her father was distant and her mother was often sick with one complaint or another. The atmosphere was depressing and when Glen found herself out of its suffocating influences and in college, she went through a couple of years of wild partying and promiscuity until a pregnancy

LEARNING TO LOVE OURSELVES

scare jolted her into thinking more seriously about how she was living her life. Since then she's been both ashamed and afraid of her sexuality. As we worked together, Glen discovered that understanding that nineteen-year-old girl who needed love and affirmation, and who had no guidance or support from her family, was crucially important. Understanding led to compassion for that lovely, confused young girl, and compassion led to acceptance and forgiveness. The whole process gave her an increased sense of strength and confidence as she realized how much she had overcome during her life. Becoming free of her secret's power allowed Glen to learn how to genuinely express her love and not to fear her sexuality.

Secrets come in many sizes and we lock them away in closets or hidden rooms where they may grow more threatening over time. A man may conceal an early homosexual relationship, a woman an early abortion, or another man the clandestine theft of money from friends. Forgiving ourselves often sounds easy on the surface. But when it comes to the kind of things we keep secret, that we lock away because they scare us or consume our self-respect in the instant it takes to remember them—well, these things are hard to forgive, and they may even make us think we aren't worth forgiving. Self-forgiveness rests on being able to understand who we were at the time and what needs, hurts, fears, and deprivations were driving us. Only then may we meet ourselves with compassion and kindness. Growth in self-knowledge brings healing, and atonement in its deepest sense means to become "at one" with who we are, to reconcile through love with our essential selves. And, our capacity to do this leads us back to the ability to say, "I am human" in its full spiritual sense.

The Great Commandment in the Old and New Testaments that begins with "Love your neighbor as yourself" captures the complex nature of love. Our capacity to genuinely love anyone else is directly related to our ability to love ourselves. Living with self-love means living with inner integrity, accepting our errors with grace rather than shame, supporting ourselves emotionally in difficult circumstances and when we have to sacrifice our immediate pleasure in the service of a deeper value. Admitting our mistakes promptly, apologizing, or acting quickly to heal problems we've caused rarely make anyone think less of us. And remembering our visions of life, the "cathedrals" that we're building, can support us through the periods when life is sad and difficult.

Love, whether of ourselves or someone else, also requires respect and courtesy and when these qualities are absent, the situation is based on power and not on love. If I drive myself like a machine no amount of self-indulgence equals love. When I am too demanding of others the same thing holds true. If I spend much time in self-criticism I'm not respecting myself. When I criticize other people relentlessly I'm not respecting them. And if I'm courteous to myself I provide an ambiance of feelings that honor the importance of my existence, and I honor other people by treating them courteously.

I love myself even knowing that there are parts in me I don't like, such as my rigidity, my aggressiveness, or my tendency to be sentimental at times. I love myself even when I know there are parts of me I'm still afraid of, the parts that sometimes give in too quickly, take on too much work, or haven't learned to say no well enough. I also love myself knowing there are parts of me I keep imprisoned, like my ability to make quick, scathing comments or to let my anger go into outbursts rather than tracking down what it is trying to tell me. But none of these things make me think I'm bad or immature. Instead, they mean I'm a complex person and that I contain all of our human potentials in some measure—including the ability to be self-destructive. I feel a kinship with some parts of myself, friendship with others, and attraction and fascination with a few. I can experience the whole range of love's possibilities within me, and I don't have to be all "nice," "together," and "normal" to care for myself.

The great paradox in this entire experience is that until we become people of substance capable of loving ourselves, we have little to offer other people and even our best efforts will carry a dark side

LEARNING TO LOVE OURSELVES

with them. But when we become people of substance our presence will be giving and renewing wherever we go and will enhance the quality and richness of our work and relationships as naturally as flowers give off their scents.

Loving ourselves is a process and while there's no exact formula for it, we've seen that it can grow as we learn more about ourselves. In general self-love evolves in the same way love is built between people. It depends upon us taking the time to cultivate our inner relationships and to learn to understand ourselves better. We have to value our relationships with ourselves enough to use some of the methods we've discussed like journaling, dialoguing, and befriending our dreams. Getting to know our shadows is also necessary. Discovering our unlived potentials, as Boss found in Zorba, opens us to enthusiasm and a clearer sense of how vigorously we can live. And, as we saw with Larry and Glen, facing our secrets and the self-understanding they can bring will lead to new self-acceptance.

If we don't learn to know ourselves, the best we can do is love a fantasy of who we are, a contrivance, an image or illusion. To know ourselves we must break free enough of the influences in our pasts to recognize the parts of ourselves we've denied and begin to accept our authentic characteristics—those we like and those we don't like.

Loving ourselves is a challenge of the heart to rediscover the feelings and the life we were forced to suppress in order to form our identities and begin our social development. To grow up, fit in, go to school, and eventually get a job we had to learn to deny much of our emotional lives. Yet it's our emotions—fear, anger, joy, and sorrow—that connect us to the experience of being alive, and alert us when our heartfelt values are being touched. The capacity to love in any form depends upon our emotional awareness. Our feelings do more however than connect us to life. They hold the key to living a life of depth, full of imagination, animation, and an awareness of being close to all life.

Emotions: The Language of the Heart

Not too long ago, Reid, the regional manager of a chain of stores, was telling me about his wife's affair and the trouble in their marriage. He went on to reveal he knew she'd had several affairs. I was struck by how impersonal he sounded, as if he was reporting the evening news on television, even though these events would be highly charged for most of us. While he was talking I continued listening carefully and paying close attention to what he was saying. He explained how patient he'd been in the past and that each time his wife would eventually come to her senses and return to the marriage. This time he was surprised because she seemed determined to leave. Our session ended before I had a chance to ask him how he felt in response to what was happening to their relationship.

That night I had a dream about Reid. In the dream we were in a polar area surrounded by ice and snow for as far as I could see. Reid seemed to be stuck in the ice and I was trying to pull him out with all of my strength. As the dream ended I was still pulling and he was still waist deep in the ice.

During our next visit I shared my dream and told him that it left me puzzled. I explained I wanted to be of help to him and after listening to his story that I'd been curious about his lack of feelings, and then I'd had this dream. I went on to ask him how he felt about the scene I'd described, where I was struggling to pull him out of the ice.

Reid paused for what seemed like several minutes. Then he told me that his wife had accused him of being cold. He began to rub his hands together and then looked up at me. "I'm afraid of feelings," he said, "I don't want to suffer." This was an important moment for him because it opened the door for us to begin exploring his fear and to awaken the consciousness of his feelings.

Emotional detachment is a defense we learn early to avoid pain and embarrassment. Being belittled, ignored, and rejected hurts, and it often seems better to shut down and feel nothing than allow ourselves to feel wounded and ashamed. Reid had followed a course many of us adopt. He shut off his feelings and acted as if he were actually superior to the situation by not getting caught up in the turmoil emotions can bring. He was waiting for his wife to "come to her senses." But this defense leaves us with a spiritual burden—the knowledge that, at some deep level, we're not who we appear to be and that the life we are living is not a reliable expression of who we are.

Several years ago, Gary, a mild-mannered minister, came to see me. Gary was recovering from a heart attack and bypass surgery. I was surprised when he opened our meeting by saying, "I want to stop being a spectator of life." When I asked him if he could explain a little more about what he meant he replied, "The terror of almost dying and being cut open may be the first time I've felt really alive in years. It woke me up. I realized that I think everyone else is living but I've just been watching and going through the motions. For years I've just gotten up and done what needed to be done without thinking too much about it. Love, fear, excitement, enthusiasm, bitterness, illness, pain—those were all things I saw in other people's lives." Gary had come to understand that without feelings our lives seem more like a movie we're watching than a process we're fully involved in.

Actually, the feelings of fear awakened by his surgery were a good place to begin his work because feelings often chain together. This fear helped Gary realize how lonely he was feeling, how much he loved his family and wanted to be loved in return, and how glad he was to have a second chance to learn how to experience life. Without educated hearts, our lives lack character and animation. The values of other people, rationality, and our culture seem more important than the aspects of our selves that are struggling to be recognized and lived. Nothing seems to arouse passion or a burning interest in us or forces a committed decision to act. Nothing, that is, until we're faced with our own mortality, as in Gary's case, or awakened to living through a desire to understand our true selves.

When a woman can't stop weeping she's usually labeled as "depressed" in the eyes of our culture and the people around her. Her relatives, friends, and colleagues will move through a short series of responses to her: sympathy to concern; concern to bafflement; bafflement to a twinge of irritation; irritation to impatience; impatience to anger. Yes, everyone wants her to get back to normal. When these situations occur I wonder if anyone's listening to the language that our bodies, through heart attacks or tears, are sometimes trying to speak for us. Crying jags are like leaky faucets—after years of holding back the pressure, they just give way; the controls burst. How can we help her or help ourselves if we don't know how to understand this language of feelings that we can't articulate and our bodies are expressing for us?

The mind-body split we hear so much about today means that we're divided within ourselves. Our minds and bodies are working independently of each other without coordination and often in apparent ignorance of what each other is doing. In the case of a heart attack or crying, the body may be expressing the emotional pain or stress that the mind is denying. It is important to remember our feelings are the connecting tissue between the mind and the body and if our minds block our emotions from awareness, we will lose the connection to our bodies. When this happens our repressed emotions may build up in our unconscious until the body expresses them. We frequently teach ourselves to widen this split without realizing it. For example, even people who seem interested in their bodies may watch television while they are walking on a treadmill without noticing they are learning to disassociate their minds from their bodies. They are distracting their minds rather than relaxing them and allowing them to focus on the experience of their bodies. Tai Chi, yoga, and some of the martial arts do just the opposite as they seek to clear the mind and help it participate in the exercises with the body. The purpose in this approach is to increase the health of the mind as well as the body, which frequently results in a feeling of peace.

Another way of thinking about our dualistic approach to ourselves is that we have two kinds of consciousness. One is of the head and the other is of the heart. The ancient Greeks called these *logos* and *eros* respectively. The consciousness of the head is centered around *reason,* and the consciousness of the heart around *feelings.* We need them both, strong and harmonized, to be complete, fully developed individuals.

But as we've seen, our society works to widen the divide by ignoring our inner development. Both reason and feelings are grounded in our inner experiences. Yet as we grow up we're taught rationality, problem solving, and information—to focus, in other words, on successful *external* living rather than learning more about what's going on within us. While our approach seems practical it may be less useful than we think. I recently read an article that said philosophy majors are doing well in business. Not, obviously, because they've been trained in business techniques, but because they have learned how to think independently and understand human nature. In the long run if we're going to continue to be competent in the external worlds, and find existence meaningful, we have to learn how to deal with our inner worlds, where we experience life. It would be helpful if our schools were able to teach mythology, literature, and art in depth, not simply in survey courses, in order to give us the understanding that there is a deeper dimension to our existence that is valuable. The currents of life are moved by the great emotional themes beneath them and we are all immersed in these forces.

As a result of the way we're conditioned, we often feel frightened any time we experience a strong emotion. Even the images and metaphors we associate with love—"I'm falling in love"—can make us feel anxious or that we're losing control. Emotions make us feel invaded by alien forces—"I don't know what came over me"—subject to compulsive urges to say and do things we wouldn't normally consider. Love, loss, pain, anger, grief, even joy can make us feel like saying, "This isn't me; I don't act this way."

Very often, we associate deep feelings with anger, whose existence either makes us feel guilty or deny we're having feelings at all. We think that anger is destructive, that it causes harm to show it, that it's wrong to express it, that "angry words can't be taken back."

We're afraid that when hurtful things are said they will stay a long time and cause wounds that don't heal. Anger, we think, is ugly and mean.

Many times when I ask people if they're feeling angry they will deny it. And in a way, they are frequently right: In many cases anger is really disguising *hurt*. Even though we haven't learned how to deal with anger very successfully as a culture, we still find it more appropriate to appear aggressive than to appear defenseless and open to attack or criticism. As a result many of us have learned to disguise our feeling of being hurt with outrage and an aggressive response. When I asked a woman in marital counseling why she didn't share her hurt instead of turning it into anger she replied, "Because it makes me feel so vulnerable." Many of us do the same thing.

Then too I remember talking with a woman who said she didn't want to fall in love. She had her career and her life planned and felt love might put her off track. In another situation, I worked with a middle-aged divorcee who was considering remarriage. "Let's face it," she told me, "at midlife marriage should be a business deal." Some people may look at marriage as an arrangement of convenience or for companionship. But it was clear in this case that beneath this practical-sounding statement was a deep fear of love and the pain she feared it could bring.

We often find ourselves feeling helpless when we need to face feelings that are unfamiliar to us or that we fear will overcome us. The truth is most of us haven't been educated in the ways of the heart. And, when we haven't been educated in feelings and don't know how to articulate them, we shouldn't be surprised that they will feel scary to us and look like what Thomas Moore calls, "a cauldron of raw emotions, suspicious desires, and disconnected images."

Educating the heart usually begins with our discovery of a need, one that is generally forced into our awareness by some kind of suffering that's clamoring for our attention. Robertson Davies, in his novel *The Manticore*, presents a character who is a well-known attorney and has gone into analysis because his life is unraveling. His analyst immediately confronts him with his intellectual arrogance and the primitive nature of his feelings. She points out how he tries to meet his needs by bludgeoning his feelings into expression and when this doesn't work, hammering the people around him by being curt and derogatory. She also explains to him that whenever he failed to live up to his own expectations he would castigate himself until he was approaching despair.

We all have primitive feelings. But simply being in touch with our feelings isn't enough. Aristotle pointed out that "anyone can become angry, that is easy. But to be angry with the right person, to the right degree, at the right time, for the right purpose, and in the right way, this is not easy." And this is true. To bring a need to full consciousness, we have to understand our feelings, where they come from, and what they mean. Only then can we experience our feelings like men and women and learn to fulfill our needs in a responsible way.

Strong emotions such as love, fear, joy, suffering, and anger are calls to begin the education of our hearts. Unfortunately what usually happens is they have to pile up until they cause an illness, depression, or broken relationship to get our attention. Considering them when they initially occur, reflecting on them, and exploring them through journaling and dialoguing is the homeschooling approach that Aristotle might recommend. This will help us prevent many painful crises and live with greater strength and exuberance.

When people come to see me professionally because of what they're experiencing, they usually have difficulty expressing themselves. They say, "I feel bad" or "I'm depressed." But either of these descriptions can also mean they feel heavy, tired, sad, withdrawn, hopeless, frustrated, fearful, and so on. Identifying what we're feeling is very important. Feeling sad and feeling withdrawn are different experiences. And the different degrees of intensity a feeling word expresses are also important. Intensity signifies the importance of the feelings. Fury means more than anger. Despair means more than sadness. Until we learn how to describe what we're experiencing, we can't begin to deal with it.

I frequently start working with someone by asking them to amplify and discuss their feelings. For instance if someone says they feel depressed I might suggest that we use "depression" as a heading and then list the feelings that come under that heading such as "sad," "weak," "confused," or "I don't feel anything." This activity helps us learn the language of our emotions and their many expressive nuances. The next step is to discover the intensity of the feelings. Does feeling sad mean feeling despairing, hopeless, devastated, upset, down, or bad? Journaling about the emotions we have during the day and their intensity, and noting the intensity of them in our dreams as well, can help us educate ourselves about the language of our hearts and how it may affect us. I'm always amazed to see how much our capacity to be passionately engaged in life improves once we've learned how to articulate our feelings accurately.

People continually ask me, "Why can't we simply put these problems behind us and move on with life?" "What good can getting angry do?" "How can it help make things better?" These are legitimate concerns. If we look at Reid's situation, where his wife is having another affair, we can ask these questions. What could happen if Reid really became angry, sad, in despair, or deeply hurt over her affair? As a beginning it would humanize him, make the events in his life more personal, and enable him to be more aware of how they are really affecting him. During our work Reid soon began to allow his feelings to emerge. His fears came true. There was a part of him that felt awful, as he remembered his early hopes and dreams and how in love he'd felt when their relationship began. But, he also realized how he had let his ambition creep into his life until it controlled him. He saw where part of this situation was his fault, but this understanding didn't keep him from becoming furious with his wife, in addition to experiencing his other feelings of sadness and regret. He thought his wife should have loved him enough to confront him with her unhappiness instead of having an affair. And from this point he became angry with himself again for not listening to her more closely for he recognized that his cool, superior persona made it difficult for her to confront him.

Did Reid suffer from this experience? Yes, of course he did, but these events also strengthened him. He and his wife had some stormy encounters with each other. With my help he struggled to keep the heat of these collisions contained, but not repressed. Part of our education is to learn to express our emotions strongly, without being destructive, and to continue to treat the other person with respect and even acknowledge their pain when it's appropriate. Once his feelings emerged, Reid was struck by the depth of his sorrow and his anger. He concluded that if he had such intense feelings, there must be, or at least had been, something he valued very much in his marriage. Reid also realized that while he had a range of feelings, he also felt cleansed, more confident of his actions, and focused on today. He and his wife went into marriage counseling in an effort to see whether love was still there, still possible, and if they could find healing and growth together.

To have the full experience of our anger doesn't mean we must spontaneously and instinctively act it out, throwing things, slamming doors, hurting ourselves, or others. Thoughtless actions aren't in keeping with the spirit of a life that is seeking to grow. Nor is the careless, fearful, or even well-intentioned repression of such a feeling. We've seen how dangerous repression can be and it's safe to guess that Reid's wife had affairs out of resentment toward him and her perceived powerlessness in the situation. The further we go along the lines of repression, the more we become detached from the life we're hoping for and our ability to genuinely experience love. Reid had to learn as Boss did, that ruling out our emotions leaves us detached, alone, and weak—weak because we don't know how to cope with life.

SACRED SELFISHNESS

Guides to Self-Love

It's ironic that the examples we search for in finding personal, fulfilling lives outside the dogmas we've been conditioned to live by have been within our view all the time. However, it generally takes an upheaval—some profound, felt experience of love, suffering, or passion that opens our eyes and urges us to try and understand our models' true messages, and to realize that these models themselves were moved by love, suffering, and visions beyond the ordinary. For instance, it was out of love for mankind that Prometheus stole the fire of consciousness from the gods. Compassion compelled Buddha to oppose the caste system and reveal the way to deal with suffering. It was out of love that Jesus opened the rigidity of tribal laws to forgiveness and declared that we should love our enemies. And other great figures such as Copernicus, Newton, Darwin, Freud, Jung, Gandhi, and Martin Luther King followed their passionate quests beyond the social character of their times and expanded the world.

From a psychological perspective the great religious leaders such as Buddha and Jesus represent archetypal models for moving beyond the limits of what we consider normal into an individual life and destiny. As models they're not to be imitated literally but are to be seen as guides showing us how to live our lives as authentically and completely as they lived theirs. When I began my inner journey it was because of the pain and restlessness I felt. My distress urged me to go beyond taking refuge in the answers of conventional wisdom and to become inner-directed rather than outer-directed. It was at this point I became aware of how many ancient myths, religions (including my own though I hadn't realized it), stories, and lives of exceptional people supported this quest.

The greatest lesson I learned from studying these models was that they moved *outside* and *beyond* the values of the social character and not against the culture in a rebellious manner. I try to keep this standard in mind every time I make a decision. I'm not interested in being a "rebel" because I believe that the values of a rebel are just as much of a trap as the values of our social character. I am committed to growing and I'm willing to accept the risks it involves. However, I want to live with social responsibility, meeting my obligations, voting, and paying my taxes, *and* pursue my individual vision of life. To go *beyond* and not *against* is one of my most important guiding principles.

Wondering where we may find even more personal guides to self-love and authenticity than our great religious models can bring us back to our consideration of Zorba and Boss. Where can we find our own "Zorbas," those galvanizing forces that initiate us into experiencing life more fully and into loving ourselves? How, in the face of a culture that drives and pushes us to experts and specialists of every kind and bombards us with information, can we reunite with the inner wisdom that has been largely educated out of our minds? The answers are within us, in our unconscious and in our emotions, dreams, reflections, and active imaginations. We can't accomplish very much if we use only one or two facets of ourselves. A diamond shines because the many facets interrelate, bounce off, and partake of each other's brilliance. Our inner Zorbas are the positive aspects and vitality of our shadows. If you remember Margaret and her dream of the gypsy woman, you can imagine that as her inner work progressed this gypsy became Margaret's inner Zorba. Margaret found that dialoguing with her proved to be a breakthrough and even more, as she realized the guide she needed was within herself.

In a poetic sense I see these images from our unconscious as inner friends who turn up in our dreams and active imaginations. If occasionally one happens to insist on being an enemy, well, our enemies often help us learn as much about ourselves as our friends do. As parts of our shadows they're archetypal and part of human nature. These images are illustrated in myths and fairy tales when the hero or heroine is aided by other figures who may range from frogs to kings and queens and shepherds to gods and goddesses, or who oppose them such as witches, scary beasts, and other villains. Nikos

Kazantzakis was a great student of mythology and it's no accident that *Zorba the Greek* is an archetypal story.

From the standpoint of psychology we might feel comfortable interpreting our dreams but still wonder how to go about dialoguing with a feeling, an illness, or a figure from a dream. We're not generally comfortable with intangibles. We don't think of ourselves as talking to images, symbols, illnesses, moods, and such things seriously, much less having them answer us. And if we do it is natural to be curious about how one of these aspects can reply to us, or to ask why we can't figure out what they mean on our own without a dialog. The answer to these questions is that the images and other things we try to dialogue with represent pieces of potential consciousness we have cut ourselves off from as we formed our identities. They're like small "exiled selves" but they have their own perspectives on us and how we're living, their own intelligence, and by recognizing them we expand our range of self-awareness. The image we're dialoguing with offers its perspective to us; it then becomes our responsibility as to how we integrate this information into our personalities. The more we dialogue with a part of ourselves—whether it be about fear or depression or pain or our shadows—the more we'll have differentiated it *from our unconscious* and *into our awareness* until we understand it well enough for it to become part of our conscious personalities. Once this has happened our personalities will grow to include this new feature and the dialogs will no longer be necessary.

Margaret, as a graphic artist, was comfortable with her imagination and had no problem dialoguing. But Jim, who had a scientific background, found this process troublesome. Yet his experience shows how important the help from our interior can be even when we're suspicious of it. Jim was skeptical of anything having to do with dreams and the imagination. He was the chairman of a large research department in the medical school of a well-known university.

LEARNING TO LOVE OURSELVES

When he began talking to me he made it clear that science—what could be seen, quantified, and measured—was his religion and he was impatient with fuzzy-headed ideas like dreamwork. As our conversation continued I learned how deeply distressed he was about his marriage and the ongoing pain he was experiencing in it. It had been hard for Jim to come see me both because of his allegiance to science and because he was a proud man, successful and well known in his profession.

Jim told me how his relationship with his wife had been a downward spiral for almost two decades as she increasingly criticized and demeaned everything about him, including his success as a scientist. Recently, he had become afraid that it was hurting his children, destroying their confidence in life and in the relationships they could expect to have one day as they drew close to adulthood. Not surprisingly Jim had at this point become obsessed with the problem of what to do about his marriage. He felt trapped between his inability to confront his wife and the fear of how a divorce could affect his reputation and his children. I assured him that I realized how complex his situation was and that we would work on it intensely. However, I added it would help us to know what light his unconscious could shed on the situation, and how that knowledge could save us time and pain.

Of course Jim was immediately leery of looking at his dreams. I shared with him that Jung considered himself a scientist, too, and had studied an astounding number of dreams, over eighty thousand, before beginning to draw conclusions about working with them, and that I had a scientific background as well. "Well, I'm like the man from Missouri; you'll have to show me, I guess," Jim said. A few meetings later he brought in a dream and was surprised by how much he learned about himself as we "befriended it." Then one day he shared a puzzling dream that included a friend from adolescence, a young man named Frank. Even after Jim had mulled the dream over and we had discussed it at length, Frank's presence in the dream remained a mystery. The only thing Jim remembered about him was that when their high school principal had accused a group of boys that included Frank and Jim of drinking at a school dance, Frank had stood up for his innocence while Jim was too scared to say anything. We were captivated by Frank's mysterious presence in a dream after all those years. Because we couldn't get much insight into why he had shown up, I suggested to Jim that he dialogue with him. As I explained the process, the "I'm from Missouri" look returned to Jim's face.

However, Jim showed up at our next meeting with a dialog in hand. Instead of opening the dialog with curiosity as I'd suggested, he'd unexpectedly jumped into a discussion with Frank concerning his problems with his wife. "I didn't want to waste our time," Jim said, "I wanted to see what he might know that I don't." The following is his short dialog and it shows how much assistance can come from an inner figure as Frank helps Jim redirect the focus of his emotional efforts.

JIM: *I need help. I'm in an awful place with my wife, Joanne, and the harder I work to try to make it better the worse it gets.*

FRANK: *Yeah, you're in a mess all right. Why don't you quit? Aren't you sick and tired of this struggle and of hurting so much?*

JIM: *You think I should get a divorce?*

FRANK: *No. You need to quit concentrating on this issue for the present and start working on other issues. You shouldn't let this problem dominate your life. It's too entangling and frustrating.*

JIM: *Are you telling me I have issues more important than my marriage?*

FRANK: *Yes, you do. If you don't figure some of them out you'll never be able to solve your problems with Joanne. You can come back to working on your marriage with greater strength.*

LEARNING TO LOVE OURSELVES

JIM: *What would give me greater strength?*

FRANK: *Well, for a beginning, more self-confidence when you're away from work, greater self-love, an understanding you're a real person who deserves more than you're getting from your personal life. Think about what we're saying and we'll talk again.*

This dialog helped Jim see that he needed to work on the basic foundation of how he felt about himself. For Jim, loving himself had become confused with rewarding himself. He thought that compensating himself with trips, good meals, and tickets to the opera showed self-love. But while such things are pleasurable they don't reflect the deeper experience of self-love that means finding the courage to listen to your whole being—the truth of your feelings—which includes your heart's requests for meaning.

This dialog and our discussion was a turning point for Jim that enabled him to stop obsessing about whether to get a divorce or not and turn toward understanding himself. Jim discovered that early in his life he learned to appear happy and to hide his feelings of sadness and anger in order to protect his parents from feeling failure or helplessness. As a child he concluded, unknowingly at the time, that his feelings were unacceptable and he became ashamed of even having them. His wife was the symphony of discontent that moved him to act. And dialoguing was the key that opened not a Pandora's box of irrational difficulties, but, as any scientist would agree, revealed the causes of his difficulties. To live and grow we must learn to find the ingredients we need within ourselves. And we grow from there into self-love.

Dialoguing is especially helpful for those of us who enjoy using and stretching ourselves through our imaginations, and many of us can do this without considering ourselves creative types. If we love science fiction, cooking, gardening, or sports we are using our imaginations. Whenever we envision an alien planet, a new menu, our spring plantings, a golf swing, or a play in football or basketball we've made a creative leap. But if we discover that dialoguing simply doesn't work for us, the other tools we've discussed probably will. By journaling, reflecting, studying our dreams, paying careful attention to our feelings, and considering how we use projections in our relationships, we can grow in personal awareness and energize our individuation processes. The guides to loving ourselves are our shadows and whatever roads we choose to pursue our journeys into them will be beneficial. As the ancient Romans used to say, "All roads lead to Rome," and whether we run into detours, heavy traffic, or bad weather once we've begun the journey, we'll discover the inner support for reaching our destinations.

Driven by Fear

Fear is a dragon we have to face and a question we have to answer again and again during a life that's being lived wholeheartedly. Just as we find that other strong feelings, or even illnesses, are the seeds for our future growth, the same is true of fear. It's something we should pay attention to, listen to, question, and reflect upon because our fears are a treasure house of self-knowledge.

When Boss in *Zorba the Greek* was attracted to the dark-eyed widow and she returned his glances, Zorba urged him to pursue her. Boss demurred, saying he was afraid he would start trouble with the other men whom she'd refused. Zorba replied, "Life is trouble, Boss," and urged him on. In mythological language, the woman symbolizes life and if Boss failed to pursue her he would be failing to become alive. The truth of myths applies to all of us, men and women alike. We must choose life. And there will be trouble. That is life, though we often have the mistaken belief that a good life is a trouble-free life. But neither God nor Buddha or any other great spiritual leader or tradition guarantees or even encourages a trouble-free life. Instead the great spiritual figures inspire us to grow through our painful experiences by seeking to understand their lessons.

We often feel it's safer to avoid trouble than to seek it. But when we do, trouble finds us anyway. I am reminded of a man in his thirties who wanted to avoid a confrontation over his wife's spending sprees. As his inner frustration grew, it began to show up as stomach pains. And when another woman in her early forties decided it was safer not to confront her partner's drinking, she found herself becoming increasingly depressed. In another situation a man continued absorbing his boss's belittling remarks out of the fear that if he confronted him he could lose his job. He too became more and more depressed. When we choose safety over self-love, the price we pay will always be higher. Would you rather pay the wholesale price today or the high retail price tomorrow—the amount that has a higher markup in disappointment, shame, and self-loathing?

Fear is seductive. In his lovely novel *The Alchemist*, Paulo Coelho has a wise old man tell the story of a young man who wanted to travel, challenge himself, discover what his dreams were, and learn what people are capable of doing with their lives. But because he felt insecure he decided he should work for a while and put some money aside. The young man wondered whether he should become a shepherd or a baker. Then he decided that people thought more highly of bakers and parents would rather see their daughters marry a baker than a shepherd. As time passed he began to think to himself that bakers slept in nice homes while travelers and seekers often had to sleep out in the open. Soon he became a respected member of the community and what people thought about him as a baker became more important than his dream of living life as a journey and an adventure. His small, practical fear about financial security had put him on a path that taught him to become afraid of how other people evaluated him and of risking the hardships pursuing his dream might have brought. Stepping onto the path of fear has its consequences. The old man concluded by saying, "He never realized that people are capable, at any time in their lives, of doing what they dream of."

If we allow fear to drive us it becomes our Satan and enables us to be seduced by the false gods of security, money, appearances, power, and all they represent. Once we give into fear we lose our control to outer forces—to what other people think, to dysfunctional relationships, to collective values, and to the addictions such as drugs, alcohol, and sex that make up the dark sides of these forces. The voice or face of fear—like the social Satans or cultural Mephistopheles that consume our lives—can hypnotize and leave us unable to think or act with clarity.

Let me give you an interesting example that has to do with fear. John wanted to write a novel but once he began he soon found himself blocked and afraid. When he dialogued with his fear he was surprised to discover that what he feared was not writing but success. As a deeply introverted person he feared the marketing aspect of publishing, the rituals of selling that would require him to give readings, talks, and appearances at book signings. Of course he also feared failing and being rejected by editors. But more than anything else he feared failing at his dream. He felt that if he failed at his dream he wouldn't have anything left to live for. Whichever way it went, the result would be the same. Publish and fail; be rejected and fail. After listening to the flood of John's fears I decided to share one of my favorite stories with him. The story is one author Sam Keen tells about himself. Once when he was talking with his friend and mentor Howard Thurman, Thurman asked him what he wanted, what his dream was. Keen, who was a successful professor at the time, answered, "I don't have any dreams right now." "Well, " Thurman replied, "you'd better start looking for one." And that is the straight-ahead answer I gave John. Cut the B.S. and get going after a dream. Part of self-love is learning how to be tough with ourselves and take the driver's seat when we need to break a fearful mood. Most of us have learned very well how to be hard on ourselves. We're really good at being self-critical, resentful, guilty, and self-depreciating—we never fail there. But being hard on ourselves is not the same as being tough with ourselves. There is a difference. Being tough means we are committed, energetic, have high standards, and tenacity. Being hard is to be perfectionistic, self-judging, self-punishing, shaming, and unaccepting of our mistakes and weaknesses. The pursuit of excellence in any domain requires toughness but is defeated by qualities that make us feel insufficient, fraudulent, unacceptable.

If we want to worship fear all our lives it will feed us all we need to keep it as our god. We can fear betrayal, fear not being taken care of, or fear not being loved; we can fear failure, fear being old or broke or in bad health, or fear success. We can fear being abandoned or criticized or looking like a fool. The list is endless. It can fill a life. Your life. Fear feeds off negative acts and negative thoughts, brings about destructive results, and destroys our ability to move confidently in the world. And yet in every life there is a Zorba or a gypsy woman within us who can lead us away from fear's embrace and teach us to laugh at failure, to persevere against the odds, to dream and to dance with joy. The stories of the mythological heroes—Psyche aided by Pan in her search for Eros, Ulysses helped through his journey by Athene, Prometheus who stole fire for humanity freed from his punishment by Heracles, and King Arthur guided by Merlin—teach in every case that once we step beyond the boundaries of accepted conventions, life will support and aid us with inner strength and help, no matter how difficult our journeys become. Our inner work can carry us beyond fear, but if we give into it we may end up hollow and haunted by our unlived potentials.

I remember in an interview that underscores these thoughts writer Erica Jong reflected, "I have not ceased being fearful, but I have ceased letting fear control me. I have accepted fear as a part of life, specifically the fear of change, the fear of the unknown, and I have gone ahead despite the pounding in the heart that says: turn back, turn back, you'll die if you venture too far."

Seeking to live and even become successful on our own terms is always scary. It means we can't, won't, or don't follow the beaten paths—and that we want more out of life than we're taught we should be satisfied with. It means other people won't understand us and may not respect us and applaud our success. Fair enough—but we will be happy. Though just how we can accomplish this breakthrough is a tougher question, one I can best answer by returning us back to Margaret and the gypsy woman she encountered in her dream, who lives in the territory beyond conventions.

The Roar of Awakening

Moving through individuation as a quest for self-knowledge becomes a process of revealing to ourselves who we really are. This revelation follows a gradual process, punctuated by startling recognitions that move us toward a deeper sense of our true identities and the possibilities inherent in them. When I first met Margaret, for example, she was outwardly a picture of poise, success, and self-assurance. However, I discovered that since college she had wanted, in fact, to be an artist. But bowing to practicality and to other values she also craved, like social position and financial security, she had set that dream aside to become a competent, successful businesswoman. When Margaret met the gypsy woman in her dream, she met a compelling shadow figure and an archetypal figure. In their encounter and by the sign on her back ("I am the way"), the gypsy woman held the key to a major transformation in Margaret's life. Let us see how.

A gypsy woman by definition can not be a prisoner of the social personality. Gypsies live outside of society's traditional values and in the realms of sensuality, music, and magic. Gypsies seem to live their passions, feelings, cultural lives, and even their religious lives spontaneously. They're fascinating, utterly mesmerizing, and threatening. Perfectly willing to relieve us of our hard-earned money, they may prey upon upright citizens, and have been rumored to snatch their children. They have their own bonds, laws, and customs. In song and story gypsies own no property, know no homeland, but camp in forest glades, close to nature. They are nature; they embody what is deep, immediate, and unknown.

It was in talking about the gypsy woman that Margaret began to reminiscence poignantly about her old desire to be an artist. For years, she had continued to paint virtually in secret. Occasionally, she would share her paintings with close friends, who praised them enthusiastically and urged her to show them. But Margaret was afraid to show her pictures, to take a step that might make her have to face her fear of living outside the mainstream. Margaret, like the young man in the story who becomes a baker, discovered that it becomes easier and easier to feel successful as part of a group, to be affirmed and validated by its standards. And whenever we're feeling threatened it seems nice to have a herd we can run back to for safety. It's harder and more scary, however, to feel successful at the margins. To be "special" or a "genius" or "different" usually means "admire but do not touch." It means being vulnerable to criticism and loneliness. We hold outstanding people like Freud, Einstein, and Madame Curie in high regard, but we also shrink away from them. They are "different," not like us—it's easier and more comfortable to succeed conventionally as one of "us."

To try and become "extra-ordinary" means to accept a vocation, a call from deep within us—not to be confused with fame and fortune, for neuroses can frequently call us to those—that compels us to emancipate ourselves from the well-worn conventional paths we think of as "normal." It means that to follow our true personalities, we must learn to obey the laws being spoken within us. It means, in other words, we must have what I called earlier *a religious attitude toward our inner lives*. It's by following this process that we become people of substance, unique and utterly individual people, our own people, whose presence will serve to give meaning to the lives of others.

By accepting the call from deep within ourselves, we release the bonds of fear, obligations, and expectations that have shaped and limited us. This brings a state of peace, of feeling centered in the midst of life's turmoil, and the ability to recognize the positive values in what appear to be the troubling, threatening moments we encounter. The more we understand that the source of our lives is within us, the easier it becomes to love life and accept its challenges as creative. The price we pay to get this is through the work necessary to keep our courage strong and taking the necessary risks.

When we talk about choices, we have to wonder if Margaret had pursued the wrong career to begin with. Could better parenting or counseling in college have put her on the path sooner to being an artist? I don't think so. I shared my own experience of growth with her and how becoming a businessman had helped me develop the strength and maturity to risk further changes and pursue new dreams. Margaret quickly understood and was relieved to discover that we rarely make the wrong choices. We make the choices necessary for our growth and she made the ones essential to her progress, to give her confidence and a broader experience of life. It had also been necessary for her to develop and appreciate her appearance, to become poised and certain of herself in order to overcome earlier experiences that had damaged her self-confidence. One of the important things she discovered through her analysis was not to be critical of her choices but to understand how they had been helpful to her total development. She needed to become a person of secular substance in order to have the strength of personality to go further. Where "further" is, is yet to be discovered.

This awakening to life reminds me of a treasured story in Jungian circles. It's "The Roar of Awakening" from Heinrich Zimmer's *Philosophies of India,* and it reveals an archetypal theme of self-realization.

The story begins with a hungry tigress, huge with her pregnancy, moving carefully alone, on a cliff in her search for food. Far below she spies a meadow and a herd of goats grazing serenely in the sunshine. The drop from the cliff to the meadow is a long one, but her hunger drives her to chance a mighty leap. As she leaps, she loses her balance and breaks her neck upon crashing to the ground. Hearing her hit the ground with an earthshaking thud, the goats flee into the forest. In her final moments the tigress gives birth to her cub. Then she dies, leaving the meadow in silence.

Slowly, one by one, the goats timidly return to the meadow. Curiously, they examine the dead tigress. Soon they discover the tiny cub close to his mother. The goats raise the cub in the only way they can, as a goat. The tiny tiger learns to eat grass and to train his voice to bleat like a goat. Living only on grass and in the company of goats causes the little tiger to appear weak and meek in a manner very unusual for tigers. One night he's lying awake while the goats sleep. Suddenly a mighty roar thunders across the meadow and the goats flee in panic. Strangely, however, the little tiger feels no fear. He remains alone in the moonlight. Majestically a fierce old male tiger slowly walks up to him, gazing in

LEARNING TO LOVE OURSELVES

astonishment at the strange young tiger facing him.

"What are you doing with the goats?" he growls in a voice the young tiger can understand.

"Baa," the young tiger bleats in response.

The old tiger grabs the cub by the scruff of his neck and carries him to a nearby pond. He forces him to look at his reflection in the moonlit water. "Look at these two faces. Can you see that your face is just like mine? We both have beautiful stripes. Why, then, do you think you are a goat, bleating and eating grass?"

The cub gazes into the water, shivering with surprise. Before he can respond, the fierce old male snatches him up, again by the scruff of his neck, and carries him to his den. There he pushes a piece of bloody meat from an earlier kill that evening toward the cub. "Eat it!" he thunders.

The young tiger shrinks back. In exasperation the old male forces some meat into the younger's mouth. To the young tiger's amazement the meat tastes strangely good. Astonished, he takes a second bite, then another and another. Each mouthful becomes more enjoyable, filling him with pleasure and strength. When he's full he gives a great stretch, lashes his tail, and yawns mightily as if he is awakening from a long, deep sleep. Then he throws back his head and gives a powerful roar. The old tiger has watched this process of transformation intently.

"Now you know who you are," he says.

When our true inner realities are expressed in our simplest and most ordinary acts, our lives become expositions of our Selves, our actual natures. We will have made a long journey out from under the dominance of behavior learned from our adaptation and all its supporting layers of illusion into individual consciousness. We will find that when we've created personalities of substance, we're no longer ships tossed about by the winds of our emotions, projections, or external trends and values. At this point our lives begin disclosing our uniqueness to others in a manner that contributes to life. Once our awakening reaches this level, it will continue throughout our lives.

PART III: Cultivating a Life of Substance

We are not unlike a particularly hardy crustacean. . . . With each passage from one stage of human growth to the next we, too, must shed a protective structure. We are left exposed and vulnerable— but also yeasty and embryonic again, capable of stretching in ways we hadn't known before. These sheddings may take several years or more. Coming out of each passage, though, we enter a longer and more stable period in which we can expect relative tranquility and a sense of equilibrium regained.
—Gail Sheehy

CHAPTER 11
Relationships of Substance

One hardly dares to say that love is the core of the relationship, though love is sought for and created in relationship; love is rather the marvel when it is there, but it is not always there, and to know another and to be known by another—that is everything.
—Florida Scott-Maxwell

"The only thing as challenging as getting tangled in the underbrush of relationships is trying to write about it," explains Thomas Moore. I couldn't say anything meaningful about love and relationships if I strayed too far from the anchor of my own personal and professional experiences. Yet, I realize we all participate in these mysterious and life-changing events in different contexts. However, exploring human experiences in general can usually help us understand our own, for beneath the surface of everyday life we all live from a deeper, common stream. As part of this stream the intense charges of attraction, love, and friendship in varying forms are trying to tell us more about ourselves and teach us about life. And, we must remember that no other relationship will ever substitute for the one we must develop with ourselves as the foundation for our individuation.

In the fifties, when my generation was young, it seemed that most of us saw marriage as a signpost pointing us into adulthood. My parents had been thrust into adult life by the Great Depression and World War II. And in my lifetime, there have been few concrete markers that, like the ancient initiation ceremonies, say to a young person "now you are a self-responsible adult." I got married in an effort to make this passage into adulthood. When I was floundering in my efforts to finish college it felt almost natural and certainly respectable to turn to marriage as a way to grow up, define myself, and begin a life I thought would sustain me. I believed that love and marriage went together automatically because I was immature and needed love. I thought love would make my life easier, more mature, and complete. It would give me the secure foundation for being an adult. Instead, it proved to make my life endlessly complicated and often troubled. But in ways I couldn't have imagined when I was young, love has made my life more mature and whole.

As time went by I discovered that my desire to get married and the manner in which I was trying to love, which had more to do with fulfilling my role as I saw it as opposed to how I felt, was a way of filling the void I carried inside. Gradually I learned that both love and relationships are forces that either compel us to face our deeper needs and desires or turn us away from the joys and vitality offered by their struggles. The obstacles that arise in love and in relationships frequently cause us to embark upon journeys of self-discovery. They often wound us, make us vulnerable, and seem to knead us emotionally, as if we were dough being prepared to rise.

As a young adult I didn't think much about love as being something different from a relationship. Early on I thought that falling in love with the right person and then acting in a responsible, loving way was all I had to do. I soon learned better. A few years of marriage taught me that psychoanalyst Erich Fromm was right when he said love is not a natural act. Love, according to Fromm, is an art that requires patience, discipline, practice, and dedication. I agree with him, but as broad as his statement sounds, I don't think it is comprehensive enough. Our lives have become so complicated that we have to consider both love and relationships as topics that are separate yet intertwined. In today's world we need for our relationships to "work," and making them do so is a matter of responsibility—both self-responsibility and responsibility to the relationship. These responsibilities include discipline, commitment, integrity, self-sacrifice, communication, respect, and courtesy.

RELATIONSHIPS OF SUBSTANCE

If love is the art, relationship is the craft of *being in life together.*

To love and be loved, to be able to deeply know and be known by another person, to be seen and understood all are treasures we seek. Without intimacy life withers away. We need each other profoundly, first to survive and then to experience the animation and well-being intimacy can bring. In love we find ourselves through the experience of another person and by learning to hold each other through both stormy and joyful times. Through love we may blossom, embrace, and discover each other as we grow. Through the craft of relationship we may also grow, and even when love seems lost we may yet discover through our commitment to the craft how to love again, or that love can be recreated on an even deeper level.

Because we come into love with different stories it's only a matter of time until our stories collide and we become immersed in the conflicts and obstacles caused by our individual differences and our need to figure them out. By understanding the nature of what's going on during these periods, we can be comforted in knowing our conflicts don't mean we've made the wrong choice. They mean that love and relationships, like practically everything else in life, require that we grow. If we refuse to grow then we've made the wrong choice. Whether we're trying to evolve alone or together we must learn to understand ourselves better, to become aware of our internal processes and to explore them carefully. During these times of struggle and efforts to grow we must treat our journeys and our relationships with kindness, patience, and compassion.

Love, patience, kindness, courtesy, commitment, work, and self-responsibility—these concepts appear to be ones whose meanings should be fairly clear. But somehow in the experience of everyday life, especially during times of conflict, they seem to become increasingly ambiguous and so does our motivation to live them in a disciplined manner. We frequently begin to think, "What about my needs?" and "What am I getting out of this?"—particularly in those moments when the person we knew and thought we loved seems like a stranger. And in most relationships, whether it's with a husband, wife, partner, lover, son, daughter, parent, friend, teacher, or associate at work, there will be those strained patches where the other person appears totally foreign to us.

More people come to see me professionally because of the distress in a relationship than for any other reason. In the privacy of my office people open their hearts and reveal their needs for love, the painful absence of intimacy in their lives, or their feelings of betrayal, of being misunderstood, mistreated, neglected, and valued less than jobs, careers, hobbies, or other friendships. Our relationships have the power to bring joy, sorrow, anxiety, and despair. Many of our great historical love stories remind us that love and the outcome of our relationships have an effect on us that can be as powerful as that of death.

An attraction often grabs us like the pull of a magnet. Suddenly we are struck by the expression on another's face—their eyes, how they speak or move, or the nature of their confidence, strength, or sensitivity. Some quality of beauty, feeling, or intelligence penetrates us and compels us to either reach out or shrink away in the fear of being overwhelmed.

When I'm working with people I'm constantly surprised at the different kinds of influence strong attractions may have on our lives. Attractions have their own meanings, almost like dreams, and if we use them to help us cultivate self-knowledge they can open our eyes to things we're missing in our daily lives and potentials we haven't realized were possible. A few years ago I was working with Alex when he had such an encounter. Alex was in his late thirties when he returned to night school to take a few courses that would enhance his career. Alex told me there was a woman in one of his classes to whom he felt immediately and strongly attracted. So far he'd shared a couple of coffee breaks with her and felt remarkably comfortable as they talked together. But, Alex was also married, and he confessed, "I still love my wife and children and don't want to do anything to hurt them."

When our commitment has become a duty or when love has been lost in the pressure and mechanics of everyday life, we shouldn't be surprised when something within us gives us a jolt toward remembering that our heart needs to have its place in how we're living.

RELATIONSHIPS OF SUBSTANCE

Alex loved his family and had a strong commitment to them, which left him confused by his new feelings. Commitments, however, begin to lose their strength when we allow them to deteriorate into obligations. A commitment that's rich with vitality must include a mutual vision based on shared values as well as love. Alex's commitment was strong but growing stale because of how busy he and his wife had become.

In the safety of my office I suggested to Alex he might open his imagination to the fantasies that could come from this attraction. Sometimes it's very informative to let ourselves wonder what we would like to do with someone we're attracted to, what we would like to feel with them and from them. Once Alex had thought about his fantasies for a while we discovered that he felt his life was dull and that his marriage had become listless. He wanted a livelier relationship and to engage in conversations that would draw him out more. He wanted to feel like his wife was deeply attracted to him and not just committed to their relationship. Alex's infatuation became a turning point in his life. It awakened him to new and deeper needs he hadn't been aware of before this experience. He also realized through our work that as we grow and become aware of our needs and desires, we need to take the responsibility for fulfilling them instead of hoping fate and our partners will do the job for us. By carefully sharing his thoughts and desires with his wife, she began to awaken, too. His infatuation with his classmate had remained just that. But by accepting and seeking to understand it, Alex began a journey with his wife that challenged them to create a relationship that was more demanding, interesting, and alive.

Stacy is another person who comes to mind when I think of the awakening power of attractions. She found herself intensely involved with a co-worker who was interested in Buddhism and the idea of life as a spiritual journey. Soon she found herself telling him the story of her life in a manner she'd never done with anyone else. He did the same and they were quickly immersed in feelings of shared intimacy and mutual affirmation. Both of them were married to other people. He had two children. Stacy had none. They began an affair and after a while Stacy left her husband. Her lover, however, didn't want to hurt his children and decided to return to his marriage.

The intense passion, joy, and suffering provoked by these events caused Stacy to begin reading everything she could about love and relationships and to talk with a few trusted friends about her experience. By the time she came to my office she'd separated from her husband, her lover had returned to his family, and she was continuing to read. She explained to me that she felt a distance from her former lover, wasn't feeling rejected, but still had agonizing moments of hope and despair.

"I understand why he had to go back. The pressure was awful." She went on to say how helpful and supportive her friends had been and then observed, "I've ended up learning so much about myself that I'm not sure whether I was looking for a lover or a guide to wake me up and start me thinking about my life."

Stacy felt that the books she was reading were like the "wise elders" in the past who brought wisdom and comfort to people based on the experience of their long lives and struggles. Her reading helped her realize what a difficult era for love and relationships we're living in. For several generations the old gods, rules, and structures in love and marriage have been crumbling and dying. While Stacy had been aware of these changes previously she hadn't realized how deeply they affected her personal life.

On the one hand we've learned to expect more from our relationships than most of our grandparents or great-grandparents would have dreamed possible. We want our relationships to be more alive, affirming, loving, and mutually fulfilling than they've ever been in the past. And an increasing number of people are wanting their relationships to become mutual journeys into self-knowledge and spiritual development. On the other hand we have no models and few guidelines to help us create the kind of relationships we're seeking. We're struggling today to map this new territory together and sometimes it's very scary and painful. Whenever we get caught up in discouragement and self-criticism we must remember to be very kind and merciful to ourselves in order not to fall back into closed, defensive states of mind.

It's easy to forget that our models for relationships are shifting and to blame ourselves for failing to meet either the old patterns we've internalized or the ideals we may have adopted to guide us. And the simple fact remains that while our culture has developed the kind of knowledge necessary for great scientific and technological advances, it has left us to find our own ways in matters of the heart and spirit. Understanding the importance of self-knowledge, relationships, and spirituality to living healthy, rewarding lives in the complicated world we've created is a major need in our society and therefore for each one of us.

Stacy had all of the fears that most of us would have in her situation. She was afraid of ending up old and alone, of not having enough money, and of having to be "out there" in the world of single people. But she said, "I've been spoiled now. I want someone I can talk about things with. I want more than just going to work and coming home. I want to be able to grow and share what's happening to me with someone who understands because they're doing the same thing. My husband just didn't, and still doesn't understand that so I can't go back to him." Stacy's attraction to her former lover lasted less than three months yet it changed how she saw herself and what she wanted from life.

The new expectations for more personal and rewarding relationships, ones that have substance beyond mere routines and obligations, are also affecting parents and children. While Valerie and her sisters were home for a holiday visit, Valerie realized the family had fallen back into the old roles they had when she was a child. As she was thinking about why this had happened, she figured out that her parents continued to see their three daughters as "the children" and continued treating them as if they weren't adults. In frustration she wrote a long letter to her parents expressing her thoughts. She said to me, "I'm thirty-four years old, and it's time they accepted who I am. I'm tired of playing this game of honoring your father and mother instead of being real."

From what Valerie has shared, she seems to have good parents who genuinely care about their children. Now what she wants is to transform their relationship from one of worn-out roles to one of mutual respect and adult appreciation of each other. I like what she's trying to do. I believe in the desire to be loved and understood for who we are; and I believe that being able to love and understand our parents is the best way to truly honor them. As a parent of grown children I also realize that if I am unwilling to give up my old role of knowledge and authority, I am burying a treasure of love in the sands of the past.

Love is something that happens to us. It's a miracle that we have no control over. No matter how empowered we think we are, we can't choose to fall in love. Love chooses us. And, as the novelist Paulo Coelho writes, "Love can consign us to hell, or to paradise, but it always takes us somewhere." While I certainly agree that love "always takes us somewhere," I'd add that we also have something to say about the journey. Even journeys to hell have meaning if we seek to learn what they're trying to teach us, as Stacy discovered.

It's also helpful to remember that if knowing ourselves is a journey then learning to know each other must likewise be a journey. The better we learn to know ourselves, the less we will project onto other people and expect them to meet our needs and expectations. And the more we'll be able to appreciate their uniqueness and the wonder of their stories. Perhaps individuation can lead us to a new kind of love that's beyond the romantic illusions and the self-limiting ideals of the past or the fragmenting struggles of the last forty years. However, we're in new territory when it comes to love and relationships, and currently the best we can do may be to continue exploring it, while remembering how rejuvenating it is to think about where we may be headed.

Eros and Psyche

Love and the way we're learning to think about our relationships began with the emergence of the ancient story of Eros and

Psyche. In his extraordinary study of love and eroticism, Octavio Paz regarded this myth as the turning point in the Western history of love, and one whose effects are still emerging and guiding our experiences. The story seems to be one of the first that pictured love as an unfolding initiation into new levels of personal growth. It opened the doors to our expectations that love can expand our souls and bring meaning and fulfillment into our lives.

Myths are treasure houses of wisdom regarding the world and the patterns of how we live. A myth like this one can be understood on many levels of experience at once. When we've sorted through our emotions and daily events, we can often discover the mythic pattern we're living that can, like a little map, help us understand our struggles or clear up some of our confusion. In addition to being a story that charts our evolving expectations of love, the story of Eros and Psyche also outlines a pattern that's lived out by two lovers. Any one of us and our partners may find our experiences following a motif similar to the one symbolized in the story. Or we can see the story line describing in symbolic terms the quest for love and unity as it tries to grow within ourselves. But, for now, let's consider it as a story symbolizing two people captured by love and their growth into a relationship of substance.

When the story opens, the lovely Psyche is having trouble finding a husband. She is the daughter of a king and her two sisters have already married. The king is troubled by Psyche's difficulty and finds her predicament hard to understand because she's so beautiful that his people have declared her the new love goddess and have stopped worshiping at the temple of Aphrodite. Because of his concern for Psyche, the king finally consults the Delphi Oracle for advice. The Oracle instructs him to prepare a magnificent wedding procession for Psyche that will take her out to a lonely mountain peak, and to leave her there. There she will be wed to a non-mortal man. Amidst great grief, Psyche is led to the crag and eventually falls asleep from exhaustion.

While these events are taking place, the goddess Aphrodite, who is angry over Psyche's beauty and popularity, orders her son, the god Eros, to dispose of Psyche by making her fall in love with a monster. However, as soon as Eros sees her on the mountain he immediately falls in love with her and takes her to his home.

I've often wondered if the venerable storyteller Aupuleius was aware of the symbolic power in this tale as he recorded it in his second-century classic, *The Golden Ass*. The word *psyche* signifies the individual soul in Greek, the heart of our personalities and individual experiences. And Eros, the god of love, is pictured as a radiant, athletic young man, personifying love's strength and power. The great goddess Aphrodite is the third major character in this story. According to Octavio Paz, she is the "faithful image of the world soul," the power of life's continuous drive for renewal. In the language of mythology we have now organized a story that can show us how the individual soul (Psyche) and love (Eros) will have to evolve when put to the test by nature's drive for continuous new growth (Aphrodite).

As the tale continues, Psyche awakens to find herself in a magnificent home where she takes up residence. Eros comes to her every night in the dark, hidden from her sight, and they enjoy their love. When she expresses a desire to see him, he refuses and tells her that it would destroy the happy life they're sharing. Soon, as such stories go, her sisters come to visit Psyche and are filled with envy by her happiness and rich surroundings. Because they're not getting along with their husbands and are jealous, they goad Psyche into trying to discover what her husband looks like. After all, they argue, he may be nothing but a hideous monster.

Finally one evening the anguished Psyche waits until her husband is asleep. Then lighting a lamp, and carrying a knife in case he really is a monster, she actually sees him. In the light she recognizes him and is overwhelmed by his beauty. While she's standing beside him transfixed, oil from her lamp spills on Eros, burning and awakening him. With a cry of despair he leaves Psyche, saying he can never return.

There are many Greek myths where gods become infatuated

with mortal women, but in none of them does an attraction for the human soul play a part as it does in this story, nor does a marriage and relationship generally follow. The story of Psyche and Eros also reveals another archetypal theme that demonstrates as soon as love is formed, it must be tested.

Many of us can identify with this crisis. We, too, approach our relationships full of hope, anticipating pleasure, joy, security, and the expectation of the enduring love our culture promises, and then, as many of us know, plummet to Earth when we encounter pain and difficulty. If our relationships don't seem to work we blame ourselves, believing we should know how to make them work or that we should have had more sense than to get involved in the first place. Older people who see our condition may simply say "the honeymoon is over." When our expectations aren't fulfilled, it's easy to become despondent and blame ourselves, our partners, or love itself.

But, the story of Eros and Psyche doesn't end here. So far we've only seen the opening movement of a journey that refines and matures the experience of love between two people. Love is an arena where fate and choice intersect. "It is a space magnetized by encounter," Paz tells us. The attractions the lovers feel must be involuntary, born from the mystery of love. At the same time it must be a choice, and the choice to pursue our destinies through love begins the journey of refining it.

In the story Psyche is devastated by what has happened and finds herself sitting by a river crying and thinking about killing herself. While she's there the nature god Pan comforts her and urges her to search for Eros. As she follows his advice she discovers that none of the other goddesses will help her. They're afraid of Aphrodite who is vengefully looking for Psyche. The difficulty of Psyche's search is increased by her newly discovered pregnancy. Soon Aphrodite finds her and imposes four seemingly impossible tasks on her as the price of her redemption.

Psyche is alone, with child, and is facing an angry fate in the form of Aphrodite and the four tasks. Eros too is alone, burned, suffering, and in despair. The myth has taken us to an unexpected place. Love and a brief look at reality have wounded both Psyche, the soul, and Eros, love. Separation and sorrow seem in opposition to our ideas of attraction and marriage, but the story shows they're actually part of the journey. Once a relationship is no longer blindly lived, we have to step back and grow further as individuals before we can come back together in a more progressive connection. For a relationship and love to continually recreate themselves, it's helpful if we understand the map this story is outlining. These experiences of coming apart and then seeking and returning to each other are as natural as the rhythmic contractions and expansions of our hearts. Understanding this pattern can help us locate the equivalent moments in our own lives; and while they may still be painful, they're less likely to destroy our love.

The structure of the myth reveals that disillusionment in love is a necessary step in an evolving journey. The stinging realization that reality doesn't match our fantasies is an important part of love's path. Hopefully this awareness can serve to help us resist the impulse to close down and protect ourselves. When the poet Rilke implores us to have patience toward the unsolved issues in our hearts, he's asking us to remember that relationships are difficult because being human is difficult and the questions of how to be in a relationship are essentially the same ones we ask about how to live.

Psyche bravely undertakes the tasks Aphrodite has set before her. In the first one she must sort a great mound of mixed seeds into separate piles before sunset. Then she has to collect a sample of the golden fleece from one of the sun god's sheep. These sheep are venomous and go dangerously mad at the sight of a person. Her third task is to collect a small crystal urn of water from the source of the river Styx, which separates the realm of the living from Hades, the land of the dead. To touch this water is fatal even to the gods, and dragons guard its source. The final task is to get a box of beauty cream from Persephone, the queen of the underworld, which lies beyond the river Styx and is guarded by the three-headed dog Cerberus.

As Psyche pursues these tasks she is aided by nature, fate, and the gods as we generally are when we face the tasks of our growth and development. Ants come to Psyche's aid in sorting the seeds. Reeds by a river whisper to her to wait for the sheep to pass and then to pick some of their fleece off of the brambles. The eagle of Zeus fills her urn from the river Styx. And finally, when she is about to throw herself off a tower in despair, the tower explains to her how to fix three cakes to placate Cerberus, find Persephone, and return.

It's important to realize that her tasks are not punishments. She, like the rest of us, must fall passionately in love in order to set her journey in motion, and be possessed by love before she can become its mistress. The tasks are necessary for her further individuation, for being able to discern her feelings and potentials, relate to her own nature, develop her own perspective, and make a successful journey into her deeper self.

While Psyche is struggling to complete her final task, Eros finds her. Then he appeals to Zeus saying they've suffered enough, and Zeus consents to making Psyche immortal. They're reconciled with Aphrodite and soon after their daughter is born, whom they name Joy. The Western concept of love believes that love refines us, that it is a journey toward a higher state of consciousness and being. The adventure begins passionately and blindly. It challenges the boundaries of common sense, thrusts us into joy and the despair of disillusionment and failure, yet fills us with hope as we face the growthful tasks it has pushed us to face.

Individuation and the journey of love combine in their efforts to awaken our consciousness and deepen our experiences of life. The lovely, dramatic story of how fate, choice, darkness, separation, trial, and reunion carry love forward to its most fulfilling level makes Eros and Psyche a tale that guides us still. If it does nothing more than remind us that life and love are made up of pleasure, bruises, and turns of fate, and our willingness to experience them is worth the price we have to pay, the story will have served us well.

The Light in the Dark

The idyllic beginning of the relationship between Eros and Psyche came to an abrupt end when their bedroom was filled with light and they could see each other clearly. Their quick glimpse of reality revealed the beauty of love and yet brought a stop to their pleasure together. However, this turning point in the story is actually the beginning of a journey that brings meaning to the myth and helps us identify the first benchmark on love's path.

Our passion is a yearning to connect with the vastness of life's experiences. The wealth of feelings we get from falling in love comes from the rich emotions, hope, confidence, and visions of the future that love stirs up in us and by the feeling of completion that another person brings into our lives. Then one day something happens to us as it did to Psyche. Some kind of discord will cause us to see our lovers in a new way. They may act impatient or critical, do something a bit untrustworthy, or want to spend more time in their own activities. Whether what they do is large or small we begin to realize that the people we are in love with are very different from what we have imagined. They may actually seem like strangers at times.

It may be helpful at this point to remember that the old cliche "opposites attract" has some truth in it. The characteristics in our lovers that once made us feel complete in the relationship are now the seeds of healing childhood wounds and new growth we need to cultivate within ourselves. Our attractions depend upon the qualities we've developed, our unhealed wounds and unrecognized needs. For example, introverted people often find that extroverted partners bring a fresh sense of vitality and involvement in the world to their lives. People who are at home with their emotions may be attracted to those who can help them bring objectivity to their perspectives, and their partners may enjoy the warmth they bring in return. There are many simple ways we can bring vitality to each other when we fall in love.

The attraction of opposites becomes more complex if we consider the ways we were wounded growing up. In these situations the attraction may be based on varying kinds of opposite or complementary needs. For example, a man may marry a woman much younger than himself. He may show the calm strength of maturity that makes her feel secure, and she may have the freshness that helps energize him and the vulnerability that brings out the tenderness in his character. Or, an older wife may provide the affirmation a younger man needs while he in return offers ardor to her in a manner that respects and takes pleasure in her maturity.

Disillusionment begins when the complementary aspects of the relationship begin wearing out. The extroverted partner becomes tired of having to initiate the couple's social life or even their conversation. The introvert begins to resent the extrovert's inability to stop talking. The thoughtful partner may become irritated at the other person's unpredictable behavior, while the more spontaneous of them in turn becomes disgusted with his or her partner's coldness.

The woman who married an older man may begin to resent how controlling he is, or feel he's smothering her, and he may become angry at the burden of her dependency and her ingratitude. The younger man may begin to act rebellious toward his older wife, who may feel angry and threatened by his adolescent behavior, which also makes her feel her age.

Similar patterns of attraction and disillusionment happen in most close relationships and it doesn't matter if they're heterosexual or homosexual. Intense relationships arouse our deep emotions when we first enter into them and the feelings are just as strong when disillusionment begins. The deeper our needs are when we come together, the deeper our distress will be when our complementary effects on each other wear out.

In *The Symposium,* Plato's great discourse on love, the author narrates a series of dialogs on love given by seven imaginary guests at a feast. Plato offers six points of view that were popular and sophisticated during his time and then presents his own perspective through the imaginary voice of his old teacher Socrates. The splendid speech Aristophanes makes is particularly memorable and tells the story of a time when human beings were complete within themselves. Originally there were three sexes: male, female, and one that was both male and female. As history evolved, Zeus decided that these complete human beings were becoming too powerful and split them into two parts. Aristophanes ends his discourse by saying that happiness in love is finding the beloved that restores us to our original feeling of completeness. Plato realizes longing for wholeness is a powerful but primitive aspect of love, and later speakers in the story eloquently explain how love must grow beyond our neediness, whether it's large or small, and must motivate us to seek beauty and aspire to divine values.

For our relationships to grow we must learn that the wholeness we're seeking is ultimately within ourselves and that our partners are mirroring the potentials within us. If we fail to realize this truth we'll remain dissatisfied in the long run. Disillusionment comes as we begin to realize our partners don't offer the completion we've longed for and that we're locked in conflict with the very characteristics that first attracted us.

I recently saw a couple who were engaged in such a clash. In addition to being highly intelligent, the woman in this couple was also very intuitive. Her partner originally loved the way she could look at a situation, size it up, and make a decision. He was also quite intelligent but was quieter and more intense. He liked to think things carefully through before making up his mind. On big decisions he didn't completely trust her intuition as a decision-making process and thought she was capable of acting impulsively. While they were trying to select a new home in a tight real estate market, they were discussing a house that she liked; he was still thinking about its good points and weak points, and weighing what kind of offer to make, and if they should even make one. As they were talking to me it became clear he felt like they were working their way methodically to a decision while she, impatient and fearful they would lose the house if they failed to act promptly, thought he was being bullheaded and naive, and wasn't paying attention to how she felt about the house. Both of them needed to back away from the conflict and learn how to communicate in a way that recognized their different styles of approaching decisions.

The couple above had been married about three years when disillusionment began to set in. It was also manifesting itself in other ways that were bringing conflict into their lovemaking, their social life, and how they handled their money. Disillusionment comes more than once and at various times in our long-term relationships; we learn inevitably that our partners are not the parents, breadwinners, or companions we hoped they would be. Nor can they always be supportive people who take the time to understand us and accept our quirks and insecurities. These realizations creep in as the initial bloom of attraction fades. And they may show up even stronger in midlife when we're reevaluating many things we've previously taken for granted. They also come to some extent at every turning point in our growth because each of these experiences leaves us seeing reality more clearly. And they challenge us to learn to love more authentically as we evolve.

To offset the effects of disillusionment we must try to learn more about ourselves and develop the characteristics we've enjoyed having our partners carry for us. Introverts may have to learn how to become more involved in life and to express themselves more spontaneously. Extroverts may need to learn how to become more quiet and reflective in order to refresh themselves. Warm, spontaneous people may need to become more thoughtful and objective at important times in their lives, while thoughtful people may find it helpful to learn how to be more open and caring. The man with the younger wife will have to accept her growth if they're going to continue in a vital relationship, and she will have to free him from the burden of her dependence. The older woman married to the younger man must foster his maturity and independence, and he must learn to reclaim his emotional needs for affirmation and recognize her maturity more fully.

When I was talking with Joyce a few years after she'd married Randy, her distress seemed almost as deep as Psyche's when she was sitting by the river crying. "He loves me," Joyce said, "I know he does. He's a good man, but he's gotten so critical: I talk too much. Why aren't I exercising more? Everyone else is. I must be lazy. Why didn't I remember to phone the repairman? I mean, I feel like everything I'm doing is wrong all of a sudden." Joyce was feeling attacked and hopeless at this point in her relationship. And, in retaliation or self-defense, she'd become very critical of Randy.

Joyce and Randy met several years after each of them had been through a painful divorce from someone else. Joyce's divorce had deeply undermined her self-confidence and Randy's had left him feeling inadequate in many ways. When they met, they started getting to know each other slowly, first as friends, then by dating and sharing activities. Soon they fell in love. Joyce's extroverted sensuality made Randy feel desired, loved, and attractive as a man. In response, he sensed in his quiet, thoughtful way when Joyce was feeling insecure and encouraged her. He helped her in other areas where she felt inadequate, such as controlling her adolescent daughter. Their sexual need for each other boosted their self-esteem after the painful rejections they had felt in their previous marriages.

Everything went well for Joyce and Randy for quite a while. Then the structure of their complementary relationship began to break down. Like the envious sisters of Psyche, doubts started creeping into Joyce's mind. She began to feel that Randy loved sex more than her. The more she thought, the more insecure and unloved she felt. Soon she started nagging Randy to show more feeling and caring. When he became angry she felt misunderstood. Meanwhile Randy was feeling rejected, trapped, and betrayed without knowing why. He responded by criticizing Joyce in her most vulnerable areas, which included her appearance and feelings of competence.

If we continue using the story of Eros and Psyche as our map, we might suppose that Joyce is now sitting by the river feeling devastated and Randy has retreated from the scene, burned and suffering after their first big experience of disillusionment. The myth shows that now is the time they must journey separately in order to grow to a point where they can come back together in a more satisfying way. It will be helpful to both of them if they can turn their energies away from each other and spend some time seeking to understand themselves better. Joyce and Randy decided their relationship was worth developing and began working on themselves. When Joyce can realize that the power for healing and affirmation is within *her*, Randy will emerge in her eyes as an individual rather than as representing the source of the help she thinks she needs. When Randy looks at Joyce and sees someone to nurture him sexually, he's also seeing her as an object to fill his needs rather than as a person, and he too must discover his capacities for healing and self-love. When both of these things happen, *then* they'll be in a position to find out if they can have a relationship of substance.

Facing our individual needs and learning to love ourselves free our relationships to be more creative, joyful, and less threatening. This doesn't mean we no longer have any needs. It means that we have created safer places for true intimacy—for learning more about the art of knowing each other deeply, and for freely expressing our love in a manner that brings joy and fulfillment to us. Then we will see our partners as someone with whom we can share our deepest values and visions of life.

When Psyche is assigned the tasks by Aphrodite, she could choose *not* to attempt them and risk losing her love forever. Or she could *choose* to grow. When disillusionment sets in so does choice. If we read the story this way, the tasks are about growth and self-discovery. Our commitment and our choice to learn about ourselves in order to recreate our love become the turning point in our process. Unfortunately, it's the pain of disillusionment that either causes us to seek help and knowledge or become bitter and discouraged. The more we learn about the craft of relationship and ourselves, the more equipped we are to make this journey a rewarding one.

Healing Our Basic Wounds

Many people form relationships to fill voids in their lives. My early marriage served to give me the purpose and direction I needed to move into adulthood. But what happens in a case like mine where a marriage or relationship has had a healing purpose and its intention has been fulfilled? In some cases new love can indeed be discovered after disillusionment has set in and the voids have been recognized, healed, or outgrown. In other situations, such as my own, the two people may have grown up as a result of their struggles to become far different from when they began, and the relationship may no longer be viable.

We need to remember that even a child who is deeply loved and wisely nurtured by a happy set of parents must pay a heavy price for this experience. In my earlier discussions, I showed how our culture and families shape our characters and identities before we have minds or wills to choose for ourselves, and how they imprint their official myths onto our personalities. The bonds that secure us also limit us. But these bonds likewise give us sufficient trust and self-confidence to eventually struggle free of them.

However if we're severely wounded, are traumatized in some way, or left with voids in our personalities, and if these wounds are basic and deep, then we'll be motivated to seek relationships that in some manner will be trying to heal and restore us. If we come back to the first lesson from *The Symposium,* we can see that the path of love begins in a manner that compels us to pursue what's missing within our makeups. Sometimes, we'll unknowingly be driven by an obsession for what is missing within ourselves into the arms of someone who is wounded in a complementary manner. Our first reaction to realizing what we've done is a wincing and withering shame. But—a big "but"—*understanding* this process can relieve us of feeling a sense of disgust and failure as we realize the problems we are encountering are part of love's efforts to help us heal and grow.

The most common wounds we encounter are the ones we receive from our mothers or fathers. Wounds from our mothers bruise our souls, what Jungians call the *anima,* the part of our personalities that is full of imagination and keeps us close to life, empathetic, and connected to people. Wounds from our fathers injure our spirits—the *animus,* which represents our deep connection to confidence, creativity, strength of purpose, and spirit.

Such wounds set up what we refer to in the jargon of psychology as a *mother complex* or a *father complex.* Frequently people with a mother complex may seem to lose their sense of equilibrium in the presence of a needy person. They may spend a lot of time in caretaking activities of varying kinds. Some people even admit they got into their relationship or stay in it because the other person needs them so badly. A woman with a father complex may be drawn to wounded, sensitive men who haven't fully matured. And a man with a mother complex may be drawn to fragile women who seem to need nurturance, protection, and guidance of a maternal kind.

In the case of a father complex, a man or woman has trouble believing in his or her own strength, competence, and importance. A woman may treat her husband, men in general, or other strong women as more important than herself. She will be drawn to men who seem strong, domineering, or even aggressive. A man with a father complex may be timid and attracted to strong, self-directed, dominating women. I once heard a woman with a father complex remark, "I'm afraid to look inside of myself for there may be nothing there." Men and women like these suffer from a loss of spirit and they are left searching for stimulation, strength, and inspiration through someone else. When we have been harshly wounded in our early lives we must find the courage to admit it to ourselves and seek healing. Otherwise our relationships will disappoint us, fail us, and may even damage us further and imprison us.

Before Carl was born his older brother had died during a minor surgical procedure. His mother went into a major depression that lasted the rest of her life. Carl received little nurturing and support from her through childhood as she barely had the strength to exist. Carl's father was a good man, a roofing contractor who had become overwhelmed by his wife's depression and his responsibilities. He went to work and took care of his family but had neither the energy nor the skills to give his wife and Carl the emotional attention they needed.

Carl was a smart young man and won a scholarship to college. But he left home with a hidden emotional void that was very strong. While in graduate school he met Lesley, who was a sophomore at the same school. Lesley's mother was somewhat cold, and her father had been a strong, cheerful, outgoing man. Lesley was their only daughter and she had two older brothers. She enjoyed the warm, joyful relationship she had had with her father before he died of a heart attack when she was eight years old. Her mother never remarried and the family had endured years of financial struggle after her father's death.

When Carl and Lesley met they felt compelled to be together. Yet, at times they both believed their relationship was a mistake and tried to break up. When he looked back on this period years later, Carl thought that when dating Lesley he secretly liked being needed so much. It made him feel solid and confident. However, he was also afraid of how possessive and controlling Lesley was. In addition, he believed that Lesley was attracted by his appearance of strength but repelled by how dependent their relationship left her feeling. However, each time they separated they soon ended up together again, and after knowing each other a couple of years they married and went on to have four children. Initially Carl felt strong in taking care of Lesley and their family, and important because of how much she needed him and deferred to him. Lesley felt protected and secure by having a successful husband.

Despite the on-again/off-again turbulence of their courtship, Carl and Lesley did not go through the normal disillusionment that many couples experience after marriage. Part of the reason was the energy it took for them to finish school and start their family. Later in his analysis, Carl said that at some level he knew he wasn't in love with Lesley when they married, but felt he couldn't change the course of what was happening. His guilt for not acting on this realization had made him try even harder to make the marriage successful. And, it almost seemed that rushing into having children and taking on financial obligations was an intended distraction, a way of avoiding becoming more self-aware in their relationship.

When he was in his late thirties, Carl had a major depression and ended up being hospitalized. Both he and Lesley were surprised at how angry, frightened, and resentful she became during his breakdown. Now their disillusionment became obvious. Both of them started analysis in order to understand and reclaim themselves. As they recognized and healed their early wounds and began taking back the parts of themselves the other person had stood for, they realized they wanted to have new and separate lives based on their restored personalities. Both of them learned a renewed respect for the person they had been married to and for the healing aspects of their relationship, but they had no desire to be in life together past this point except for dealing responsibly with their children.

From the standpoint of our societal values, their marriage was a failure. From a psychological standpoint, it was a blessing that allowed them to see that their conflicts and failures were symptoms calling for more extensive healing than simply trying to fix a marriage. Their marriage had served to get them into adulthood and to a level of maturity strong enough to enable them to face the healing they needed. Once Carl's depression began to bring the pain of their disillusionment into the open, they had to learn how to face the failure of their relationship with authenticity and mutual esteem rather than continue a marriage that would have been a destructive charade. We must be willing to take emotional risks and trust that our experiences can teach us, heal us, and bring us to a feeling of inner completion. Life is a process of becoming and is never limited to simply making proper choices, no matter how informed we may think they are. Learning to have the strength and courage to face ourselves and get the help we need when we're stuck and suffering is the stuff of a loving and fulfilling life.

Turning the Corner

Relationships are crucibles for growth, and the most important ones are the ones within ourselves. Intimate relationships stir our emotions and push us to see ourselves more clearly. But this isn't to imply we must have special partners to grow. Being single doesn't mean we don't have any relationships. Many of the ones we have with friends, family, children, and mentors can also be important to our growth and frequently very intense. You may remember, for example, that the love based on a growing friendship between Zorba and Boss became inspiring and beautiful. Such bonds result when two people can move toward each other and neither of them tries to dominate the other one. All relationships are a dance of coming together and going apart.

The same kind of thing happens in my professional relationships. A person comes to see me, we work together in a very individual way, and as he or she evolves we face a time of separation. A few months ago, Margaret, the businesswoman with the gypsy woman dream, and I began our process of growing apart. During our final session we were reflecting upon the process we'd gone through and I remembered the very different Margaret of not so long before.

"As I look back I can see how restless I was and how hard I was trying to deny it because my life seemed so good," Margaret began. "Now I realize I was searching. During the first part of our work I thought I was searching for intimacy and a sense of being loved. Then I began to understand I was searching for much more than that. I needed to discover the path that was my life."

Margaret had been caught in the familiar paradox of seeming to have a good life and yet knowing it wasn't working for her. We may feel restless, as she did, depressed, or simply drained. The dream appearance of the gypsy woman opened Margaret to the unrealized potentials she had for new growth, which led her to quit her job and become an artist.

But like most of us, Margaret had to revisit her past in order to uncover some of the old patterns that were controlling her life. "I spent, oh, I don't know how long, twenty or thirty years, more probably, trying to prove to my parents that I was special and lovable by behaving and living in a way they would approve of," she continued. "Actually, I suppose a lot of that time was spent, out of habit, trying to prove it to myself—to the parental attitudes I'd internalized. Naturally I expected Fred [her husband] to furnish me with that affirmation by making me feel loved and admired. It took me over twenty years of adult life and analysis to build the foundation I needed to move into my real life."

I also recalled that Margaret's journey hadn't been an easy experience for Fred. Initially he hadn't understood her unhappiness or why painting part-time wasn't enough to satisfy her. Plus he resented the financial strain that leaving her job brought on the family. At times they had argued furiously about money. Fred accused Margaret of being selfish, thoughtless, and childish and she blamed him for not being loving and supportive, and for caring more about his lifestyle than about her. Both of them charged the other with abandoning their love, and at times their sex life became another battlefield. When things became unbearable they separated for a while. But both of them seemed to retain some hope for their future and Fred went into analysis himself.

Throughout a period of turmoil that lasted several years, their teenage children were obviously worried at times but continued to function fairly well. Because Margaret and Fred had been open with them, they were able to understand both sides of their parents' struggle. They continued their pattern of growing up, making good grades, playing sports, and acting responsibly. As their parents worked through their arguments into a more growth-oriented stage, the children became fascinated with Margaret's and Fred's new ideas about how to live in a more personally satisfying manner. Children usually do OK when their parents own their struggles and seek to work them out instead of suppressing them and then using the children as pawns in an undeclared war.

There was no doubt that Margaret's growth forced several crises in the marriage and compelled Fred to face himself and make some changes. Fred had to see a Margaret he had never imagined and learn to either take pleasure in her growth and change, or dissolve the marriage. However, once he got over the shock of seeing things alter that he had thought were stable—their financial status, plans for the future, and even their personalities—he began to feel a new sense of freedom and that he could ask more from life than he had believed he could in the past. During our final meeting when I asked Margaret how Fred was doing, she responded and went on to explain that she was sorry for some of the arguments they had "as I tried to make him play out my parental conflicts with me." Then she paused thoughtfully and said, "But I don't feel guilty. He had his own list of things he needed to work through in our dance. I'm just sorry for the times we hurt each other."

Through these experiences and their analysis Margaret and Fred learned that while being angry was perfectly human and often appropriate, we still have to maintain a sense of courtesy and respect for each other. When we can do this, it becomes easier to reflect upon our arguments because we're not so caught up in our hurt and resentful feelings that we push our relationships over a precipice. This reflection can help us look at our parts in what has happened in the past as well as to see other people more clearly and realistically—who they are with their hopes, dreams, fears, plans, and disappointments; how we are hurting, scaring, or inspiring them; and how we can work together with more respect for each other. "We don't fight much anymore," she said, "I think we've learned that relationships aren't all sweetness and light and they must be grounded in something solid like honesty and respect."

As our hour was coming to a close Margaret leaned forward and said, "Looking inward has helped me feel the presence of love in my life. That something has been interested in me all along, guiding my life, supporting it, in some strange way. Trying to become known by me. It's somewhere within myself. It seems funny I had to seek it while at the same time allow it to find me. It brings a sense of peace, or serenity, no matter what hardships I have to face."

RELATIONSHIPS OF SUBSTANCE

When speaking of alchemy an ancient Chinese writer once said, "They believed that it was a matter of turning lead into gold; was this not madness?" To the practical mind, allowing ourselves to be transformed by the powers of love on its many levels may in fact seem like madness. I've thought so more than once myself. And yet, the ancient alchemists pursued their craft with devotion, separating base materials, refining them, and attempting to bring them back together in a new form.

Margaret learned to live this pattern as a model for her inner work and in her outer relationships. And she discovered, as we all can, a deeper level of being at peace with herself, of experiencing love—of turning ordinary life into gold.

CHAPTER 12
Living the Choice

Wonder and despair are two sides of a spinning coin. When you open yourself to one, you open yourself to the other. You discover a capacity for joy that wasn't in you before. Wonder is the promise of restoration: as deeply as you dive, so may you rise.
—Christina Baldwin

"But when you think about what people are actually undergoing in our civilization, you realize it's a very grim thing to be a modern human being," the great mythologist Joseph Campbell said in an interview with public television commentator Bill Moyers. We live in frightening times because we've outgrown ourselves. Our outer knowledge has outstripped our inner knowledge; and our philosophies, educational and religious institutions, and societal customs are rarely able to guide us to fulfilling lives. If we want to live authentic, heartfelt lives we are going to have to rely on our own resources.

The other side of this equation is that we live in challenging and exciting times. Because the old gods are crumbling, and our old models are failing us, we can explore new ways of living, understanding ourselves, and growing that may result in opportunities that are more unique, personal, fulfilling, and loving than ever before. The choice is up to us and depends on whether we're willing to take our journeys into inner knowledge seriously enough to balance the power of society's influences on our lives.

We haven't arrived at this point overnight. It's been building since the industrial revolution. Our advances in technology, science, and marketing have put us in the position of either living in a sickly selfish, impersonal manner as part of the herd or taking up the quest of becoming sacredly selfish individuals of substance. This quest helps us learn how to live in our modern world without being victims of it. Joseph Campbell thought that myths and legends could help us in our quests by teaching us how we can understand our experiences of life and the meanings behind them. One of his favorite lesson plans for modern life came from the legendary quests for the Holy Grail that I mentioned in the beginning of this book. These quests parallel the individuation process in many ways because the Grail represents the highest fulfillment of human life. The quest for the Grail became a necessity in a kingdom where life had become a *wasteland*, withering and dying, and where its people were starving. When writing or speaking of the Grail, Campbell was usually careful to point out that its seekers began their quests alone by entering the forest where it was the thickest and where there were no paths.

When we apply this legend to modern life it becomes clear that wherever there's a path it represents someone else's way; be it the collective path of our families or culture, it cannot lead us to fulfilled lives at their most satisfying levels. In the Grail story, every knight (symbolizing each of us—whether man or woman because symbols aren't restricted by our current notion of gender) had to enter the forest where it was dense and mysterious and follow the lead of his own experience and intuition. This personal journey did not remove knights from collective life: They were still knights, members of the kingdom, serving the king, but through their personal quests they were trying to redeem a lost world. In Campbell's rendition of the legend, whenever a knight saw the trail of another knight, thought that knight might be getting close to the Grail and so began to follow his trail, he would go astray entirely.

The wisdom in the legend reveals that each of our quests must be an individual one seeking to bring forth our unique potentials, which are different from anyone else's. This means that for each of us there is a life force that can be refined and translated by us into actions and love. Because we're unique, this expression can't be duplicated and if we fail to develop it, meaning to refine it beyond the limits of society's roles, it will never exist and will be lost for all time. While each knight had to journey alone he was still a member of the Round Table, a community of seekers. Today, our Round Table of support may be those very people like ourselves who are seeking more fulfilling lives. Still, individuation will always be a personal journey based on our increasing self-knowledge as individual men and women. And in most cases we will have to develop the ability to function in the world, our secular substance, as a foundation for the quest, just as each knight had to become a knight in order to begin the search for the Grail. Several schools of psychology, mythology, and the mystic branches of religion (the branches most interested in developing spiritual consciousness) recognize that every person is charged with an individual destiny, a destination of completeness in his or her life; and it's this realization alone that makes sense of our existence.

My major purpose in these pages has been to show how learning more about who we really are can bring us to an experience of love and wholeness. The mystics believe that the search for self-knowledge ultimately leads to an experience of knowing God, the name they give to the absolute or transcendent dimensions of life. In Jungian psychology this assertion is true because it leads to the knowledge of our greater Selves and our relationships with them. The Self is the image of God or the transcendent within us—that aspect of each one of us that makes us feel centered, at home within ourselves, and with a unique value and purpose for being alive. In our daily lives we're pushed and pulled by many outside forces that stir up a profusion of conflicting emotions, needs, desires, and obligations. But in those special moments of joy, peace, reflection, and even sadness we may experience a brief glimpse that everything fits together within us, or between us and life, like the pieces in a mosaic. When we experience the interrelatedness and the inter-dependence of the different aspects of our selves we'll soon go on to have the same experiences between ourselves and other people, and life in general. The journey into self-knowledge, the quest for the Grail, leads us into the recognition of things coming together and being interrelated, which is an experience of the Self and love at its highest level. The more we seek to fulfill our potentials for wholeness, the further it will lead us in our psychological and spiritual development—into relationships with other people that are creative and loving.

The Self acts like the hub of a wheel centering our life force, arranging our potentials and fostering their development like the carefully spaced spokes that reach from the hub to the rim of the wheel. The rim acts like our personalities, supporting our progress and movement through life, yet its support rests on the center, the Self. Taoist writings state that "the sage is he who has attained the central point of the Wheel and remains bound . . . in indissoluble union with the Origin." When people have made this connection and are aware of the importance of their inner lives, we experience them as having a presence that is liberating and healing. I explained in chapter 9 how physician and author Rachel Naomi Remen experienced Carl Rogers this way. Many of us have such people in our lives who were turning points. I often think about my grandfather who was willing to take the risk and follow his dream of founding a school. The image of his courage, love, and determination has stood like a beacon throughout my life. We might remember a coach, a teacher, or a mentor who in a special moment drew us out of ourselves and affirmed what was emerging rather than simply directing us in some task. Distinguished author bell hooks still recalls the man who gave her Rilke's *Letters to a Young Poet,* the book that sustained her through a dark adolescence and changed her life for the better.

People who have experienced life and its potential wholeness have an impact on the others around them like a stone thrown in a pond. Vitality and growth emanate from them like circles that ripple across the water.

The more we search for self-knowledge, the more our efforts

become pilgrimages to the center of our beings and the more our personalities come into harmony, enabling us to reach beyond ourselves. We might consider this a growing expression of our true Selves as everything we do becomes an increasingly authentic expression of who we are. This is the experience of illuminated consciousness, to return for a moment to the use of psychological language. Or more simply, we might say we're polishing the stones that represent our essences. Studying them, turning them around, we become aware of their many facets and buffing them further, we finally have diamonds in our hands that are unique, radiant, and beautiful.

Life Against Death

The imperative of life is to grow and if we're going to grow as human beings, we must ally ourselves with life, love, and courage and face the struggles that growth entails. Easier to say than to do, you might think. But if we keep life's basic purpose in mind, alive in our reflections, these allegiances may take root within us sooner than we expect. And if instead we fail to grow, we will stagnate and begin to deteriorate, no matter how good we are at presenting the public faces we might be hiding behind. Loren Eisely, a great anthropologist with the heart of a poet, explains how life has always been a fight, how it began by absorbing the energy of the sun until plants burst into existence. He says that life "began like a war with strange chemicals seething under a sky lacking in oxygen; it was waged through long ages until the first green plants learned to harness the light of the nearest star, our sun. The human brain, so frail, so perishable, so full of inexhaustible dreams and hungers, burns by the power of the leaf." Our self-knowledge grows in a similar manner, often out of sight until it comes into our awareness through a building up of tensions, which ultimately are seeking to break through our former limits. We've seen many examples of this process in the stories I've shared with you, with Margaret and Fred who struggled to grow and have their marriage grow, with Janice who woke up to her own strength through her depression, with Rob who discovered a new beginning at midlife, and with many more. Like them, if we cannot stand the strain of our growthful passages, we end up falling back, which usually means falling back into rigidity and eventually into a wasteland of the heart.

The archetypal images from ancient Greece that picture the illicit affair between Ares, the god of war, and Aphrodite, the goddess of love, show that behind our best public appearances love and war are structured into our natures. In other words if we're going to embrace life and live passionately, we must be able to hold the tension between the limiting effects of old values, obligations, and others' expectations and our need to progress, and be able to endure the inner and outer conflicts this causes. Ares and Aphrodite represent the passionate forces of life, our need to be able to struggle and love as a normal part of existence. They had three children that represented the outcomes of these forces and their effects on us. Wisely, the Greeks named the children Fear, Discord, and Harmony, showing us that living passionately means facing our fears and the troubles we encounter in order to eventually achieve a state of inner harmony. If we're unable to live passionately, we'll have the tendency to repress our strong emotions and project our conflicts outside of ourselves, where they may eventually erupt into violence. These conflicts represent a desire for life that has been blocked by some other force. When an adolescent gets into a major confrontation with an overly rigid parent they are fighting for the freedom they feel the parent is blocking. The rigid stance and the vicious retorts of the parent may reflect how fear has impeded their own desires for independence and opportunity. Such conflicts also take place between lovers, neighbors, business colleagues, classes of people, or between nations, and the principle is frequently the same.

Many centuries ago Aristotle made it very clear that *courage* is the most important of all the virtues because without it we can't practice any of the others. Courage is the nearest star, the sunlight that can fuel our growth. Maya Angelou says we must be courageous about facing and exploring our personal histories. We must find the courage to care and to create internally as well as externally, and, as she says, we need the courage "to create ourselves daily as Christians, as Jews, as Muslims, as thinking, caring, laughing, loving human beings."

During the journey of growth we may have to confront the structure of values we've been living by, the relationships and jobs we're in. Growth is not risk-free or guaranteed to be joyful. We may have to make some major changes; we may hurt or disappoint people near to us. Taking such risks is painful and scary. Margaret and Fred discovered they had to redefine themselves and their marriage. Deep down, first Margaret and then Fred wanted to break free of the lives they had been living and the ways they felt limited, but not from each other. While they knew they were suffering and hurting each other, they had to work to see if staying together, setting new boundaries, and opening up their future was possible. The answer to these questions took months of effort to arrive at.

But if we're in jobs or relationships into which we cannot successfully bring love, then they will depress our spirits, erode our self-esteem, and eventually cause us to dislike ourselves. It's better to take the risk and suffer the needed losses if there are influences or aspects of our lives of which we must break free. In the long run, breaking free of the forces that imprison our souls is empowering. Living years of useless virtue, inertia, and cowardice—unhappy martyrdom—helps no one. It's much better to say that all of our conscious lives and energies—all that time lost and reclaimed now—have been dedicated to the growth and liberation of the human spirit, and that the work began with ourselves.

When I drive to work every day I see a tree that is growing in what appears to be an impossible place. Year after year I've watched it climb out of a stone wall by an old building. I love to see it and imagine it as a triumph of life over death, of *eros* over *thanatos*, the terms Freud used to define the pull of life against the force of death. Our natures are like that tree. They push us toward growth, and our societal values, conventional wisdom, and fear pull us toward the seeming security of refusing to grow, or denying its possibility. Erich Fromm personalized these forces and summed them up as either *a love of life* or *a love of death*. He felt that society inevitably pushes us into a love of death because it urges us to live dutifully and by the values of the culture, rather than to live authentically and creatively.

Two paths, then, with two ends. Which will you choose? The path that leads into the wasteland, however rich and seductive it appears? Or the path through the forest, the path of loving life that begins with self-knowledge? The latter is the only way you can learn to create the conditions for love to take place. If you choose this path, like a faithful knight, you must then take up your sword and shield and seek to enter the forest of your unknown interior. And while this quest is a noble one it's also an attainable one. It isn't about seeking lofty ideals, gaining extraordinary powers, or attaining a special condition. It is, like the legends, tales, and myths you've read about, finally a story, *your* story, simple, inexorable, and as natural as the beating of a heart. It is about finding a way to live fully, by living wholeheartedly.

Weaving Our Tapestries

When cultivating a life of substance we're invited to choose for ourselves and take responsibility for our choices. In this way we bring our stories as contributions to the greater story of human emergence—out of darkness and into creative fullness.

A few weeks ago a friend wanted to share an intense dream with me that he felt had opened his eyes to a new way of thinking about himself. (He's a well-respected professor who was preparing a series of lectures on the psychology of Eastern thought.) He told me that as the dream began he was walking into an ancient stone church. The blocks of stone were large and covered with moss. As he walked up the center aisle through the dim light, he saw that the altar was surrounded by the flames of many candles. As he drew closer he saw there were nuns in old-fashioned habits on the right of the altar and monks in cassocks on the left, and they were chanting together in a moving chorus of masculine and feminine voices.

While he was speaking I remembered that he wasn't raised a Catholic, but somehow his unconscious was choosing this symbolism from several centuries in the past. He went on to explain how he had knelt in the first row with his head bowed. Then he said, "Slowly I looked up toward the altar and Althea was the priest preparing for communion." I knew that Althea had been his first great love, whom he hadn't seen since high school but who had become over the years a kind of inner feminine companion in his dreams and fantasies.

"As the service continued," he said, "she lifted the chalice into the air toward the large crucifix that was hanging from the ceiling. My eyes followed it upward to the crucifix. As I made out the features on the cross, I found, with a shock of amazement, that I was looking directly into my own face.

"The dream has taught me something important," he continued. "For the first time in my life, I'm beginning to understand the meaning of passion. This process is extremely personal; it's my crucifixion, my transformation, my communion, myself in life in relationship to eternity—my death. When I awoke, I felt as if I'd discovered some lost purpose in my life—one I didn't even realize was lost."

Such dreams as this are gifts, reminding us during our hours of sleep that every moment of our lives is a moment of personal meaning that when understood will lead us closer to the true gold, the imperishable meaning of life. And when we try to understand ourselves and face our inner and outer lives with love and courage, we'll find something deep within us coming to our support.

In many mythologies, weaving women or goddesses open and close the cycles of human life and even of civilizations. In the tradition of ancient Islam the weaver's loom symbolizes the structure and motion of the universe. The framework with its upper and lower rollers shows the configuration of life. The upper roller is known as the heavenly roller and the lower one stands for the earth. In most of the old traditions weaving is a work of creation and a bringing to birth. For centuries we've envisioned our lives as tapestries being woven by our experiences and our responses to these occurrences. In the tradition of the Near East, the shimmering fabric of the world stands out against the background of human suffering and struggle. Philosophers like Shopenhauer and mystics like Padre Pio have compared life to a tapestry whose pattern we cannot see until it is near completion.

I like to imagine that life is like such a tapestry that's being woven carefully day by day, year after year. It's a fabric of relationships, woven together, with one side representing the many relationships we have with ourselves and the other side reflecting the ones we have with other people.

In the old myths of Greece the fates wove and controlled the patterns of our lives, their content, form, and length; and even today most things that form our early experiences are beyond our control. But we hope that the important years that take us into adulthood are woven of broad cloth, of sturdy cotton lightly threaded with gold and iron strands. Think of the durable cotton as experiences that pull together the common relationships of education, work, and social skills we need for the ordinary tasks of living; and the threads of iron as the strength of our families and society's traditional values, which initially support our growth. In the long run, the wear and tear of life will weaken these threads, and either the water of tears or of the spirit will rust them away. This is as it should be. If the iron threading is too heavy and does not wear away, we can end up harsh and rigid, or as the ancient Greek writer Hesiod tells us, hard and materialistic. Next to the threads of iron are those of gold. Though they're few in number they are pure and strong, flexible—and able to bend to the events we encounter and the growth and change that must take place.

Frequently, there will be threads of copper woven close to the threads of gold, and if we're lucky at first and experience even a little love and safety, and are committed to life later on, they'll be many in number. These are the flecks of thread that carry the electric sparks of passion that often burn and then disappear. But these threads once woven into life are always ready, and when touched they charge our lives with tension like the sharp point of an arrow fired by Eros.

Finally there are elegant, gossamer threads of silk woven by the small events in our lives. They're strong and beautiful, the result of self-knowledge clearly earned by living. We feel these silken threads in the smoothness of mature love, and in the soft welcoming texture of life beckoning before us.

We seem to have such difficulty overcoming our images of how things are, of how we are or should be, of how we want things to be. Yet we appear, nevertheless, to be in the hands of a weaver who spins us lessons in the dark, through our relationships, diseases, and other experiences, to open us to the mysteries of love and the possibilities within ourselves and life. Let us value our existence, and value our opportunities enough to listen and to learn from the sources deep within us in a manner that helps us choose the threads that will create a pattern that reflects our love of life.

SUGGESTIONS FOR FURTHER READING

Books have been teachers and mentors throughout my life. My debt to the following authors is especially keen. Their thinking and the things they awakened in me led me into the rich journey of writing this book.

Campbell, Joseph. *Transformation of Myth Through Time.* New York: Harper and Row, 1990.

Davies, Robertson. *The Merry Heart: Reflections on Reading, Writing and the World of Books.* New York: Penguin, 1996.

Fromm, Erich. *The Essential Fromm: Life Between Having and Being.* Edited by Rainer Funk. New York: Continuum, 1995.

Hillman, James. *Insearch: Psychology and Religion.* Dallas: Spring Publications, 1967.

Johnson, Robert A. *Inner Work: Using Dreams and Active Imagination for Personal Growth.* San Francisco: Harper and Row, 1986.

Jung, C. G. *Memories, Dreams, Reflections.* Edited by Aniela Jaffé and translated by Richard and Clara Winston. New York: Pantheon, 1973.

———. *Modern Man in Search of a Soul.* Translated by W. S. Dell and Cary F. Baynes. New York: Harcourt Brace and Company, 1933.

Moore, Thomas. *Care of the Soul: A Guide for Cultivating Depth and Sacredness in Everyday Life.* New York: Harper Collins, 1992.

Paz, Octavio. *The Other Voice: Essays on Modern Poetry.* Translated by Helen Lane. New York: Harcourt Brace Jovanovich, 1990.

Rilke, Rainer Maria. *Letters to a Young Poet.* Translated by Stephen Mitchell. New York: Random House, 1984.

———. *Rilke on Love and Other Difficulties.* Translations and considerations by John J. L. Mood. New York: Norton, 1975.

INDEX

Abraham, 87
addictions, 81
Adler, 12
advertising messages, 18, 43, 89, 96, 97, 105, 128–29
Aeneas, 8
Aeneid, 196
The Alchemist, 295
alchemy, 99–100, 276, 331
alienation, 93
    See also self-alienation
American Dream, 6, 7, 42, 187
analysis, 82
ancient civilizations, 62, 80–81, 196–97
Anderson, Hans Christian, 249–51, 271
Angelou, Maya, 338
anger, 175–79, 284, 287
anima, 325
animus, 325
Aphrodite, 314–15, 317, 338
Apollo, 78
Aquinas, Thomas, 19

Ares, 338
Aristophanes, 320
Aristotle, 338
The Artist's Way, 60–61, 158
Aspects of the Novel, 22
attic roles, 140–41
attractions, 309
    opposites, 318–19
Auden, W. H., 142
Aupuleius, 314
Auschwitz, 88
authenticity, 62
awakening, 298–301
Awakening at Midlife, 246

Bacchus, 77
Baldwin, Christina, 333
Baudelaire, 112
"Beauty and the Beast," 86, 114
biological characteristics, 40–41
Bird by Bird, 182
Bishop Sybnesius, 197
Blake, William, 158
"Bluebeard," 83–86

INDEX

bodily needs, 119–20
Brehony, Kathleen, 246
Bronte, Emily, 219
Buber, Martin, 215
Buddha, 19, 36–37, 86, 288
    dreams, 197

Calvin and Hobbes, 17
Calvino, Italo, 39, 101
Cameron, Julia, 61, 158, 175, 227
Campbell, Joseph, 5, 7, 36, 73, 76, 82, 106, 250, 333–334
capitalism, 11
Care of the Soul, 20
career choices, 63
Catholicism, 74
challenges, 248
change, 53–55, 99
character, 1
Charles, Prince, 18
childhood, 41, 73, 257
    dreams, 232
    revisiting, 203–6
    wounds, 125–26
Christ, 19, 36–37, 288
    birth story, 86, 197, 248
    suffering of, 81
Churchill, Winston, 166–67, 215–16
Cicero, 196
"Cinderella," 86
classical studies, 20
Coelho, Paulo, 295, 312
collective unconscious, 106–7, 133
commitments, 309
competition, 95, 96
conflict, 70
conforming, 105
conscious relationship, 139
consciousness, 133, 134, 215
    complex consciousness, 28–32, 40, 67, 100, 117, 215, 249
    conventional consciousness, 71
    four stages of, 27, 40
    illuminated consciousness, 38–40
    individual consciousness, 32–38, 40, 67, 73–75, 117–18
    simple consciousness, 27–28, 40
consumer spending, 42–44, 128–29
courage, 65–66, 338
creativity, 158
cultural influences, 24, 97
culture, 129
Curie, Madame, 299

Dachau, 88
Daedalus, 234
Daniel, 196
dark attitude, 86
"Dark Night of the Soul," 87
dark side, 243–69
Davies, Robertson, 47, 102, 106, 158, 209, 285
"The Deadliest of the Sins," 209
Death in Venice, 112
defense mechanism, 263
Delphi Oracle, 313
depression, 80, 93, 166, 170–73, 235
dialoging, 157–91, 292–93
    purpose of, 191
    suggestions for, 173–75
diary, 149
discernment process, 70
Dostoevsky, 112
Dr. Jekyll and Mr. Hyde, 112, 252
dragons, 116–18
dreams, 67–68, 82, 135–37, 193–96, 254, 258
    ancient civilizations, 196–97
    befriending, 219–42
    biblical, 197
    of Buddha, 197
    dark dreams, 230–31
    falling, 234–35

INDEX

interpretations, 224
journals, 154–55
life decisions, 241
listening to, 227–28
meanings, 223
nightmares, 232
paying attention, 225–27
purpose of, 236–37
pursuit, 232–33
questioning, 228–29
reflecting, 229
shadows, 255–56
stories, 236
story form, 222
symbolic language, 194–95
writing down, 225–26
duty, 308

Eckhart, Meister, 19
economic system, 96
Edinger, Edward, 37
Edison, Thomas, 220
efficiency, 80
ego, 211, 215
Ego and Archetype, 37
ego-development, 28, 29
egotism, 1
Ehrenfeld, David, 197
Einstein, Albert, 59, 157, 299
Eisley, Loren, 226, 337
Eliot, T. S., 6, 118
Emerson, Ralph Waldo, 1
emotional detachment, 280
emotional maturity, 52
emotions, 58, 280–84
    See also feelings
"The Emperor's New Clothes," 102–3
eros, 283, 312–18, 339
exhaustion, 93

failure, 7–8

fairy tales, 38–39, 82, 83, 85–86, 101–4, 106
faith, 65–66
family influences, 24, 30
father complex, 325
fear, 161–65, 294–97
feelings, 58, 209–10, 283
    denial of, 126
    See also emotions
"The Fisherman's Wife," 120–21
Forster, E. M., 22
Frank, Arthur, 170
Frankl, Viktor, 88
Freud, Sigmund, 12, 47, 79, 93, 299, 339
    iceberg analogy, 133–34
    patients, 105
    unconscious realm, 105
"The Frog Prince," 86
Fromm, Erich, 12, 17, 31, 79, 306, 340

Gift from the Sea, 156
Goethe, 19
gold, 99–100
The Golden Ass, 314
golden mean, 78
Gorbachev, Mikhail, 263
Grach, Judith, 133
Grail legend, 7
Greene, Graham, 243
growth, 274

Hammarskjöld, Dag, 133, 142, 143, 144, 147
Hanh, Thich Nhat, 60, 160–61, 166
happiness, 17–19
Harris, Massimilla M., 271
healing forces, 62
heart disease, 78
Hemingway, Ernest, 268
Heracles, 248

INDEX

Heraclitus, 9
Herod, 86
The Hero with a Thousand Faces, 7, 106
Hillman, James, 36, 220
Holocaust, 88, 109
Holy Grail, 335–36
Homer, 196
hooks, bell, 336
Hotchner, A. E., 268
hurt, 284

Icarus, 234
identities, 30, 33, 114, 257, 265–66
idolatry, 11
Ignatius of Loyola, Saint, 74
illness, 81, 167, 170
image, 105
imagination, 157–60
Inanna, 8, 114
independence, 95
individualism, 1
individuality, 48, 95
individuation process, 5, 61, 265, 305
    cultural influences, 97
    guide to life, 26–27, 53, 143
    illness, 167
    journey of, 66
    Jung, 21, 138
    love, 312, 317
    religion, 36, 62
    self-knowledge, 298
inner artist, 187–90
inner critic, 93, 182–87
inner substance. *See* personal substance
inner transformation, 114
Insearch: Psychology and Religion, 220
interbeing, 217
The Interior Castle, 101
intimacy, 307
Isaac, 87
Islam, 197, 341

island analogy, 133
Ivanhoe, 113

Jesus. *See* Christ
Johnson, Robert, 26, 106–8, 116, 157
Jonah, 135
Jong, Erica, 297
journaling, 133–56
    dreams, 154–55
    elements of, 154–55
    imagination, 159
    religious attention, 142–47
    writing tips, 155–56
judging ourselves, 127–28
Julien of Norwich, 144
Jung, C. G., 1, 5, 12, 20–21, 36, 62, 79, 88
    active imagination, 159–60
    alchemy, 99
    children, 103
    collective unconscious, 106
    consciousness, 215
    dialoging, 174
    dreams, 135, 198, 234, 236, 241, 256, 291
    individuation process, 138
    patients, 105
    regressive restoration, 115
    religious outlook, 58–61
    success, 53
    unconscious, 108–9

Kazantzakis, Nikos, 271, 290
Keen, Sam, 149, 161, 167, 210, 296
Kierkegaard, Soren, 78
King Herod, 248
Kitchen Table Wisdom, 266

Lamed Vovniks, 81
Lamott, Anne, 182
Lao-tze, 19
legends, 82

INDEX

Letters to a Young Poet, 336
lifestyle, 104
Lindbergh, Anne Morrow, 144, 156
listening, 211
Living Buddha, Living Christ, 160
Loeb, Sophie, 224
logos, 283
love, 277–79, 284, 305–7, 312, 335
    attractions, 308–11
    historical love stories, 308
    love of death, 340
    love of life, 340
    personal growth, 313
Lucretious, 196

Mann, Thomas, 112
Man's Search for Meaning, 88
The Manticore, 285
Markings, 142
martial arts, 282
mastering oursleves, 142
maturity, 52
McLaughlin, Mignon, 67
medicine, 81
Merton, Thomas, 132, 144–46
Metamorphoses, 77–78
Metzger, Deena, 99
Midas, King, 77–78
midlife, 33, 34, 67, 198–203, 249, 253, 257
Mier, C. A., 80
mind-body split, 282
mindfulness, 60
Moore, Thomas, 20, 86, 109, 147, 284, 305
Moses, 36
mother complex, 325
Moyers, Bill, 333
musicians, 220
mystics, 74, 335
mythology, 106, 234, 294, 313, 341, 342

myths, 82

Nebuchadnezzar, 196
needs, 120–23
Nietzsche, Friedrich, 166
Nin, Anaïs, 193
normalcy, 17–21, 61, 94–95, 299
    defined, 45, 47
    society's illusion of, 40–46
Norman, Marsha, 219

Odysseus, 8
The Odyssey, 114, 196
The Old Man and the Sea, 268
original mind, 107
Ornish, Dean, 78–79, 93
The Other Voice, 195
overweight, 179–82
Ovid, 77–78

Pan, 78
parables, 82
Paracelsus, 19
parents, 55
    honoring, 58
paying attention, 60, 211
Paz, Octavio, 194–95, 313–14
Peck, Scott, 134
perfectionism, 182–87
performance, 80
persona, 29
personal choice, 138
personal reflection, 259
personal substance, 193–218
personalities, 139
perversion, 111–12
philosopher's stone, 99
Philosophies of India, 300
Pio, Padre, 342
Plath, Sylvia, 112
Plato, 196, 319–20
power of the imagination, 159

351

INDEX

Price, Reynolds, 72–73, 168, 172
primitive feelings, 285
projection, 246, 262–65
prospective function of dreams, 241
psyche, 312–18
psychological growth, 22, 36
    See also individuation process
psychological maturity, 268
psychotherapy, 13, 82
public face, 29, 252

The Quest for the Holy Grail, 118–19
quest stories, 4–6
questioning, 211, 213

racism, 109
Reagan, Ronald, 263
reason, 283
reflecting, 74, 211, 213–14
relationships, 18, 139, 305–32, 328
    attractions, 319
    disillusionment, 319
    distress in, 308
religion, 9, 11, 21, 58–61, 100–101
    institutions, 96
    organized, 59
religious figures, 86–87
religious stories, 87
Remen, Rachel Naomi, 127, 266, 275, 336
The Right to Create, 133
The Right to Write, 227
Rilke, Rainer Maria, 75, 77, 203, 243, 249, 272, 316, 336
The Road Less Traveled, 134
"The Roar of Awakening," 300
Robin Hood, 113
Rogers, Carl, 266, 268, 275, 336
Round Table, 335

sacred selfishness, 10, 142, 271–302
    defined, 1

sacred substance, 100, 114, 242
Sadat, Anwar, 144
Sand, George, 151
Sarton, May, 144, 149
Scott-Maxwell, Florida, 305
secrets, 277
secular substance, 100–101, 242
Self, 23, 26–27, 36, 75, 336
self-alienation, 93, 127
    See also alienation
self-awareness, 121, 265
self-containment, 96
self-destructive attitudes, 93
self-doubt, 67
self-esteem, 10–11
self-examination, 74
self-images, 68
self-knowledge, 101, 190, 298, 335–37
self-loathing, 67
self-love, 273, 277–79
    guides to, 288
selfishness, 1, 274
Sellby, Hubert, 112
"The Shadow", 249–51, 271
shadows, 108–9, 243–69
    power of, 109–13
    projection, 262–65
    substance, 113–16
    uncovering, 265
Shakespeare, William, 230
Sheehy, Gail, 304
Shopenhauer, 342
sickly selfishness, 1
"Silent for Seven Years," 39
slaughter of the innocents, 248
social character, 31–32, 42, 45, 73, 79, 95, 209
Socrates, 19, 196, 320
The Star Thrower, 226
Stevens, Anthony, 198
Stevenson, Robert Louis, 112, 252

INDEX

stories, 59, 82
Storr, Anthony, 167
substance, 7–9
success, 53
support groups, 81, 93
The Symposium, 319–20, 324

Tai Chi, 282
Talmud, 196
Tao, 336
Teresa of Avila, Saint, 101
Tertullian, 197
thanatos, 339
thievery, 111
Thoreau, Henry David, 16
Thurman, Howard, 296
Tillich, Paul, 36, 106
To a Dancing God, 149, 161–65, 210
Tolstoy, 112
transformation periods, 73
The Twelve Labors of Heracles, 248

Ulysses, 113–16
unconscious, 106–7, 109, 133–34
values, 48, 53, 61, 79, 94, 138
    awareness of, 62

Van der Post, Sir Laurens, 36
vices, 265–67
Virgil, 196
virtues, 265–67

waking sleep, 215
"The Waste Land," 6
Waterson, Bill, 17
weight, 179–82
wholeness, 335
A Whole New Life, 72, 168
willpower, 142, 143
Woolf, Virginia, 144
The Wounded Storyteller: Body, Illness and Ethics, 170
Wuthering Heights, 219

yoga, 282

Zeus, 317, 320
Zimmer, Heinrich, 300
Zorba the Greek, 271–74, 289–90, 294

AUTHOR'S BIO

Bud Harris, Ph.D., originally became a businessman and successfully owned his own business before returning to school to become a psychotherapist. After earning his Ph.D. in psychology and practicing as a psychotherapist and psychologist, he experienced the call to further his growth and become a Jungian analyst. He then moved to Zürich, Switzerland where he trained for over five years and graduated from the C. G. Jung Institute. He is the author of ten books, lectures widely, and practices as a Jungian analyst in Asheville, North Carolina. For additional information about his practice and work, visit: www.budharris.com.

Made in the USA
Coppell, TX
03 June 2021

56806124R10215